2/2010

TECHNICAL ANALYSIS

SFO Personal Investor Series:
TECHNICAL ANALYSIS

INTRODUCTION BY:
RUSSELL R. WASENDORF, SR.

EDITED BY:
LAURA SETHER

PUBLISHING

P.O. Box 849, Cedar Falls, Iowa 50613
www.w-apublishing.com

Library of Congress Control Number: 2007924420
ISBN-13: 978-1-934354-01-8
ISBN-10: 1-93434-01-5

Printed in the United States of America.

10 9 8 7 6 5 4 3 2 1

The principles of successful stock speculation are based on the supposition that people will continue in the future to make the mistakes that they have made in the past.

— Edwin LeFevre, Reminiscences of a Stock Operator

CONTENTS

INTRODUCTION

BY RUSSELL R. WASENDORF, SR.

Give a man a fish and you feed him for a day.
Teach a man to fish and you feed him for a lifetime.
                                                    –Chinese proverb

The purpose of this book is to teach personal investors about tools, which can enable them to make informed and potentially profitable trading decisions on their own. No longer do individual traders need to rely on a broker for the latest hot tip. The advent of the electronic age has smashed the paradigm of trading from yesteryear. Over the last decade, the door has swung open wide for personal investors to participate on a level playing field in the world of global finance from the comfort of their home computer.

However, in order to trade and invest successfully, one must develop and fine-tune a strategy. Within the arena of market analysis there are two major approaches: *fundamental analysis* and *technical analysis*. The fundamental method for stocks focuses on the study of a company's financial statements and involves analysis of profit-to-earnings ratios, revenues, expenses, assets and liabilities, management teams, and new product offerings in the pipeline. In the commodities arena, fundamental traders zero in on economic reports, supply/demand figures, and production and consumption data.

The focus of this book is the latter method, referred to as technical analysis, which is the analysis of price and price history. There is an old market axiom, *"It is all the in charts."* That idiom reflects the important concept that all known fundamental factors are reflected in the current price of a financial instrument. So, a trader may not need to know the specifics about the latest monetary policy decision out of the Bank of Japan in order to execute a successful dollar/yen trade, if he is studying the charts. Technical traders point out that it is virtually impossible for an individual investor, or even a team of researchers at a big Wall Street firm, to identify and understand every fundamental factor, which is impacting price. The three main tenets of technical analysis include the concept that all known news is discounted in price, the idea that price moves in trends, and the truism that history repeats itself.

Varying forms of charting and technical analysis have been utilized for hundreds of years. Early methods of charting can be traced to Japan, where rice traders in the 1700s etched "candlesticks" on paper in order to track price movement. In the United States, technical analysis can be traced back to the 1880s. The so-called tape readers of that time were in actuality implementing a form of price study. Today, there are myriad charting software programs and trading platforms, which provide personal investors easy access to technical indicators and price charts.

However, technical analysis wasn't always popular and in fact there was a time when this method of study was shunned on Wall Street. In the '60s and '70s, chart watchers were pushed to the back rooms of major New York brokerage firms to conduct technical work. Then, the results of their technical studies would be offered up to clients under the guise of fundamental recommendations. The veil was lifted with the advent of the personal computer, which changed everything. Not only did personal investors gain direct access to markets, but also the rise of the computer age has seen a resurgence in reliance on technical analysis. Extensive charting software and back testing capability have created a world in which personal investors can now do their own market studies at home and on their own schedule.

The backbone and essential building block for technical analysis is, of course, the chart. This is a graphic representation of price history over a time period chosen by the trader, such as 5-minute, hourly, daily, weekly or monthly. There are bar charts, point and figure charts, candlestick charts and line charts to name a few. This book will highlight the pros and cons of various chart types in order to help individuals determine what will work best for them.

A market can go up, it can go down, or it can go sideways. Even beginning traders have heard the adage "*the trend is your friend.*" Technical analysis can help traders define the trend and then determine specific entry and exit points for trading opportunities. There are two major types of technical indicators: trend-following tools and oscillators, which are useful in non-trending markets. Beginning traders can often find themselves overwhelmed with the array of choices available on many charting software pull-down menus. Traders would be well served to take it slowly and experiment with various indicators before diving in and utilizing them to make trading decisions.

Traders need to take the time to do their homework and understand the technical tools they are relying on in order to implement them amid appropriate market conditions. Examples of trend-following tools include moving averages, Bollinger bands, and trend lines. But, for those times when a market is consolidating in a sideways fashion, indicators such as stochastics, the relative strength index, and moving average convergence divergence (MACD) can be useful.

Another form of technical analysis is pattern recognition. The rationale behind this area is that history repeats itself. Fear and greed have created many a bottom and top in markets throughout history. Price often evolves in recognizable patterns around market turns or while a market is resting and consolidating a move. This book will introduce several patterns, which offer tradable opportunities with specific entry points and profit objectives. Patterns also offer traders a clear "when you are wrong" point, which can help determine the all-important stop-loss placement level.

Technical analysis is a universal market tool. It doesn't matter if you trade ETFs, individual stocks, spot forex, or orange juice futures. The principles of technical analysis work across all markets and all time frames. It is equally valuable for intraday traders whose positions may last seconds to minutes, as well as longer-term investors who rely on TA to identify specific entry and exit price points.

What you have in your hands is a treasure trove of information. We have chosen the 'best of the best' articles from the *SFO* volumes. However, it takes time, research, homework, and perhaps even paper trading to become successful at trading. There is no holy grail. My mission is and has been for many years to provide personal investors the information that they need to make successful self-directed trading decisions. Since its inception in 2001, *SFO* has become the most widely distributed monthly publication specializing in stocks, futures & options, and we are proud to offer you this collection. Good luck with your study and trading.

By Russell R. Wasendorf, Sr. is chairman and CEO of Peregrine Financial Group, Inc., publisher of *SFO* and author of *The Complete Guide to Single Stock Futures* and *All About Futures*

SECTION ONE
Where It Came from and Why It Works

Technical analysis, once the red-headed stepchild of market analysis, has become the standard-bearer of prediction tools among the current generation of professional and home-based market analysts. Once a bona fide dirty word in the investment world, technical analysis is now one of the most commonly used forecasting tools for traders. The reason behind this is simple: it works.

Technical analysis is actually the oldest form of market analysis, dating back to 17th century Japan. We'll take you through its long, storied past and evolution from a top secret charting tool hidden in the back rooms of brokerages to the mainstream success it has earned today. You'll learn how the Market Technician's Association, a fledgling group of technicians in the early 1970s, played a major role in bringing technicals to the forefront of a fundamental trading world. The group now boasts a worldwide membership in the thousands.

Dow theory, the foundation for modern technical analysis, developed from a series of editorials in the *Wall Street Journal* by Charles Dow in the late 19th century. His intention at the time was not to found a major school of market analysis, but his insights into price action have stood the test of time. The basic tenets of trend analysis from more than one hundred years ago—lessons such as trends persist, trends are confirmed by volume, and stock market increases confirm each other—can improve your trading today.

The observation that crowds behave in predicable ways is at the core of technical analysis. The key is knowing how to recognize the repeating patterns that foretell price signals for the future. Learning the technical indicators will give you the tools you need to recognize price signals. Once you've mastered that you're well on your way to becoming a more effective trader.

IT'S ALL IN THE CHARTS

BY KIRA MCCAFFREY BRECHT

Most investors are familiar with concepts such as the price-to-earnings ratio or quarterly profit reports, but if the terms double bottom, Fibonacci levels, or head and shoulder top sound a bit more foreign, you are not alone. While cash flow analysis and the price-to-earnings ratio fall under the category of fundamental analysis, the latter fall under the category of technical analysis. This chapter is a basic introduction to the subject of technical analysis. Perhaps, after reading these few pages, you'll be interested in learning how to trade breakout points for yourself.

To the average investor, technical analysis may not be standard cocktail-hour conversation, but it is a methodology that market players have utilized for hundreds of years. In recent times, with the advent of the personal computer and the Internet, and as more day traders have become active in the financial markets, technical analysis has come out of the closet and is becoming more well known even among individual investors.

But, what exactly is technical analysis? Before attempting to define and explain technical analysis, it is probably worthwhile to briefly define fundamental analysis, as these are the two major forms of analysis that market watchers utilize in an attempt to determine future direction of price. Fundamental analysis relies on the use of economic numbers, including supply and demand figures, production, and consumption numbers to determine the worth of a stock or commodity. Or in the case of individual stock analysis, analysts examine the financial books of a company, evaluate management and cash flows and dividends, and consider new product launches and overall competitiveness in the marketplace.

"Fundamental analysis deals with companies and economies, while technical analysis deals with stocks and markets. They are not the same thing," said Philip Roth, chief technical analyst at Miller Tabak + Co. "The company and the stock are not the same thing. Fundamentalists look at the company—is the management good, are the products good? But, we are not buying the company. We just buy one teeny bit of the company. One hundred shares can trade off the psychology of the marketplace. The technician analyzes supply/demand relationships in the market and the psychology of the participants. The charts have memories. They represent actions of investors in the past."

Price Is the Key Indicator

The technical analyst will say there is no way that one person, or perhaps even a team of researchers can identify and pinpoint every known fundamental supply and demand factor in the marketplace. Therefore, a major tenet of technical analysis is that "it is all in the charts." The current price of a stock index future, a commodity, or an individual stock reflects the current opinion of all of the players in the marketplace. In other words, all currently known fundamental information is reflected by buyers and sellers to push the security to the current price—"it's all in the charts."

Technical analysis simply put is remembering prices. It is the study of prices and price history, in an effort to gauge current and future trends. Technical analysts rely on three major tenets: all news is discounted in the price, price moves in a trend, and history tends to repeat itself.

In his book, *How Technical Analysis Works* (New York Institute of Finance, 2003), author Bruce Kamich says, "The prices of goods and raw commodities—silk, spices, gold, rice, horses, cattle—have been followed for centuries. People remembered the prices of last season, the extreme highs and lows, and more. For centuries, farmers have had a vital interest in following prices; the result of a whole season of sweat and toil will come down to the price they are able to get in the marketplace. If your livelihood depends on being paid for one crop of tobacco, coffee, or rice, you will have a strong interest in price."

One basic element in technical analysis is the concept of price resistance and support. Miller Tabak's Roth explains it as "if I buy a stock at 50, but then it goes down to 40—I'm thinking—please just get back to 50 so I can get even—that becomes a resistance area. Or, if I buy a stock at 40 and then it goes to 50, I'll remember that 40 was an attractive price. If it goes back down to 40, I may buy it again, which becomes a support level. Support and resistance are basically established because of the psychological component. People remember past successes and failures."

The Oldest Form of Market Analysis

Technical analysis, or analyzing price, is the oldest known form of market analysis, originating back to the rice markets in Japan in the 17th century. Even here in the U.S., early technicians were simply "tape readers," or those who watched prices go up and down on the ticker tape, which was introduced in 1867. The point and figure type of charting can be traced back to the 1880s here in the U.S. It wasn't until the 1930s that fundamental analysis first emerged as a market discipline.

The basic tool of the technical analyst is the price chart. One of the most widely used types of charts is simply a bar chart. In the case of a daily bar chart, the line will represent the price high, low, and close for the day. Depending on the trading or investment timeframe, you could utilize an intra-day chart (such as an hourly or 15-minute) if you are a very short-term trader, or a weekly or monthly chart if you are a longer-term investor.

The idea of trend is pivotal to developing a basic understanding of technical analysis. There are many old-market expressions, "the trend is your friend" and "never buck the trend." A basic definition of trend is simply the direction in which prices are moving. While many people tend to think of the market in two directions—a bull or a bear—there are actually three types of trends: an up-trend, a down-trend, and a sideways or a range-trade trend. Looking at a price chart, a technical analyst would need to see a series of higher price highs, in order to confirm an uptrend. On the flip side, a series of lower price lows reveals a downtrend. Trend can also be classified in terms of time frame. For example, the longer-term trend could be down, but the shorter-term trend could be up, which would be called a corrective upmove in a downtrend.

John Murphy, long-time market technician and author of what many consider to be the bible of technical analysis, *Technical Analysis of the Financial Markets*, rev. ed. (New York Institute of Finance, 1999), said that "all technicians are trying to do is measure the trend of the market."

Murphy, currently the chief technical analyst at Stockcharts.com, adds, "technical analysis tells you what the market is actually doing, as opposed to what people think the market might be doing. The market is always looking to the future. If the market is telling us what is going to happen six months in the future, if you don't look at the charts, you'll always be behind the curve." (Economists tend to believe that the stock market is a leading indicator of the economy and that current stock market prices tend to reflect expectations for the economy and companies six months out.)

Fear and Greed Make Tops and Bottoms

If you've ever done any trading or investing, you may have experienced common feelings of fear and greed. Market bottoms tend to be made during extreme periods of investor and trader fear, while market tops tend to occur during times of extreme greed. A case can be made that the bubble-like top in the Nasdaq index, scored in March 2000, was made amid investor greed. More and more individuals bought into tech stocks because they had seen a brother-in-law double his money in a matter of months—and they wanted in on the game too. Miller Tabak's Roth explains it as, "a long-lasting market advance will eventually lead to feelings of greed. Tops are made from buying excesses. Conversely, market bottoms occur amid panic, when people can't take the pain (of losses) anymore."

Human psychology really hasn't changed much over the centuries. Markets move from greed at a top to fear at a bottom, and unless people learn to control those emotions, markets will continue to move up and down.

Within the field of technical analysis, there are hundreds of different indicators and tools. However, in the early days of technical analysis, price and volume were the two main factors that traders analyzed. Now, with the advent of calculators and computers, traders have devised mathematical formulas which automatically measure such things as how fast a market moves up or down—is it overbought or oversold? There is pattern recognition, which simply is a visual read of a chart looking for certain patterns, such as double tops or double bottoms.

One long-time market technician explained the likely evolution of the double top pattern as this: "Somebody was watching the tape and they'd see General Motors rally to 110 and pull back. Then they'd see it rally again, but fail at 110. By empirical observation, the trader can say that after it fails the second time and closes under the intervening low price, there are good odds that a top has formed."

Relating to the human psychology and emotions, technical analysis offers tools to gauge investor sentiment. Stockcharts.com's Murphy notes, "markets tend to overreact in both directions. Like, right now—everyone is very pessimistic (on stocks). Traders can use technical indicators, such as the put/call ratio to measure sentiment. When the put/call ratio gets too high—generally a reading over 1—that means that people are too pessimistic, and this is often associated with market bottoms. Or when the put/call ratio gets too low, under .5, it means people are too optimistic, which tends to occur around market tops."

Many innovations in technical analysis actually evolved from the futures side of the markets, not the stock trading side. Murphy estimates that 80 to 90 percent of futures traders rely on technical indicators in their trading, as "futures trading tends to be very short-term oriented and is very highly leveraged. It's all timing. If you are 90 percent leveraged, timing is extremely critical, and you have to be right. The shorter term you are, the more you have to rely on technicals. If you are buying and holding for three years into the future, it doesn't matter as much."

Tools to Tell You When You Are Wrong

You may have heard the old market saying, "let your profits run and cut your losses short." Getting out of losers—and getting out quickly is key to capital preservation, especially in fast-moving and highly leveraged futures markets. A major advantage that technical analysis offers over fundamental analysis is that "it tells you very quickly when you've made a mistake," says Murphy.

How does this work? One traditional buy type of signal in technical analysis is when a single stock futures contract rallies above a previous peak, or resistance point on the chart—that is considered a breakout to the upside, or a buy signal. Traders could use that breakout to initiate a long position. However, the charts offer a clear "I'm wrong" level with that breakout point. If the single stock future retreated back below the breakout point, the trader would know that something had gone awry—it had been a false breakout—and the trader could quickly exit the position, thus preventing serious losses.

Cut Your Losses Short

Murphy notes a key to success in trading is "never let a small loss turn into a big loss," and the charts offer specific price levels that let you know when you are wrong. Many profitable futures traders actually say that they have more losing trades than winning trades. How is that so, you ask? It goes back to the old saying, "let your profits ride and cut your losses short." If you rely on technical price points to get out when you are wrong, thus keeping losses to a minimum, and on the flip side—when you are right—let a winning position ride a trend, you can be profitable.

Murphy notes that when a fundamental analyst recommends a stock as a "buy," the stock may actually lose 50 percent of its value before the fundamental analyst changes his outlook. "With fundamentals, there is no fail-safe mechanism for getting out."

Technical analysis can be as simple or as complex as you make it. While there are sophisticated computer programs and books that burgeoning technical traders can read and study, the experienced market watchers say "keep it simple." Murphy says, "all of technical analysis is extremely simple. If a line is moving up, that is good and you want to participate. If the line is moving down, that's a negative sign for a market."

Many old-timers—traders who were active several decades ago before the heavy reliance on computer trading—actually recommend charting by hand. BC (before computers), traders would compile their own daily bar charts, or point and figure charts, by hand. The actual physical act of drawing the line on a piece of graph paper or putting in a number every day after the close offered a type of feel for the market that may be missing in the computer-dependent trading world of today. While computer charts are clearly easier, it may not be as easy to catch the innate feel or momentum of a market without the touchy-feely process of yesteryear.

If you are interested in learning more about technical analysis, there are a variety of books and seminars available. Or you may want to check out the Market Technicians Association at www.mta.org. This organization offers the Chartered Market Technician (CMT) accreditation program. There are three different exams to pass, and studying for the exams is an excellent way to learn about the field.

Overall, it is important to remember that technical analysis is the study of market action mainly through the use of price charts, in order to identify future price trends. Patterns on the charts can offer price objectives and clear stop-out points. Momentum tools can measure overbought and oversold status, and investor sentiment gauges can help determine when a major trend may be nearing an end. No method of analysis is perfect. No method of analysis is right all the time. But, technicals can be valuable tools to a trader, especially one who is active in the fast-moving futures arena.

Kira McCaffrey Brecht is senior editor at *SFO magazine*. She has been writing about the financial markets for sixteen years. Posts during her career include Chicago bureau chief at *Futures World News,* market analyst at *Bridge News,* and technical analyst at MMS International. She has passed Level I and Level II of the MTA's MCT exams. McCaffrey Brecht holds a degree in political science from Brown University. This article originally appeared in *SFO* in March 2003.

PROFITING FROM PROBABILITIES: The Value of Technical Analysis

BY MICHAEL KAHN

You are surrounded by flickering screens. Dozens of red and green lights flashing on one. News headlines scrolling across another. A famous analyst is speaking in the television window of yet a third screen. It's almost as if you can see the electromagnetic waves emanating from your being, flooding your senses, and drowning your perception of just what is going on in boardrooms across the country, in the markets of Chicago or on the trading floors of New York.

Earnings are up, should I buy?

Wait! Earnings are not up as much as the gang of Wall Street analysts said they should be, so should I sell?

Ben Bernanke is about to address Congress. And what about the war on terrorism?

If you look at the business of trading as a war in its own right, then you are ahead of the pack. Would you send in your financial troops for an attack without a map of the battleground? As you confront the enemy, wouldn't you want to know if they are heading toward you or away from you? In other words, just knowing where the "enemy" (the market) is right now tells you nothing about its speed, power and direction. You need a map, and you need to track it over time.

A Chart Can Help

This is what many floor traders can do in their heads, but if you are off the floor, as most traders are, and are trying to keep track of more than just a few contracts, then you need help. That help comes in the form of a simple plot of price changes over time—a chart.

This simple yet elegant tool allows you to see not only where your market is, but also how it got there and even how fast it is moving. You have heard that past price performance has no value in predicting future price movements, and on behalf of the thousands of trading professionals that use nothing but charts to make their decisions, I say "bunk!"

Charts do not predict the future, just like a weather map does not predict what you will see on your weekend picnic. They both lay out probabilities for what might happen based on what has happened in the past in similar circumstances. From there, you plan your picnic in the park or you look for an indoor venue. From there, you decide to buy or look for an alternative plan (sell or hold).

Technical analysis is simply the study of the markets using only data generated by the market itself and the actions of people in the market. In other words, company data like earnings and sales, and economic data like housing reports, are not used. There are no estimates and no revisions of data. While extremely useful in making forecasts of market action, the bottom line is to make the buy, sell or hold decision and nothing more. Technical analysis will invariably miss the absolute high and the absolute low, but when applied properly, it will allow the user to capture the lion's share of any price move. More importantly, it will alert the user very quickly if the analysis was incorrect to minimize losses.

Technicians analyze the market like a psychologist analyzes a patient. They assess the market's health using indicators. They can profile market behavior based on past behaviors and use probabilities to determine what kind of future behavior can be expected. What does a technician analyze? Market psychology and the behavior of crowds. Crowds, after all, make up the entity we call the market.

It is reliable to the extent that it is based on experience and objectivity. What constitutes some technical conditions is subjective at times. However, when applied consistently, it will yield more winners than losers, and then it is up to money management to lock in the profits. A significant part of technical analysis involves knowing when to acknowledge losers and locking in profits on winners.

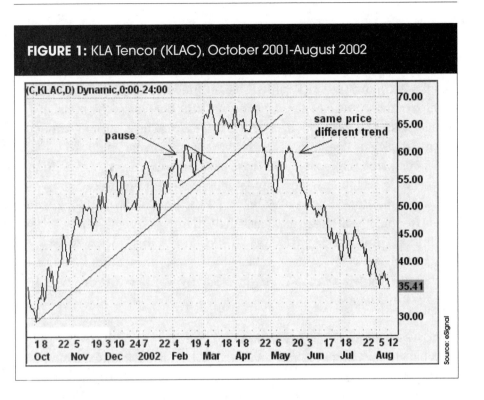

FIGURE 1: KLA Tencor (KLAC), October 2001-August 2002

What Exactly Is a Chart?

A picture is worth a thousand words. This is not just some cliché you heard at your grandmother's dinner table, but a real concept that can help a trader assimilate thousands of data points literally into a picture of the market with no more that a simple glance. It does not take long to figure out if a price is cheap or dear when you can see where it was an hour ago, a day ago or a year ago. If you are trading more than just a few stocks or futures contracts, then the chart becomes an extension of your own brain. It is like an extra memory card for your human computer where you can recall history at the click of a mouse.

What good is that? In the very simplest of terms, knowing if a market is moving up or moving down helps traders trade only those contracts that have the odds stacked in their favor.

Supply and Demand

The bottom line in all markets, whether they be financial, real estate, or breakfast cereal, is that when demand is greater than supply, prices will rise. A chart with a positively sloped price line is exhibiting excess demand. It stands to reason that it is far better to be long the market when demand is greater than supply than the other way around.

In *Figure 1* of KLA Tencor (KLAC) this is illustrated well. From the October 2001 low, the stock rallied sharply and was a top performer. A rising trend became clear, and by February 2002 it was in the midst of a second push higher following a pause. Prices were near 60, and demand for this stock was keeping pressure on the bears to give up.

When price peaked near 70, those skeptics who missed buying in the 50s were kicking themselves. Fundamentals were supposedly improving, and when the stock dipped back below 60 once again it looked like a good buy. After all, it was cheap at 60 just a few months earlier. Right?

But this time, the rising trend was broken and this stock was not cheap at 60. It was not even cheap at 40, no matter what the fundamentals might have argued. Demand was gone. Supply was flooding the market to drive prices lower still.

Trends Persist and Patterns Repeat

Let's backtrack a bit to the concept of trend, because it is crucially important whether you believe in technical analysis to the max or not. If you take just one concept to heart, it should be that trends persist. This is not only true in the world of physics, where a body in motion tends to stay in motion unless acted upon by an outside force. In the trading world, trends continue until the weight of evidence, in the form of supply and demand, tells us these trends have ended.

Why do trends persist? It is because information flow in the markets is not perfect. If everyone knew all that was to be known about a stock, interest rates or evolving business laws, then prices would jump instantly from one level to another to reflect that information. The truth is that prices do not jump like that, even when prices gap up or down at the open. Information spreads through the marketplace at different speeds, and it is assimilated by market participants at different rates. Did the thought of the equities bear market sink in faster for you, for your neighbor across the street, or for your colleague across the trading desk?

Know the Trend and Stack the Deck in Your Favor

Patterns that develop on price charts are the next bread-and-butter tool used by technical analysts. Because markets do not travel in straight lines for very long, analyzing how they pause helps analysts

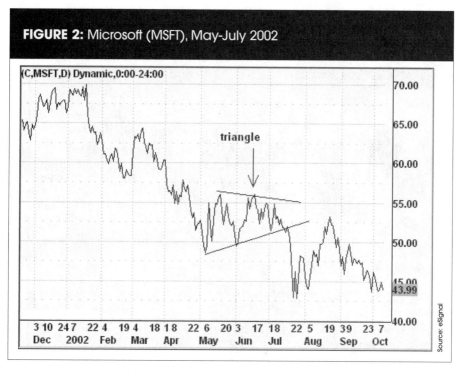

FIGURE 2: Microsoft (MSFT), May-July 2002

take the market's vital signs and, more importantly, tells them when things are about to get going again. In other words, will the trend continue or turn around? Or will it just end and leave the market flat?

The names of these patterns range from the very descriptive "triangle" to the Picasso-like "head-and-shoulders." Flags, horns, rectangles, double bottoms, saucers—the list goes on, but the bottom line is that the market was trending, and now supply and demand are more in equilibrium. Bulls and bears are squaring positions and jockeying for control.

When prices move out from these patterns, whether higher or lower, it means that supply and demand have once again changed. Perceptions of value held by market participants have changed, and a new trend begins as this paradigm filters out to the masses.

We can see a clear triangle pattern in Microsoft (MSFT) from May through July of last year (*Figure 2*). Prices bounced around in a range until something happened, and what was a good buy was not perceived as a good sell.

These patterns repeat themselves across time, time frame and market. They outline the probability of what is to come, because market participants faced with similar market conditions will act in similar ways.

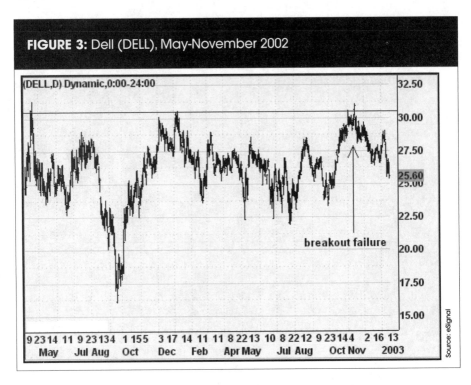

FIGURE 3: Dell (DELL), May-November 2002

Source: eSignal

We can delve into the psychology of crowds, but for the purposes of this discussion it suffices to say that this is an observable phenomenon, and following its clues stacks the odds even further in our favor.

Early Warning for Mistakes

This is no crystal ball into the future, and anyone who tells you that he or she can predict the future from patterns is mistaken, to say the least. What we take from this are probabilities that the market will move a certain way. We also get an early warning system to tell us that we have made a mistake, either in the analysis or the market deciding to buck the odds this time around.

Technical analysis not only helps you forecast, but it gives you a level at which you know it is time to admit defeat and move on to the next trade. Top professional traders know where they will close a position before they open it. Top technical analysts can see or calculate those levels based on the patterns on the charts.

Did you buy because a pattern was broken to the upside? If prices dip back into that pattern, clearly the breakout was not what you thought, and it is time to reevaluate.

A clear example of this can be seen in Dell (DELL) in November 2002 (*Figure 3*). It had traded through a long-term resistance, partially as good news was released, but it could not hold at that level. There were other technical patterns at play to confirm this failure, but the point is that we knew right away that this stock was not breaking out to the upside. It was all downhill from there.

Did you sell because an earnings report was not so good? If the stock does not react as expected, then the market is telling you something and it might be wise to cover. Perhaps all of the bad news was already priced into the market. Perhaps the report was expected to be even worse than analyst consensus and the bears were spooked by the news. Whatever the reason, the charts tell you that all is not what it seems.

Again, if a technical pattern or market event does not result in the price movement it is supposed to drive, you will know it sooner rather than later, and this can help you avoid large losses. Money management is just as important as vehicle selection.

Risk vs. Reward

Another key aspect of technical patterns is that they give you guidelines for target setting. Just like they tell you when to close a position when you are wrong, they tell you when to close a position when you are right.

This, once again, refers back to crowd behavior and how supply and demand factor in. In a technical pattern, a trading range develops. True, each pattern has a different slant on that range, but the bottom line is that prices bounce around without making real progress up or down. Support and resistance levels develop where demand and supply, respectively, are strong, and things stay that way until something happens to change that equilibrium.

Whatever the spark may be, prices emerge from the range, up for example. Here, what was rich is not considered to be cheap. What was once a price that brought out the sellers in droves is now a price that brings out the buyers and the market begins to move higher.

The interesting component of all of this is that markets tend to move in a quantitized manner for a while after the patterns break. In other words, if the trading range were from 50 to 60, then the first upside target would be 70, the height of the range projected up from the breakout point. If the trend were strong, then 80 would be the next target, the second integral multiple of the range height.

Look back at the Microsoft example we saw earlier. The breakdown led quickly to a move equivalent to the height of the broken pattern.

There is a lot more to setting price targets than this, but when these price targets coincide with other technical, quantitative, or fundamental targets, then you know the odds of a successful trade are high.

What It All Means

Technical analysis is not voodoo, and it does not pretend to predict where the market will be at any point in time. It is only an investment decision-making tool. It can give you a framework for where the market will be, but it's a probabilities game, just like human behavior.

It's not about being right, being smart or, as previously mentioned, predicting the future. It's all about making the buy, sell, or hold decision. It works in bull markets, bear markets, and, most importantly, in sideways markets and puts the market on your side as an ally, not as an adversary.

But technical analysis is not always right. Nothing is. Every technical tool in the world can agree that Joe's Customized Research Company is a stock on the verge of its great bull market when a little thing like the Internet comes along to change the rules of the game. Technical analysis will quickly point out that the original forecast was wrong.

It is not the Holy Grail but rather it is a tool. Treat it as such, and it will help you build your own trading success story.

Michael Kahn is a well respected technical analyst. He writes the *Getting Technical* column for Barron's Online (www.barrons.com) and the daily *Quick Takes Pro* technical newsletter (www.QuickTakesPro.net). Kahn is the author of two books on technical analysis, most recently *Technical Analysis Plain and Simple: Charting the Markets in Your Language* (Financial Times Prentice Hall, 2006), and was chief technical analyst for BridgeNews. He also is on the board of directors of the Market Technicians Association (www.mta.org). This article originally appeared in *SFO* in April 2003.

DOW THEORY:
The Time-Tested Foundation

BY CHRISTOPHER TERRY

The challenge of the stock and futures markets is multi-faceted. Each trader has his own interpretation of the trend, individual reasoning as to what support and resistance levels may be, what continuation patterns and reversals are, and what constitutes a meaningful chart formation versus what does not.

The Dow theory, first developed approximately one hundred years ago, offers an incredible wealth of information for the technical trader that is as valid today as it was back at the turn of the 20th century.

Dow Theory and Technical Analysis

Until his death in 1902, Charles H. Dow wrote editorials in the *Wall Street Journal* outlining his theories observing that averages of both the primary industrial and the rail stocks acted as a barometer for the nation's economy. Dow's successor, William P. Hamilton, continued the development of Dow's theories and principles for the next twenty-seven years and crystallized them into his own version of what we know today as the Dow theory.

The pioneering work of Dow and Hamilton became the foundation of the discipline that led to the groundbreaking work that helped launch the technical analysis revolution. Richard Schabacker's *Technical Analysis and Stock Market Profits* (1932) paved the way for Edwards and Magee's *Technical Analysis of Stock Trends* (1948). Their books have stood the test of time and are considered to be some of the most important work ever on technical analysis.

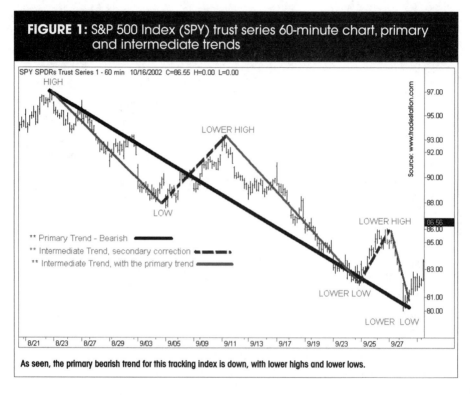

FIGURE 1: S&P 500 Index (SPY) trust series 60-minute chart, primary and intermediate trends

As seen, the primary bearish trend for this tracking index is down, with lower highs and lower lows.

Technical analysis in its purest form, of course, is the study of price and the use of charts as a tool to discover patterns and to learn the trend of a market. The first visions that come to mind when considering technical analysis are various types of chart patterns, both continuations and reversals. Some of the more popular are triangles, wedges, head and shoulders, flags, and pennants.

The Theory and Foundation of Trends

Realizing stock and futures prices quite often trade in trends, a basic understanding of what makes up those trends will provide the foundation necessary for a trader to identify the type of market in which he is trading. By gaining a broad understanding of the Dow theory and technical analysis, a trader will gain confidence in chart reading and, ultimately, will enhance his ability to spot and trade trends successfully.

The Dow theory concentrates on three types of trends: primary, secondary, and minor. The most easily understood definition of trends, of course, is that an up-trend exhibits higher highs and higher lows, and a down-trend exhibits lower lows and lower highs.

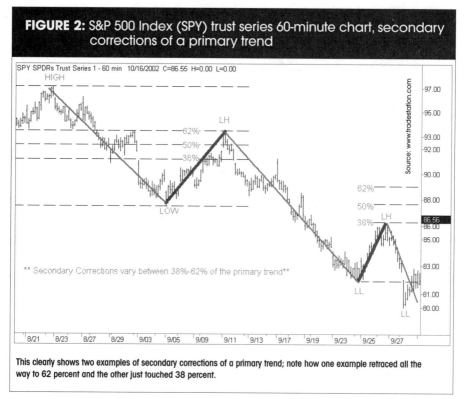

FIGURE 2: S&P 500 Index (SPY) trust series 60-minute chart, secondary corrections of a primary trend

This clearly shows two examples of secondary corrections of a primary trend; note how one example retraced all the way to 62 percent and the other just touched 38 percent.

When each intermediate rally (advance in price) rises above the high of the prior rally (higher highs), and each correction down or secondary reaction stops above the low of the previous correction and price reverses back up (higher lows), the primary trend is up. This is bullish.

When each intermediate decline (decrease in price) takes prices below the low of the previous decline (lower lows), and each rally or secondary reaction stops below the high of the previous rally and price reverses back down (lower highs), the primary trend is down. This is bearish. *Figure 1* shows this very clearly.

The original theory refers to the primary trend on a very large time frame, but today traders can and do utilize multiple time frame analyses to qualify a primary trend. For example, a primary trend could be on a daily chart, with the secondary trend on a 60-minute chart. Or a primary trend could be a 60-minute chart, with the secondary trend on a 15-minute chart. There is ample flexibility to determine a trend using multiple timeframe chart analyses.

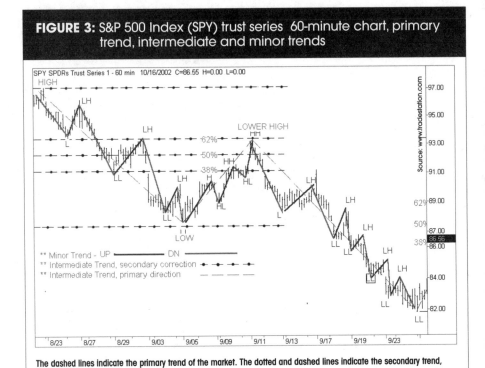

FIGURE 3: S&P 500 Index (SPY) trust series 60-minute chart, primary trend, intermediate and minor trends

The dashed lines indicate the primary trend of the market. The dotted and dashed lines indicate the secondary trend, which is considered a corrective price retracement within the primary trend. The solid lines indicate minor trends, which are typically a series of shorter-term waves that occur within both the primary and secondary trends. See *Figure 4* for a 15-minute timeframe example detailing a segment from this chart.

Secondary trends are significant reactions that disrupt the development of the primary direction. These reactions are the declines in a bullish trend and rallies in a bearish trend, also known as retracements.

An intermediate trend is also considered a smaller segment of the primary trend. For example, if you break down a primary trend into two components, each of those intermediate-term segments—whether primary or secondary in direction—is an intermediate trend.

Typically, the retracement levels for these secondary trends are a minimum of 38 percent to a maximum of 62 percent, and many times they stop at around 50 percent. These retracement levels are just probabilities because, for instance, there are times in which prices never reach the 38-percent level and also times in which prices correct more than 62 percent.

Very simply, minor or short-term trends are a series of three or more distinguishable short-term waves that make up an intermediate swing, within either the primary or the secondary trend.

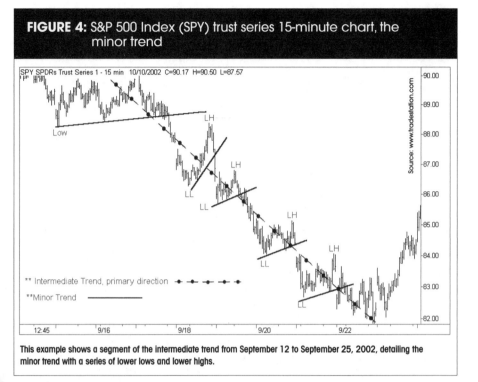

FIGURE 4: S&P 500 Index (SPY) trust series 15-minute chart, the minor trend

This example shows a segment of the intermediate trend from September 12 to September 25, 2002, detailing the minor trend with a series of lower lows and lower highs.

Figure 3 shows that minor trends within the direction of the primary trend have lower lows and lower highs and, conversely, that minor trends within the secondary trend have higher highs and higher lows.

A trader would generally assume that a minor trend rally within the scope of a down primary trend would have a high probability of failing and continuing lower and, thus, minor trend retracements in the secondary trend would have a high probability of failing and continuing higher.

A trader must also be aware of the primary trend when trading the minor trends. Also in *Figure 3,* one can see that trading minor waves in the direction of the secondary trend holds a greater risk as the primary trend can resume at any time.

Dow Theory Compares the Ocean's Tide to the Market's Trend

The tide, the wave, and the ripple represent, respectively, the primary or major, the secondary or intermediate, and the minor trends of the market.[1]

Though this may be a bit trite, it's nonetheless apropos of market trends in their various states of importance. If we take a close look at the

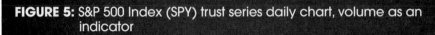

FIGURE 5: S&P 500 Index (SPY) trust series daily chart, volume as an indicator

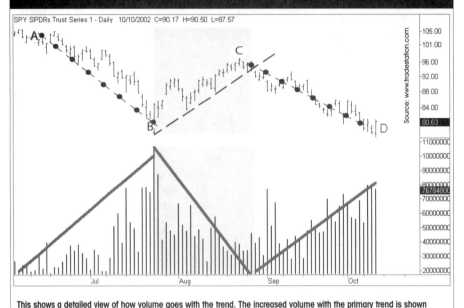

This shows a detailed view of how volume goes with the trend. The increased volume with the primary trend is shown between points A and B and between points C and D. Volume dries up on its secondary reaction (B to C).

market's primary trend, it is similar in respect to the ocean's tide. The bullish market can be compared to a rising tide, where the waves continue to push further up the beach each time the water rises until a high tide sets in. The reverse is true for a bearish market or an ebb tide, where the ocean's tide continues to recede, and each push of waves onto the beach falls short of the mark of the last preceding wave.

The intermediate or secondary trend is compared to waves. Each wave is an intermediate trend, either primary or secondary depending on whether its movement is with or against the direction of the tide. And, finally, a minor trend, the shortest type of trend, can be likened to the surface water being constantly agitated by wavelets, ripples, and cat paws moving with or against or across the trend of the waves.

> *Like a carpenter who uses blueprints and a wide assortment of tools to properly build a house, a trader also needs the proper tools to do his job correctly. A trader uses these tools to determine recognizable chart patterns and spot trends across multiple time frames as short as a one-minute chart or as long a weekly chart.*[2]

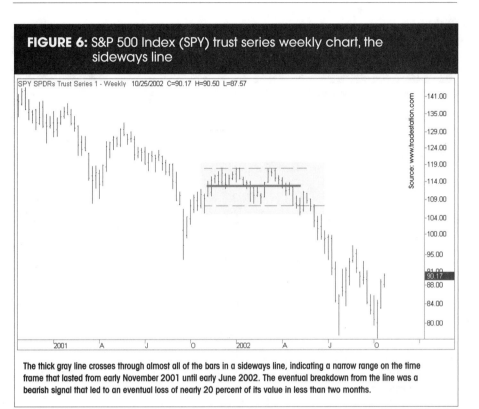

FIGURE 6: S&P 500 Index (SPY) trust series weekly chart, the sideways line

The thick gray line crosses through almost all of the bars in a sideways line, indicating a narrow range on the time frame that lasted from early November 2001 until early June 2002. The eventual breakdown from the line was a bearish signal that led to an eventual loss of nearly 20 percent of its value in less than two months.

Pivot highs and pivot lows are important chart points. The time frame will determine that chart's pivot high or low. Twenty-day highs and lows are considered important chart points, as well as weekly highs and lows for showing major chart point support and resistance levels. A basic example is shown in *Figure 1*, in which each high or higher high and low or lower low are pivot highs and lows.

Regarding retracement levels, today's charting program trend line tools allow the trader to plot support and resistance—these are 38-50-62-percent lines plotted on the chart from significant highs and lows. (*Figure 2* shows the use of these retracement levels.)

Patterns, Volume, and Confirmation

The trader's toolbox includes a good variety of tools that can be used in combination or individually. Some are used more than others. Dow theory considers trading volume and its relationship to price, indexes, and their relationship to each other, reversal and confirmation patterns,

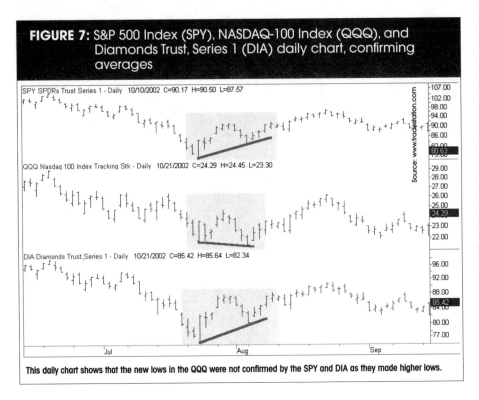

FIGURE 7: S&P 500 Index (SPY), NASDAQ-100 Index (QQQ), and Diamonds Trust, Series 1 (DIA) daily chart, confirming averages

This daily chart shows that the new lows in the QQQ were not confirmed by the SPY and DIA as they made higher lows.

and chart patterns to help analyze the trend. In later charts, we'll put all of these tools into play, but initially, let's take the four of them one at a time.

Volume goes with the trend,[3]

Trading volume is one of the best tools to help confirm a trend, but also is one of more misunderstood areas of technical analysis. In a bullish-trending market, as prices rise, volume increases to confirm the advance in prices for the direction of the primary trend. The reverse is true for a bearish-trending market. As prices decline, volume will rise to confirm the bearish trend. In a secondary correction of a bullish trend, prices decline against the primary trend and volume typically dries up. In a bearish trend, secondary recoveries or rallies in price will see the same decrease in volume. (*Figure 5* shows this very vividly.)

Lines may substitute for secondaries[4]

24

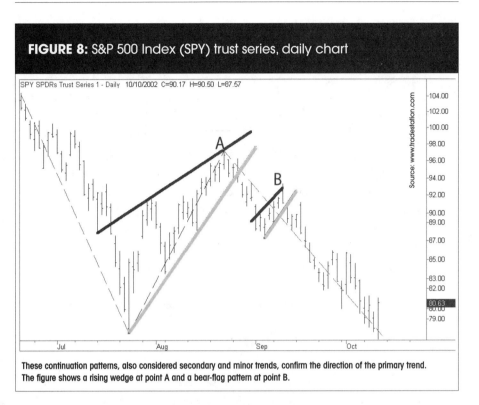

FIGURE 8: S&P 500 Index (SPY) trust series, daily chart

SPY SPDRs Trust Series 1 - Daily 10/10/2002 C=90.17 H=90.50 L=87.57

Source: www.tradestation.com

These continuation patterns, also considered secondary and minor trends, confirm the direction of the primary trend. The figure shows a rising wedge at point A and a bear-flag pattern at point B.

A line in terms of the Dow theory is considered a sideways movement in which prices trend in a narrow range for an extended period of time. For instance, a daily chart may trend sideways in a line from as little as two weeks to as much as three months. If using a shorter-term time frame, a 15-minute chart, for example, the time frame of the line would be hours sideways in a narrow range. The longer and narrower the line is, the greater the possibility for a more substantial breakout. Lines may occur at tops or bottoms, but typically they take place during consolidation areas in the progress of an established primary trend. A line may form in lieu of a normal secondary reaction. One average, the NASDAQ, for example, may form a line, while the S&P has a normal secondary reaction. A breakout up through the line is bullish, and a break down though the line is bearish. It's hard to predict in most cases the direction of the breakout of the line in advance *(see Figure 6)*.

The two averages must confirm[5]

The Dow Average

Most suppose that Charles Dow, who posthumously was credited as the inventor of the Dow theory, was either a financier or a high-powered corporate executive. In fact, he was neither, confining his business talents to anonymous journalism in the Wall Street Journal and a way to make sense of a confusing market.

In 1884, he began his "stock average" with a dozen stocks, mostly railroads, since the iron horses were the sturdy leaders of the day. By 1896, he had introduced the industrial average as well. His theory, which really was seated in the fundamental school, was that if industrial stocks were headed upward, investors must have seen the potential. Likewise, if the railroad stocks were rising, the potential for them was good, too. And, the two were linked, he reasoned, because the railroads were in the business of transporting products of industry. Pretty simple stuff, actually.

Over the years, of course, the average has changed dramatically just as railways have given way to airplanes. The number of components included in the average has increased from 12 to 20 to 30 as the U.S. economy has expanded. Further, the Dow's focus has shifted from agricultural products and basic materials such as coal, iron, lead, rubber, and leather to technology companies, financial services providers, manufacturers, and retailers. And while some question the composition of the unweighted Dow as not being broad enough to be representative of the market, it does indeed represent each important sector in the stock market.

Had Dow lived a longer life, he might have been surprised to see that his namesake today includes no transportation issues.

This theory was based upon the primary industrial average and the railroad average around the turn of the century. The present day primary indexes, the Dow, S&P, and NASDAQ, are used in terms of confirmation and non-confirmation of the primary trend. Confirmation would be the three indexes all making new highs or lows together. Non-confirmation would be one index not confirming the other two. For example, the Dow and the NASDAQ make new highs and S&P does not. Non-confirmation of indexes is also called a price divergence *(see Figure 7)*.

Then there are the continuation and reversal patterns. *A trend should be assumed to continue in effect until such time as its reversal has been definitely signaled*,[6] is perhaps one of the most important lynchpins in the entire Dow theory. Many a trader has heard the term, "the trend is your friend" or "don't buck the trend." Therefore, a trend with momentum has a greater probability of continuing, as opposed to failing and revers-

FIGURE 9: S&P 500 Index (SPY) trust series 60-minute chart, head & shoulders

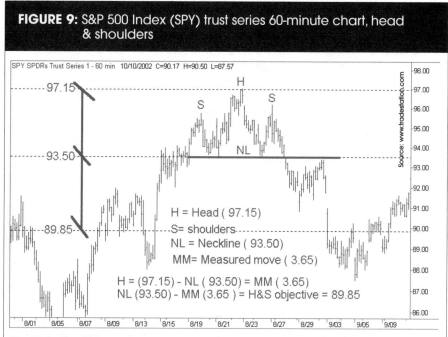

A head & shoulders (H&S) pattern is a reversal pattern and can be used for both tops and bottoms of a trend. H&S patterns forecast a measured move, for a topping pattern, using the high of the head (in this case 97.15), subtracting the value of the neckline (93.50), with the resulting number, in this case, 3.65. Subtracting that number from the neckline will give a measured move objective; in this case, it is 89.85.

ing sharply. Some examples of continuation patterns are bull flags, bear flags, bull pennants, bear pennants, and rising and falling wedges. Some examples of reversal patterns are broadening, head and shoulders, and double tops and bottoms. (See *Figure 8* for a continuation pattern and *Figure 9* for a reversal pattern.)

The Dow Theory at Work

The following charts will show how the trader could improve his market timing using the concepts we have discussed.

By combining a few tools, such as a retracement zone of 38 to 62 percent, volume, a bearish chart pattern, and a shorter-term reversal pattern, the trader will have an easier time of effectively timing the market turning points with increased accuracy, or it will allow him to enter into the direction of the trend properly once the market turns in favor of the primary trend again.

In *Figure 11*, letters A though C illustrate chart points from which the chart reader can take away a wealth of information.

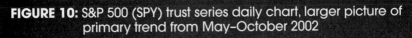

FIGURE 10: S&P 500 (SPY) trust series daily chart, larger picture of primary trend from May–October 2002

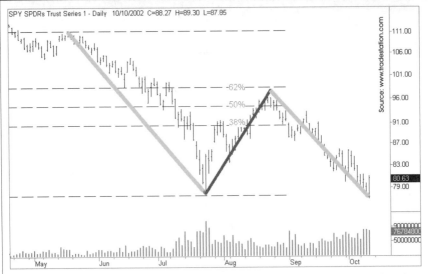

The larger-term primary trend from May 2002 into October 2002. The gray lines indicate that the primary trend was down, and the black line indicates that the secondary trend was up. *Figures 11* and *12* illustrate more detailed views of this chart.

A reference to each chart point with the notes below give a detailed breakdown, based on the tenets of the Dow theory.

A few notes on *Figure 11*:

• A to B is a secondary correction against the primary trend; B to C is an intermediate trend in the direction of the primary trend.

• A is an important pivot low; leading to that low, there was increased volume that confirms the primary trend, and the price low also had the highest volume day in months.

• At B the market retraces up to around the 50-percent retracement level of its previous secondary trend high.

• A to B shows a rising wedge pattern (from *Figure 8* and *Figure 11*), and the highlighted area B is a head and shoulders topping pattern on a 60-minute chart (from *Figures 9* and *12*).

• C shows the retest of the pivot low, support from A.

• D shows that volume increased into pivot low A and subsequently dried up as prices rose into B, and again increased as prices tested into C.

• H-1 shows a segment of the primary trend, as originally detailed in *Figures 1, 2,* and *3*.

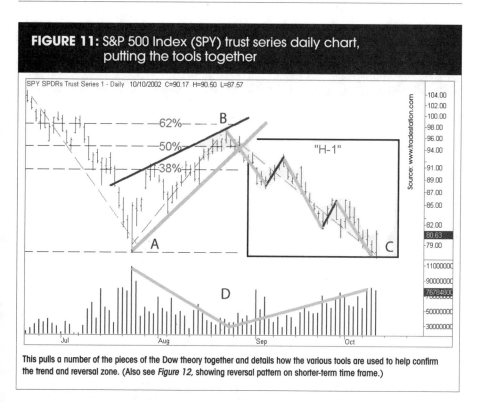

FIGURE 11: S&P 500 Index (SPY) trust series daily chart, putting the tools together

SPY SPDRs Trust Series 1 - Daily   10/10/2002 C=90.17 H=90.50 L=87.57

This pulls a number of the pieces of the Dow theory together and details how the various tools are used to help confirm the trend and reversal zone. (Also see *Figure 12*, showing reversal pattern on shorter-term time frame.)

It would be a massive undertaking to give a chart example and an explanation for each and every rule of the Dow theory. My intention, though an abbreviated one, was simply to give an overview of the Dow theory and to educate the reader on its basic concepts, as well as to give various examples of some of these rules and show how they can be applied in multiple time frames. In essence, these principles should assist traders in their chart analysis. Credit for the analysis of these time-tested technical principles is given to *Technical Analysis of Stock Trends*, 7th Edition, by Robert Edwards and John Magee (Amacom Books, 1997), a book that outlines the Dow theory. These concepts serve for the basis of my trading and for the trading of countless others.

Before applying any of these concepts and risking trading capital, readers must have a full understanding of the tools they are using, the timeframe or frames involved and a feel for market conditions. Armed with that knowledge, they should have a considerably easier time making sense of their charts and what those might portend.

FIGURE 12: S&P 500 Index (SPY) trust series 60-minute chart, head & shoulders pattern (from Figure 9) combined with larger-term chart pattern and rising wedge (from Figure 8).

This shows a head & shoulders topping pattern, a reversal pattern on a shorter-term 60-minute chart. Combine this with a rising wedge (bearish) on a larger-time frame—i.e., daily—and see how the two time frames and patterns mesh to give traders some market direction.

Christopher Terry is a full-time professional trader in both the index futures and equities markets. He speaks regularly at derivative conferences and has written many trading articles for publication. Terry has traveled extensively and spoken on the psychological approach to achieving success, recently focusing on technical analysis and trading methodologies. In addition to trading, Mr. Terry and his partner, New Market Wizard Linda Bradford Raschke, provide free educational information for both stock and futures traders at www.lbrgroup.com. This article originally appeared in *SFO* in December 2002.

1, Technical Analysis of Stock Trends, 7th Edition, by Robert Edwards and John Magee (Amacom Books, 1997).
2. Ibid., 3. Ibid., 4. Ibid., 5. Ibid., 6. Ibid.

TECHNICAL ANALYSIS THROUGH TIME

BY KIRA MCCAFFREY BRECHT & MICHAEL KAHN

There's a bullish divergence on momentum readings. The tick
indicator hit an extreme. The stock broke out of a sideways trading
range. These days, technical analysis of stocks and commodities
is commonplace and in widespread usage. In fact, most active traders rely on technical tools to aid them in their buying and selling.
For many intraday or day traders, fundamental news is almost of
no consequence.

But, today's widespread acceptance of technical analysis wasn't
always the case.

In fact, many of the top technicians on Wall Street today remember the late '60s and '70s, days when chartists were shunted off in
back rooms, and clients weren't told that buy and sell recommendations were emanating from the charts. While fundamentals were
considered king, a group of young technicians banded together to
form the Market Technician's Association (MTA), which promoted
education of technical analysis throughout the industry and may
well have helped technical analysis come out of the closet. "There is
no question in my mind that technical analysis would not be where
it is today without the MTA," says John Brooks, a founding member
and current vice president at The Lowry's Report, which has offered
a daily market comment since 1938.

The Chartered Market Technician Exams

The CMT exams are given twice a year at hundreds of locations around the world. The CMT designation is earned in three stages:

Level 1: Definition

The CMT level 1 exam measures basic, entry-level competence and understanding on the part of the candidate. Candidates need to have a working knowledge of the basic tools of the technical analyst.

Level 2: Application

The CMT level 2 exam requires the candidate to demonstrate a greater depth of competency in a variety of fields of expertise. Candidates are expected to demonstrate proficiency in applying more advanced analytical techniques.

Level 3: Integration

For CMT level 3, the candidate may choose to take an exam or write a research paper. The exam tests the candidate on the formation of well-thought-out research opinions, portfolio strategies or trading decisions based on a wide range of charts and technical data. Candidates who choose to write a research paper are expected to demonstrate a sound mastery of research techniques as applied to the practice of technical analysis. The conclusions reached should extend the body of knowledge in the field of technical analysis.

Astrology or Chart Reading?

Forty years ago, "technical analysis or the reading of charts on stocks was looked upon as a form of astrology and tea leaf reading," comments Alan Shaw, managing director at Smith Barney, a division of Citigroup, and a forty-five-year veteran of the business. Shaw remembers making his rounds to meet with portfolio managers to offer his technical views, and "they realized we weren't charlatans. I'd say 'See, I didn't come in here on a broom or with a pointed hat.'" Brooks, a forty-year veteran of the business, agrees that, in the early days of his career, technicians had a tough road to hoe. He called the environment for technical analysis "hostile," adding "nobody wanted to admit they had technical analysts at their shops."

Shaw and other long-time technicians point out that technical analysis has been practiced in the U.S. since the late 1800s—actually before fundamental analysis took hold as a mainstream discipline. "Fundamental analysis in those days was income statements and balance sheets. If they were available, they weren't necessarily reliable," Shaw notes. But, price—

the foundation for technical analysis—was, of course, always available. "In price there is knowledge," Shaw says.

In the late 1960s, fundamentals dominated Wall Street, and the New York Society of Security Analysts was the group. "That was the bastion of fundamentalists, and that is where corporate America met Wall Street," reflects Ralph Acampora, Jr., charter member of the MTA and current managing director at Prudential Securities. "To get a ticket to that luncheon was the biggest thing in the world—it was very exciting. But, what were they doing for technicians? Nothing. I bumped into Brooksie [John Brooks] and said, 'Why don't we meet?'" Once the MTA officially formed in 1973, "it gave technicians a place to gather and talk about indicators and what was going on in their shops," says Brooks. Total membership in the MTA today numbers more than 2,000 members and affiliate members.

However, Brooks recalls early resistance to the formation of a society of technical analysts, which he blames on the dubious reputation of "Tip and Clip" clubs, popular in the 1940s and 1950s. "Somebody would host a lunch for other technicians—some independent stock broker, a con artist type, and he would say, 'It looks like IBM is going to break out and go substantially higher.' Basically, he'd generate buying at the lunch, and then he'd go back to his office and sell into the buying. There was a big scandal about this on Wall Street in the early '50s," Brooks remembers. "So when Ralph and I started making phone calls to people thirty years our senior, we were just considered pains in the neck. They didn't want a technical group that just got together to talk about what the next hot idea was."

Perhaps because of those Tip and Clip clubs, early MTA members focused on education as the foremost purpose of the organization. "People would come in and show an indicator and we would discuss it," Brooks says. Back in the days without computers to crunch numbers everything was done in pencil. "People would come in and share real research." Some of the early indicators that charter MTA members would study and discuss were the advance/decline line, new high/new low list, short interest [short interest is simply the total number of shares of a stock that have been sold short and not yet covered], and interest rates.

Pros and Cons of Screens

Don't forget, in those days, if one wanted to see the moving average or overbought/oversold oscillators, there simply were no computers to generate the information. Traders and analysts calculated the numbers

The MTA...It Worked For Me

After cutting my teeth in the futures markets for several years, working on the Chicago Board of Trade bond floor in the early 1990s, I moved into an analytical position at the Chicago office of a financial markets advisory firm. While I was well versed on the bond market's reaction to the monthly employment report and just about any other economic news, charts and technical analysis were all Greek to me.

Of course, I had seen many floor traders studying their daily charts and had even read a book on Japanese candlesticks, upon the recommendation of a friend. But, I was still a fundamentalist by and large. I was on top of those daily bits of economic news and every rumor and joke that would drive T-bond prices up and down several ticks during the slow times of the trading day.

At my new job, my boss handed me John Murphy's book, *Technical Analysis of the Futures Market*, rev. ed. (New York Institute of Finance, 1999), and said, "Learn this." I dutifully read the book and several days later told him I was done. He said, "No, you really need to learn this." So, I embarked on a several-year journey studying technical analysis. And, now I do know it. A great help to me in this process was the Market Technician's Association (MTA)'s CMT exams. I joined as an affiliate member and started studying. After my first year, I took and passed Level I of the CMT and, after the second year, launched into and passed Level II. (I never did Level III—back in those days you had to write an original research paper and I ummm....just never got around to that.).

But, the actual process of studying for the exams helped me master many areas of technical analysis. I found the process to be invaluable and would recommend this course of study to any beginning trader interested in learning more about technical analysis. Simply having to study for a test forces one to cover both the basics and more advanced aspects of technical analysis. Also, for traders who are interested in camaraderie, the MTA offers monthly get-togethers in many cities. For those traders who work for themselves at home, just getting out to meet with other traders and analysts and converse about indicators and markets can be a welcome opportunity.

So...it's been a while since you've taken a test. Aww....you can do it. And, the knowledge that you gain will be well worth the studying.

—Kira McCaffrey Brecht

manually and etched daily bar charts by hand. Some technicians have suggested that while today's technology has allowed for traders to monitor a much wider variety of markets and indicators, something is lost via the computer screen. In the late '60s, "a good technician could walk around with six hundred chart patterns in his head—because they were doing them by hand," says Brooks. He remembers in his first job, he had to manually post daily updates to four thousand point-and-figure stock charts before the open.

"A lot of what we did was read the charts in a human way. It was interpretative and subjective, and that was the art," says Smith Barney's Shaw.

Manually updating a chart by hand allows one "to get know exactly what the market was doing. You really get into the rhythm of the chart pattern. You lose that familiarity of the chart just by looking at it (on the computer), as opposed to building it yourself," Brooks adds.

There are huge upsides to the advances in technology, of course. "The computer has allowed us to think about the craft of technical analysis in a more quantitative and scientific way," says Shaw. "Now you can optimize and backtest to find, for example, the profitable moving average point."

"Technology has allowed us to see more things. I can flip a chart of Zimbabwe, corn, lead, and bonds, if I want," volunteers Brooks. Back then, technical analysts had to go to the federal government to get a chart on corn. There probably were some traders at the Chicago Board of Trade keeping corn charts by hand, but who knew how to find them? Nowadays, technology allows the techs to do more inter-market connections. "But," adds Brooks, "you do lose the personal touch of knowing which way the market will be going because of the four thousand charts that you just did that morning."

Despite technology, chartists at Smith Barney in New York, even today, do some of their work by hand. Shaw notes the chart room at the firm boasts a chart fifty feet long and nine feet tall. While the data for the myriad indicators charted, including volume, VIX, the advance/decline line, and tick and the arms index (TRIN)[1], are all generated via computer, analysts plot this data daily onto the giant charts on the wall. On the weekly wall, Shaw notes there is forty years of market history on display. The charts are arranged on sliding panels to allow for a daily, weekly, and monthly chart. "When you step ten feet back from the wall, you see a lot repetition of certain patterns throughout the years," Shaw notes. He points to Smith Barney as having the best chart room on the sell side, but says Fidelity in Boston boasts the best chart room on the buy side of the business.

Technical Resources

In 1975, the MTA started the first library of its kind in the world, housing strictly books on technical analysis. However, because the former offices of the MTA were on the forty-fourth floor of the World Trade Center, priceless photos of master technicians and the entire MTA library were lost on September 11. Fortunately, the staff in the office at the time of the attacks all were able to safely evacuate down the stairs. Due to the generosity of publishers and members of the MTA, the library reopened in Woodbridge, New Jersey, and some books are also available in the Broadway Avenue MTA office in Manhattan.

For those beginning traders interested in becoming more competent in the field of technical analysis, the MTA offers a three-year exam, which culminates in the Chartered Market Technician (CMT) designation, first awarded in 1989. The CMT is the most widely accepted certification of competency in technical analysis and has become a standard for excellence among market professionals. Through studying for the exam, technicians and traders gain proficiency in the field.

Taking the MTA's core mission of education to the next level, in 1993 the MTA Educational Foundation was formed to sponsor and promote the for-credit teaching of technical analysis at the university level. The foundation developed a series of lectures and took them on the road to universities and colleges, with an offer to teach a class on technical analysis in their respective schools of finance. These efforts have paid off, and there now are for-credit courses being taught in dozens of schools across the country.

Also each year, the MTA, along with Dow Jones newswires and Barron's, sponsors the Charles H. Dow Award for excellence in technical analysis. Technicians are invited to submit papers on work that breaks new ground in the field or makes innovative use of established techniques, in the spirit of the pioneering market technician, Charles H. Dow.

Todd Campbell, president of EB Capital Markets, LLC, joined the MTA to help market his firm and discovered technical analysis gurus and disciples who were willing to educate and be educated. "Frankly," says Campbell, "the MTA is the information superhighway of technical analysis. I think the greatest enemy of profits is the unwillingness to learn and evolve, and the MTA provides, quite simply, the best landscape for becoming a better trader and investor."

Affiliate membership in the MTA is open to anyone with an interest in technical analysis. But, in order to achieve full member status, individuals also must demonstrate professional standing in the financial community. While most of these members and affiliates are located in the U.S., fifty-six countries are represented. Members and affiliates work as technical analysts, portfolio managers, traders, investment advisors, and market letter writers across all asset classes and derivatives. For more information, please visit www.mta.org where you can read about the various committees, the CMT program, and meetings.

Kira McCaffrey Brecht is senior editor at *SFO magazine*. She has been writing about the financial markets for sixteen years. Posts during her career include Chicago bureau chief at Futures World News, market analyst at Bridge News, and technical analyst at MMS International. She has passed Level I and Level II of the MTA's MCT exams. McCaffrey Brecht holds a degree in political science from Brown University.

Michael Kahn is a well respected technical analyst. He writes the *Getting Technical* column for Barron's Online (www.barrons.com) and the daily *Quick Takes Pro* technical newsletter (www.Quick-TakesPro.net). Kahn is the author of two books on technical analysis, most recently *Technical Analysis Plain and Simple: Charting the Markets in Your Language* (Financial Times Prentice Hall, 2006), and was chief technical analyst for BridgeNews. He also is on the board of directors of the Market Technicians Association (www.mta.org). This article originally appeared in *SFO* in December 2003.

[1]Tick reveals the number of NYSE stocks whose most recent price change was uptick or downtick, and TRIN measures the ratio of advancing issue to declining issues divided by up volume to down volume.

SECTION TWO
Chart Construction

Years ago, dedicated chartists had to plot all their charts laboriously by hand. These days, technical traders rely on computers to generate Byzantine charts with megabytes of information in nanoseconds. However, even if you're a whiz with electronically generated charts, you'll improve your trading by learning how to draw the lines yourself.

Hand-constructed charts can give you an intrinsic feel for the trend and can make you look at price charts in a new way. Electronic charting has an inherent impermanence, with the constantly changing monitor in front of you. Drawing a chart on paper gives you a tactile connection to the graph and an easily accessible history of the trend.

This section includes information on myriad types of price charting. You'll learn the basics of constructing a simple high-low-close bar chart. You'll broaden your horizons by learning about point and figure charts (Xs and Os), which are based solely on price action. Removing time factors from the chart eliminates some of the meaningless noise of a time-based bar chart and better reflects dynamic markets and the shifting balance of supply and demand.

Steve Nison, the Western world's leading authority on candle charts, introduced candles to the West in the early 1990s, and they have quickly become one of the most widely used tools in the technical charting world. Nison and Tracy Knudsen will show you how integrating candles into your toolbox can improve your timing and preserve your capital. And using candlestick charts most effectively—combining Eastern candles with traditional Western technical tools—can help spot early market turns that can make the difference in your trading practice.

GRAB A PENCIL AND RULER:
The Case for
Hand-Constructed Charts

BY KEN SHALEEN

Conventional wisdom has shown over and over again that an investor or speculator who keeps his or her own charts by hand will have a much better feel for the market. And now that computer-plotting packages have teamed up with online quotes, the case is even more compelling for a trader to keep at least one chart by hand.

Obviously, an equity trader with a universe of two hundred-plus possible candidates for a portfolio cannot and does not want to be chained to a drafting table every afternoon. But it does make sense to isolate a stock deemed to be a bellwether of the overall market or industry and interact with this chart on a daily basis.

For example, two price points define a trend line on a chart. Whenever a legitimate trend line is placed on a chart, it should never be erased. Sure, subsequent price activity may render the trend line useless, but its presence will keep the trader aware of what could have been happening at the time. How often are lines on a computer-constructed chart kept on the screen? Typically, not very long. Therefore, by definition, the trader has no sense of history.

Futures Traders Take Note

Let's focus on the futures market, which is an especially difficult charting environment.

Futures traders have considerably more reasons than a stock chartist to keep the chart of the most active contract by hand. Here's a simple example: in the Chicago Mercantile Exchange's charting class a new student will show me a freshly printed, computer-generated, high-low-close daily futures bar chart. What do you think the response is to the following questions asked of the student?

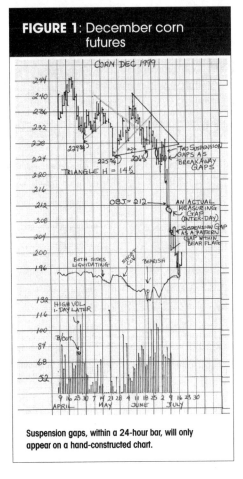

FIGURE 1: December corn futures

Suspension gaps, within a 24-hour bar, will only appear on a hand-constructed chart.

• Is the chart of electronic trading only?

• Is the chart of pit trading only (if applicable)?

• Is the chart a combination of electronic and pit trading showing the highest high and the lowest low for the (almost) 24-hour futures trading day?

• Is the volume the total of all contracts, all months, or is it just the single contract?

• Is the open interest total, or only the single contract month?

• Does electronic trading after the pit close occur? If so, at what time is the tic-mark for the close taken?

How about, "I don't know" as an answer to all of the above questions?

Conclusion: G.I.G.O.—Garbage In Garbage Out.

Know the Defaults

The answers to all of the questions posed need to be known before a trader can intelligently utilize the graphical picture presented. How many chartists will refer to the help manual for the computerized charting package? What are the default parameters the program uses?

Periodically, a futures chartist must very carefully check the contract specifications.

• Does the future have dual symbols, one for pit trading and a different symbol for electronic dealing?

• What are the specific trading hours for each venue?

• Does "side-by-side" (simultaneous electronic and open outcry) trading occur?

• Does electronic dealing continue after the pit closes?

• What time is the closing tic mark posted?

The next step is to think about what the trader wants to see and whether or not the electronic charting package can produce this output.

Ideal Daily High-Low-Close Futures Bar Chart

The ideal daily high-low-close futures bar chart would include the following three items:

• High and low price: The highest high and the lowest low for the (almost) 24-hour futures day. The assumption is that the new "day" begins with electronic dealing when the sun is moving toward the International Date Line in the middle of the Pacific Ocean. The new day begins with New Zealand, Australian and Asian dealing and ends in the Americas.

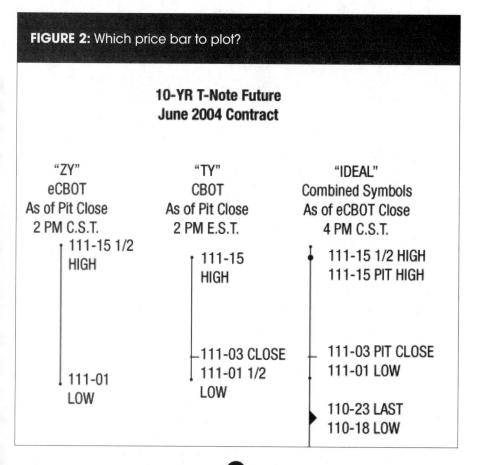

FIGURE 2: Which price bar to plot?

10-YR T-Note Future
June 2004 Contract

"ZY" eCBOT As of Pit Close 2 PM C.S.T.	"TY" CBOT As of Pit Close 2 PM E.S.T.	"IDEAL" Combined Symbols As of eCBOT Close 4 PM C.S.T.
111-15 1/2 HIGH	111-15 HIGH	111-15 1/2 HIGH 111-15 PIT HIGH
	111-03 CLOSE 111-01 1/2 LOW	111-03 PIT CLOSE 111-01 LOW
111-01 LOW		110-23 LAST 110-18 LOW

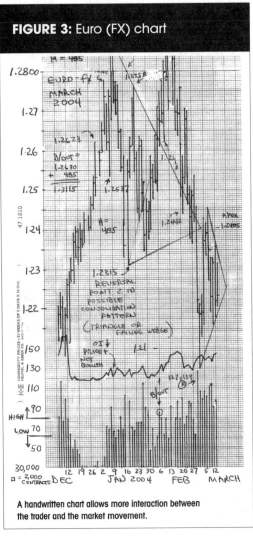

FIGURE 3: Euro (FX) chart

A handwritten chart allows more interaction between the trader and the market movement.

If the electronic and pit sessions are separated in time by a suspension of electronic dealing and then a resumption of pit trading, the possibility exists that a suspension gap will occur in between the two sessions. Ideally this gap would be visible within the daily bar. A good example of this exists with the Chicago Board of Trade's grain futures, where a fundamental report is released in the time period between the two trading sessions. *Figure 1*, a December corn futures chart, shows how a technical trader can identify the suspension gaps within the daily bar on a hand-constructed chart.

• Closing tic mark: The clearing house for the two large futures exchanges in Chicago uses the pit close as the price that clears the market for margin purposes. If electronic dealing continues after the traditional close, it would be instructive to have another tic mark indicating where the market was trading at the end of the entire "day." Constructing a chart by hand allows this functionality without much difficulty. Try to program the computer to post two closes. *Figure 2* shows how two closes could be placed on a chart.

• Volume and open interest: Total volume, including all contracts and all months, should be plotted. The same is true for total open interest. This allows the general rule for a healthy price trend on a futures chart to be used. Volume and open interest should increase as prices move in the direction of the major price trend. *Figures 1* and *3* both contain a plot of total volume and total open interest.

The Euro (FX) chart in *Figure 3* is an example of how a trader interacts with the chart. Note the following:

• All trend lines are drawn with a hard pencil;
• Important prices, especially support and resistance levels, are written on the chart;
• Vertical heights of the price patterns are noted;
• The calculation of the measuring objective is hand written on the chart;
• High and low volume parameters are drawn (in pencil) at the left margin;
• Extremely high (blow-off) volume is noted;
• Volume on a price breakout is circled; and
• The open interest scale is functional—meaning day-to-day changes can be seen.

The Chicago Mercantile Exchange clearing house realizes that quote vendors are wrestling with the problem of disseminating data in a fashion that lends itself to the chartist's organizational needs. Although there are no plans to change the current convention, the electronic marketplace is evolving. Until the computer programmers are told what to do, the best computer is the brain of the chartist.

Ken Shaleen has been teaching technical analysis for the Chicago Mercantile Exchange since 1974. The students are still required to submit a hand-constructed chart in lieu of a final exam. Shaleen is the founder of Chartwatch (www.chartwatch.com), a company that produces weekly technical research reports and daily telephone market updates covering selected financial instruments and grain futures. He is the author of technical analysis classics *Volume and Open Interest* (Probus, 1991, 1997) and *Technical Analysis and Options Strategies* (Probus, 1992). This article originally appeared in *SFO* in August 2004.

GETTING A FEEL FOR YOUR CHARTS

BY PHILIP GOTTHELF

Gone are the days when chartists bonded with their hand-drawn charts. Today, your time frame, vertical axis, and screen size, among other factors, offer challenges to electronic charting.

Most traders are familiar with two predictive approaches. Traditionally, price potential is measured through supply and demand relationships. In the case of equities, circumstances that determine supply and demand can be extremely complex. As a brief example, college texts reference such things as products or services, product maturity, product position, financial structure, price-to-earnings ratios, leadership, number of shares outstanding, competition, location, and a host of other fundamental conditions that can influence the stock's desirability. For real estate, price-determining factors begin with location and include interest rates, economic activity, local real estate taxes, schools, public services, land use, public facilities, and other fundamental considerations. Commodity markets revolve around production, consumption, and fundamental influences that may include natural effects like weather or man-made circumstances like politics and regulations.

From the investment perspective, supply relates to the particular investment vehicle rather than operational elements. In other words, equity supplies deal with the fixed number of shares authorized for each company rather than the supply of a particular company's products or services. In real estate, we focus upon land availability and zoning. Commodity markets experience changes in the commitments between buyers and sellers, called open interest. Debt securities flow from government or corporate borrowing. In each case, the investment vehicle is one step removed from the underlying entity. For example, stock certificates represent ownership, but have little to do with corporate products or services. A commodity contract calls for delivery of an underlying commodity without regard for the actual supply of that commodity.

This initial understanding is important because it forms the basis for using fundamental or technical analysis. Since the advent of inexpensive computing power, research has been conducted to distinguish between analysis of the investment vehicle and the fundamental vehicle. This is most apparent when we see that a corporation can release profitable earnings results while the associated stock can plunge. Why? Because earnings might not be as anticipated.

This disassociation between reality and perception has fostered new respect for a once-taboo approach: technical analysis. Rather than evaluate intricate details of corporate performance, technicians concentrate on the frenzy to buy or sell stock. Thus, it is the demand for certificates relative to the shares issued that determines price direction. For commodities, it is the same. It is not how much wheat farmers plant, it is how much wheat we think we will have at some point in the future when delivery takes place.

To determine who wants what and when, investors increasingly have relied upon charts. Interestingly, the art or science of charting has become another function of computer technology, rather than its traditional magic of human interpretation. In the old days, charts were drawn by hand. This created an historical intimacy between chart and chartist. There was a feel for a market derived from familiarity with historical price behavior. Equally important, virtually every chartist bought his or her paper from Keuffel & Esser (K&E), a Morristown, New Jersey, company dealing in standard 11 x 16 1/2-inch, ten-point and eight-point grids. There were other papers, but K&E was the standard.

Consistency and Distortion

So, technical analysis was integrally linked to subjective intuition, coupled with a common media. At the very least, patterns and formations looked the same because they shared the same universal scale established by K&E chart paper. But, technology marched forward.

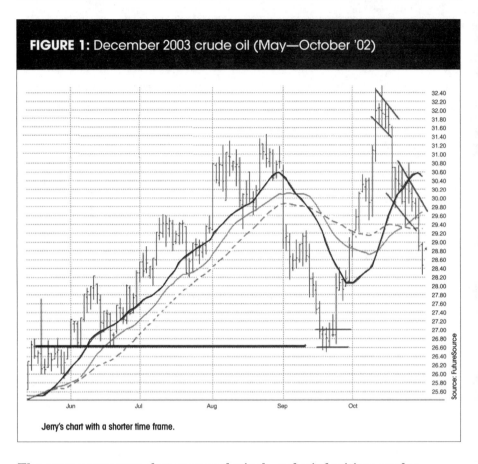

FIGURE 1: December 2003 crude oil (May—October '02)

Source: FutureSource

Jerry's chart with a shorter time frame.

The very computers that gave technical analysis legitimacy also distorted the standard. Virtually every quote system and analytical product available on today's computers can configure charts and technical studies. Alas, subscribers to these services are a diversified bunch with everything from 10-inch micro laptop screens to giant 61-inch plasma displays.

With this diversity comes flexibility. With flexibility comes the question, "When is a chart not a chart?" The answer might be, "When it's electronic." Some readers may already sympathetically or empathetically know what this means. Harry sits across from Jerry and yells, "Did you see that bearish flag in December crude?" Jerry replies, "What flag?" Harry retorts, "Are we lookin' at the same chart?" Alas, they are not.

Figure 1 and *Figure 2* are both December crude oil for 2003, but the scales and time frames are different. Consolidations appear flat on the wide view and more pronounced in the more condensed version. Thus,

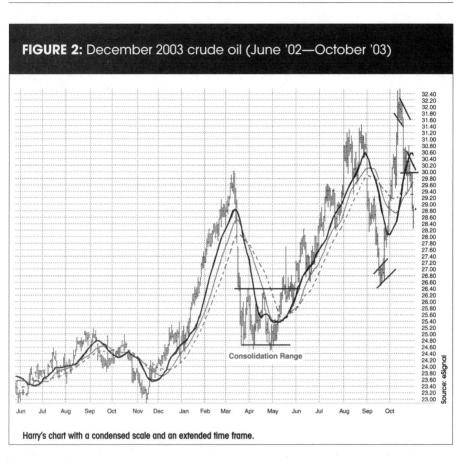

FIGURE 2: December 2003 crude oil (June '02—October '03)

Consolidation Range

Source: eSignal

Harry's chart with a condensed scale and an extended time frame.

Harry and Jerry may see different formations and draw different conclusions. Assuming Harry is looking at the more condensed scale and extended timeframe, he has access to the consolidation trading range for a reference. He may interpret the September upward flag as a continuation pattern that anticipates a further dip (continuation) to test the March through June consolidation range.

Jerry is not influenced by that consolidation because it is not on his chart. Further, he sees a flat consolidation in September, from which an upside breakout occurs. He sees this as a test of the support or resistance seen in December and January from which a new high is projected. Jerry is right, and Harry is wrong. Yet this is with the benefit of hindsight.

In the Eye of the Beholder

This drawback to electronic display has become particularly apparent during presentations at events like investment trade shows.

Charts are projected onto large screens as various experts attempt to educate knowledge-thirsty attendees in the ways of sophisticated chart analysis. Interestingly, when enthusiastic listeners go back to some of the selling booths, the presentations are reformatted to accommodate 15-inch computer screens. The large-scale definition becomes diminished along with the ability to duplicate prior pattern recognition.

No doubt, many charting advocates will take exception to the argument that electronic formatting can and will impinge upon proper chart analysis. The question already has been tested among chartists who debate the efficacy of using anything but an approved scale. In other words, don't dilute the image with an unrealistic format. Anything less than six months for reference is invalid.

Indeed, the ease of electronic formatting should carry a discipline. However, there are no proven standards for establishing how charts should be displayed. We must accept the fact that computer screens have different capacities, resolutions, and configurations. When combined with software, the combinations and permutations for the same chart can seem unlimited.

Chart Analysis

This is not to cast aspersions on the use of electronic charts. For example, the following chart analysis (see *Figure 3*) was conducted contemporaneously.

It appeared in my book, *Currency Trading: How to Access and Trade the World's Biggest Market* (John Wiley & Sons, 2002). With almost surgical precision, each chart-based forecast fell into place. The scale seemed just right. The following is an excerpt from the book. Though lengthy, it makes several points that get to the crux of the situation:

Putting it all together usually requires a vast search of hundreds of charts to illustrate each unique pattern. However, Figure 3 packs most of the popular patterns into a single euro currency chart over just one year. This exceptional example of conformity enables us to take each pattern and demonstrate how it may be applied to (hopefully) work. In this particular example, the pattern recognition was actually conducted in real time without the benefit of 20/20 hindsight. The identification

FIGURE 3: Popular chart patterns (euro)

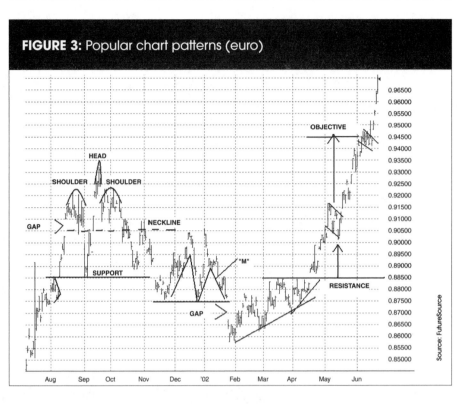

was used to advise traders who subscribed to the Commodity Futures Forecast Service during 2001 and 2002.

Moving from left to right, the first pattern in Figure 3 consists of a rapid rise culminating in a triangular consolidation. Alone, this pennant does not provide insight into the next direction. If the price had fallen below 0.87000, we would predict a setback to 0.86000 if the initial bust below the 0.87500 bottom of the consolidation did not instantly achieve the 0.86000 objective. However, there was a powerful breakout above 0.88500. Measuring the distance from 0.85000 to 0.87500, we get 150 points. A crude, but popular method of calculating an objective is to add the 150 to the top of the consolidation, which gives 0.90000.

Gaps. As we can see, prices did touch 0.90000, but extended further to a high above 0.92000. In the process, a more radical dislocation between buyers and sellers gapped prices to a new consolidation between 0.90500 and 0.92000. The rule on gaps is that they eventually fill. That is, what goes up eventually comes down, and vice versa. There are two types of gaps: breakaway and exhaustion. As the names imply, *breakaway gaps see a continuation in the direction of the gap, whereas exhaustion gaps usually have a consolidation and a retracement. Many skeptics contend that gap identification is post facto. You don't know what it is until it's been. In Figure 3, prices consolidate and decline just enough to fill the gap. Once filled, bulls can regain confidence that the price will move higher. But how high?*

Gaps are considered useful for answering this question. The term measuring gap is used to project to a new high or low. The distance traveled from the first gap is approximately 150 points. By adding this to the consolidation high, we get 0.93500 as our next upward goal. Amazingly, the next breakout above the gap achieves this lofty figure, but not before testing all the way down to 0.88500. The powerful bounce from 0.88500 signifies support that is identified by the breakout from the triangle and subsequent inability to fall below this same price level. The severity of each event also has significance. It means buyers are strongly opinionated about 0.88500 being a good parity for the euro against the dollar.

To be precise, the 0.88500 test violated an important subsequent level of 0.90500. Notice in the left consolidation labeled "shoulder" that prices touched just below 0.90500 and moved higher. We have a hint that 0.90500 also represents support. At this stage, a review of the appropriate action helps clarify the exercise.

The breakout from the August pennant results in the following decision: buy September euro currency at market using an 0.87500 stop. Move stop to entry after 0.90000 (0.88500 1 150). Raise stop to 0.90000 after 0.91500.

We see how the buying decision was generated and how we arrived at placing and moving protection. When prices fell below 0.90500, this position was stopped out with a 150-point profit from 0.88500 to 0.90000.

When prices dropped to 0.88500 and supported, there was not action. Perhaps another chartist might have identified some alternative action, but this interpretation was directionless. After supporting, however, there was a new incentive to buy. With prices jumping from 0.88500 to 0.89500, the action is: buy long December euro currency at market using an 0.88500 stop. Move stop to entry after 0.90500. Increase stop to 0.90500 after 0.92000. Raise stop to 0.92000 after 0.93500.

The rationale behind this action should be identifiable on the chart. Rather than offer a step-by-step explanation, trace the logic to see if you would have come to the same conclusions.

This resulted in another stop out at 0.92000. We see this head floating between 0.92000 and 0.93500. From there, the price gaps lower and the right shoulder fills the gap. At this point, we are not necessarily able to determine a new strategy. However, there is significance to 0.90500 as support. The appearance of two shoulders with a higher exhaustion head alerts to the possibility that 9500 is a neckline. The problem with this interpretation is the rise to the head takes place in September after already violating this alleged neckline. Thus, purists would deny the existence of a true head-and-shoulders formation. However, real-world applications find us bastardizing charting rules all the time. We bend and make exceptions because other aspects of trading action suggest such liberties. Hence, charting is far from an exact science or even a disciplined art.

The distance from the top of the head at 0.93500 to the neckline of 0.90500 is 300 points. This measures for our downside objective that is 0.90500 less 300, or 0.87500. The next downside would subtract another points to produce 0.84500. The strategy is as follows: sell short December euro currency at approximately 0.90500 using 0.91500 stop (150 points). Lower stop to entry after 0.89000 (150 points). Drop stop to 0.89500 after reaching 0.88500 former support (in case support holds and a rally follows). Take profits at 0.87500, canceling stop.

Penetration Adjustments. At this stage, we can introduce the concept of penetration adjustments. Although the term and practice may sound like an excuse for missed transaction, it is actually a widely applied technique for adjusting objectives. Generally, objectives appear to line up with the chart grid. Chart grids, by nature, divide the vertical into even numbers falling at regular intervals. This can tease the eye and mind into selecting exact grid numbers such as 0.80500. To overcome this propensity, chartists apply an adjustment for penetration. Usually, it is in the conservative direction when setting profit goals while allowing some extra leeway when setting stops. Assume the euro adjustment was five points. Instead of seeking 0.87500 exactly, we would look for 0.87550.

In our example, we would have taken our profits at 0.87550 in late November. If no adjustment was made, we would have been stopped at 0.89500 for a 100-point gain. With the adjustment, we achieved our objective.

The move above 0.88500 brings us back long with an 0.87500 stop. We move stop to entry after reaching 0.90500 (or 0.90450 with adjustment). After the market retreats, we are stopped at our entry for a breakeven plus costs. Now, the market supports at 0.87500 again. Here, we are on the sidelines waiting to see if 0.90500 offers resistance. If it does, we sell seeking 0.88500 as a first goal (former support) and 0.87500 as a second goal.

A more astute chartist might have bought on a breakout above 0.88500 (former support assumed to be new resistance) using an 0.87500 stop. The first objective to move stop to entry would have been the 0.90500 neckline that is assumed to be resistance. The result would probably have been a breakeven after the setback. However, a breakout above the neckline would have generated a handsome profit as the stop was ratcheted higher.

The January 2002 decline became a challenge of 0.87500 support. This converts 0.88500 former support into the resistance line. We have an "M" pattern that says a dip below 0.87500 will result in a drop to 50 percent of the distance from 0.90500 resistance as a first goal. Indeed, prices gapped below 0.87500 and touched below 0.86000, right on target. Unfortunately, the gap foreclosed our participation.

M Pattern and W Formation. It is worth mentioning that an "M" pattern is obviously a double top, whereas a "W" formation is a double bottom. The significance is at the extremes, that is, the tops of the M or bottoms of the W and the base of the M or height of the W. A bust below or breakout above either level is considered a continuation, with the first objective equal to 50 percent of the height of either pattern. Although the letter may not be perfectly symmetrical, the tops and bottoms should conform. Once the downside objective of 0.86000 is achieved, we wait to see the next pattern. Our new assumptions are that 0.87500 will offer resistance, the bottom of the M. This leads to a sell if 0.87500 holds and a buy if it is exceeded. The buy would have been stopped at 0.86500 for a 100-point loss. The sell would have succeeded. Which would you have *done? Try to be honest with yourself. Remember as Shakespeare said, "to thine own self be true."*

The decline below 0.87500 stops just below 0.86500 and rallies just under 0.88500 resistance. We can identify a pattern of increasing lows and highs. At the end of March, the dip to 0.87000 provides the points necessary to construct a trendline. From March through mid-April, 0.88500 resistance continues holding to form an asymmetrical triangle. Our anticipation is a breakout above resistance with the following strategy:

Buy at 0.88450/50 using 0.87000 stop. Move stop to entry after making 0.90000 (0.88500, 1150 points). Raise stop to 0.89950 (0.90000 adjusted by 5) after reaching 0.91450 (0.91500 adjusted by 5).

When we reach 0.90000, buyers and sellers have a brief argument where sellers bring the price down to 0.90000 in a downward sloping flag. This behavior reflects the anticipation of the 0.90000 and 0.91500 objectives. Some buyers (longs) who set their exit objective at 0.91500 added to selling liquidity. In the meantime, other buyers are waiting for the dip to 0.90000 to reenter, enter for the first time, or add to existing positions. It is also worth noting that the 0.90000/0.91500 range correlates with the head-and-shoulders neckline assumed to be 0.90500.

This becomes a continuation pattern as long as the 0.90000 support holds, which it did. The projection is to 0.94500 that measures the distance from 0.88590 former resistance (the breakout from the asymmetrical triangle) to 0.91500 (the top of the flagpole). Behold! The next leg higher does stop at approximately 0.94500 and we see the same type of consolidation, probably for the same reasons. The next projection is 0.97500, moving the stop up by the full objective plus 50 percent.

I have always believed that chart analysis should become part of a medical school's department of psychology curriculum. What we are doing is making predictions based on mass psychology patterns reflected in chart formations. We see areas where buyers or seller become reluctant to participate. We understand that measurements made by John could be the same as those of Mary, who is following the advice of Jane, who was talking to her husband's broker, Bob. Whatever the se-

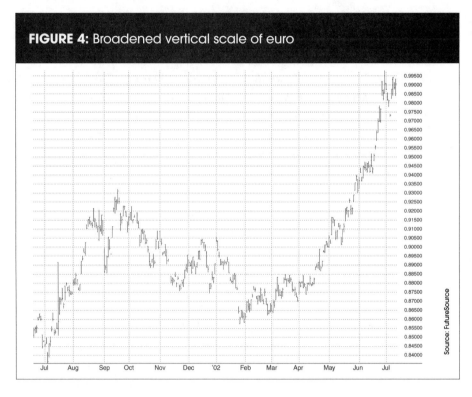

FIGURE 4: Broadened vertical scale of euro

quence that leads to the reflected behavior, we assume these formations and patterns have consistency.

Charting is as much a mental exercise as a method of trading. Talk to any chartist and you will find he or she takes as much pleasure in the exercise as in the results. This is why so many chartists who consistently lose continue their practice in the hopes that some day they will get it perfect. In the meantime, they enjoy the process.

Inconsistent Vertical Scales Skew the View

When the market in *Figure 3* was being evaluated, screen dimensions and scaling were the same. However, when we examine the same euro chart using a broadened vertical scale (see *Figure 4*), look what happens.

The data is the same, but the more refined vertical perspective condenses the height of each alleged pattern. Where is the August-October head and shoulders? Yes, the benefit of the previous chart shows us where and what to look for. Yet, an honest gaze might easily have missed several of the seemingly obvious patterns and formations annotated in the currency book example. Perhaps it was simply luck to have fallen upon the right scaling for making that remarkable string of chart interpretations and measurements.

Thus, not only is the horizontal resolution critical, but the vertical may pose an even greater threat to our pattern recognition. Try to realistically match the patterns identified in the annotated chart (*Figure 3*) with the plain chart (*Figure 4*). The difficulty should be obvious.

More an Art than a Science

The electronic dilemma stems from the requirement for subjective interpretation. What is the solution? A general rule of chart analysis is "the more the better." This means more data provides better reference points and a more accurate assessment. Although our very first example with Harry and Jerry refutes this rule, theirs was an anomaly rather than the norm.

Armed with sufficient data (represented along the horizontal axis), the vertical axis should be sufficient to reflect a minimal 12-month price range and a maximum 18-month range. Taking a continuous chart like the cash Dow Jones Industrial Index or 30-year T-bonds and moving the time scale forward and backward can demonstrate the reason for the range limitation. The more pronounced volatility experienced over the past decade or two causes the scaling to leap and contract over time because the vertical screen size is fixed.

In the old days, these leaps were tackled simply by pasting a piece of chart paper on top of or below the top and bottom borders. Some old-timers may recall how manual charts were like massive foldouts with scraps of paper protruding from multiple folds. It is frightening to think such sprawls were the basis for trading decisions!

Keep in mind that these parameters of 12 to 18 months are not fixed in stone because a techie chartist with the new Apple 17-inch-wide screen notebook is going to see a different picture with the same scaling than the trader sporting an old 12-inch screen.

Much will depend upon the individual eye for patterns and formations. So, every trader must experiment and find a scale that is right for his or her needs. Once a working format is found, of course, it's important to be consistent. Make the format a template that you can always use.

It is sufficient simply to be aware of the inconsistencies of electronic formatting to avoid the pitfalls. The potential for bogus patterns and formations is significant. Perhaps all electronic charting platforms should come with a disclaimer: "warning: charting can be hazardous to your wealth!"

Of course, electronic systems are not limited to subjective chart interpretation. There are objective parameters that can be applied to help implement proper analysis. For example, ratios like Fibonacci and Gann squares can quantify turning points on charts. Differential equations can standardize slope measurements and define trendlines. Still, the majority of chart analysis is done by eye. That is why the question, "When is a chart a chart?" is so important.

Philip Gotthelf is publisher of the COMMODEX, the longest-running daily futures trading system published anywhere, and president of EQUIDEX Inc. and EQUIDEX Brokerage Group. Known for his extensive work in the futures industry, Gotthelf's works have appeared in major industry and business publications. He is quoted regularly in *Barron's*, the *Wall Street Journal*, the *New York Times, Fortune, and Forbes*, among others. Gotthelf also has written several books, including *Currency Trading: How to Access and Trade the World's Biggest Market* (John Wiley & Sons, 2002), *The New Precious Metals Market* (McGraw-Hill, 1998), and *Techno Fundamental Trading* (Probus Press/McGraw-Hill, 1994). This article originally appeared in *SFO* in March 2004.

THE ABCs OF POINT AND FIGURE CHARTS

BY KEN TOWER

OK, let's start out making one thing clear: point and figure charts are different. How? Quite simply, they are based entirely on price activity and not at all based on time. When you think about it, this makes a lot of sense—there can be some tremendous advantages to ignoring time. But the charts look funny because there's no time on the horizontal scale, and that puts some people off. Stick with me for a few moments, and you'll learn why our country's oldest form of charting has survived into the modern era.

All Days Are Not Created Equal

You know it's true—some days are more important than others. Yet the charts on which most traders rely make it difficult to see. That's because time-based charts add a fixed amount for each period. For example, a daily chart adds the same amount of horizontal space every day. It doesn't matter whether there was a lot of news or no news, whether it was a volatile day or a dull day—the chart adds the same amount of data. That's true of all time-based charts, whether they're one-minute, daily, or monthly charts.

Point and figure charts (P&F) adapt to changing market conditions. By focusing on price action, not time, they can better reflect the shifting balance of supply and demand, which is crucial information to traders and investors. So on a day when there is a great deal of turmoil, a P&F chart will reflect that turmoil with a lot of updates, while on a dull day, there will be few, if any, updates required.

FIGURE 1: Point and figure chart

Trading activity differs from day to day. P&F charts adapt to the market's changing conditions, yielding varying amounts of data, as noted over a four-day period on this chart. Day one begins (solid gray box in the column below the number one) with prices falling sharply (most likely due to overnight news). The news created a great deal of turmoil, which is reflected in the many chart postings on that day. Day two (solid black box) is less volatile, as traders/investors react to the news, and day three (solid black box) shows volatility back to normal.

Source: CyberTrader

This responsiveness is illustrated by *Figure 1*, which follows the action of a stock over four trading days. The beginning price for each day is signified by a solid box. An X reflects upward price movement while an O reflects downward moves. Day one begins with a very long column of Os. This is almost certainly a gap down that occurred in response to disappointing news released overnight. Trading was frenetic that day as traders and investors tried to sort out the implications of the surprising news. This furious trading produces thirteen columns of data for day one.

Each column represents a period when either the buyers (a column of Xs), or sellers (a column of Os) were dominant. Postings remain in the same column until there is a shift in price action. When price action shifts from up to down or down to up, the P&F chart moves one column to the right and enters the new posting. The fluid nature of that day's market is reflected in the thirteen columns of data, each of which reflects a shift between periods when buyers dominated ("Maybe this news isn't so bad.") and sellers dominated ("This is awful—get me out of this thing!") over the course of that single day.

Day two is less volatile, with only eight columns of price action. Day three contains only two columns of data, indicating that the market had pretty well digested day one's news, and volatility had dropped back to normal levels.

On a daily bar chart, of course, each day would occupy the same amount of space. One would have to look for the gap down or a spike in volume to determine that day one was any different from days two or three. Therein lies the difference between point and figure and the others.

History of P&F

The inventor of P&F charts is unknown. Charles Dow referred to them nearly one hundred years ago in the *Wall Street Journal*, and they apparently were invented sometime around 1880. Victor de Villiers generally is credited with giving them the name "point and figure" in the 1920s when they gained popularity during the great bull market of that decade.

It is easy to see why they were popular then and why they still are popular today among traders—they offer a method of keeping track of buyers and sellers without having to post each and every trade. By tracking fixed price increments, they simplify the process of monitoring price activity.

Getting back to *Figure 1*, one can see this type of chart does more than simply track price action; it reveals what's going on inside a particular day. Sure, an intra-day chart also would show more details of trading activity than a daily chart, but again, each day would occupy the same amount of space. There would be little to highlight the turmoil that took place on day one while the P&F chart automatically adapts to changing market conditions. The adaptability of the P&F chart combines the best attributes of a daily and intra-day bar chart.

Construction Details

To understand how the P&F chart reflects the changing dynamics of the market, we need to delve a bit more into its construction. Data added to a P&F chart is commonly referred to as a posting. A posting reflects a price movement of a user-specified amount. In *Figure 1*, each posting represents a move of $0.25. This is a one-box reversal chart, which means that we post each price move of the specified amount (in this case $0.25). It is this focus on price movement that provides P&F charts with their adaptability. On a day with many sharp price moves, there will be a lot of postings, reflecting the rapid shifts in the market. On a dull day, there will be few, perhaps zero, price moves of $0.25. That's a day that can be pretty well ignored.

Let's examine the action just after the opening gap down on *Figure 1*. We've just had a sharp decline in the stock price (a column of Os), and now the price begins to rally. Until the price rallies to a point $0.25 or more above the previous price posting, we don't touch the chart. Once that $0.25 threshold is crossed, we need to reflect that price action with an X. We must then move over one column to the right in order to avoid writing over a posting already on the chart. If subsequent price action continues to rise, we will mark each new $0.25 posting in that column. One will note that there are five Xs in that column. That means the price moved up $1.25 (5 x $0.25) before it fell by $0.25. If it had continued rising without that $0.25 decline, there would have been no reason to change columns. Thus, the rule is to stay in the same column unless a new posting would overwrite another posting, in which case the trader places the new posting one column to the right.

Ease of Use

In *Figure 2*, readers can see how the P&F chart, by automatically adjusting to trading activity, provides extra information for a trader. Soon after the opening gap, prices stabilize. Rallies terminating at a similar price form a resistance level that is highlighted by the line marked A. There are eight columns beneath that resistance line indicating eight distinct shifts in price action. Then the price breaks out to the upside (point B). An upside breakout in price—on any kind of chart—is a signal that the forces of supply and demand have shifted in favor of the bulls. Because the P&F chart works in fixed price increments, support and resistance levels are particularly easy to see. As trading volatility dies down over the next few days, the number of columns of data shrinks and returns to a more normal level. Thus, when trading was normal, the P&F chart gave much the same information as a daily bar chart, but when trading revved up, it gave trading details about significant intra-day reversals that a daily chart wouldn't show.

Indicators

While few software programs accommodate them, indicators work on P&F charts in much the same way as on bar charts. The upside breakout at point B occurs just after the price has moved through the ten-column moving average. This moving average then provided support to the up-trend over the next few days. At this point I commonly hear,

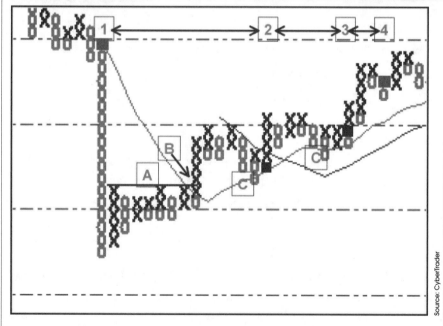

FIGURE 2: Point and figure adapts to changing conditions

Source: Cybertrader

Notice that a resistance level forms early in day one (point A). This reflects early analysis on the part of buyers and sellers as they grapple to determine the significance of the previously released bad news. The price then breaks through that resistance area, signaling a shift in the forces of supply and demand, from balanced to one favoring the buyers (point B). That breakout occurs just as the price moves through its ten-column moving average. That moving average then provides support for the up-trend that continues over the next few days (points C).

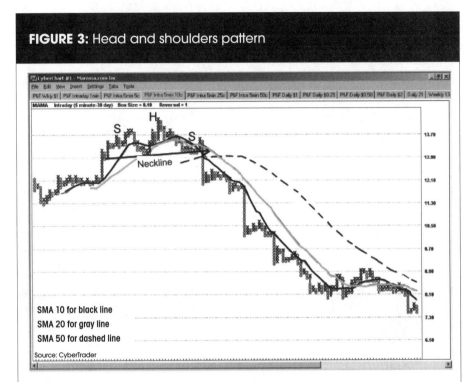

FIGURE 3: Head and shoulders pattern

A classic head and shoulders top forms on this $0.10 reversal chart and is followed by a significant decline over the next six days. The ten-column moving average solid black line does a nice job highlighting resistance on the way down. A second head and shoulders forms at the end of this chart.

"What's that you say? ten-column moving average? Did you mean to say ten-day moving average?" No, column is correct. P&F charts don't work in time, but move across the page (or screen) in columns reflecting periods of rising and falling prices. A moving average is just a technique for smoothing out jagged price action. It works just as well on a P&F chart as on a bar chart.

Price Patterns

Most of the common price patterns also appear on P&F charts. *Figure 3* shows an example of one of the most popular of all reversal patterns: the head and shoulders pattern. This one is on a $0.10 reversal chart covering a twenty-day trading period. After the breakdown, you'll note that the ten-column moving average does a nice job of containing any rally attempts. Nearly all popular bar chart reversal patterns appear with only minor variations on P&F charts. The one missing element is volume. Traditionally, P&F charts have not included volume, and it is not shown here, but some analysts are starting to include it more frequently.

Bottom Line

Buy and sell signals, indicators and price patterns are all similar on bar and point and figure charts. Like bar charts, P&F charts may be tailored for both short- and long-term use. The adaptability of P&F charts gives them a capability that bar chart users envy.

Countless hours and articles have been devoted to researching a variable-length moving average technique for bar charts. It's the changing nature of markets that make such a moving average so desirable. P&F is by its very nature a dynamic method of chart construction. As such, indicators based on its postings are inherently adaptable. This adaptability in both chart and indicator construction offers the trader and the investor an often unique insight into market action.

Ken Tower, CMT, is a former chief market strategist at CyberTrader, Inc., a Charles Schwab Company. He has more than two decades of experience in market analysis, is a former president of the Market Technicians Association, and is a frequent lecturer on technical analysis. His research is available at www.kentowerreport.com. This article originally appeared in *SFO* in November 2004.

SECRETS OF THE ORIENT: Candle Charts Help Spot Early Turning Signals

BY STEVE NISON & TRACY KNUDSEN

Candle charts are Japan's oldest form of technical analysis. They are older than point-and-figure and bar charts, which were more dominant here in the West. Amazingly, candlestick charting techniques, used for generations in the Far East, were unknown to western technicians and market watchers until Steve revealed them in his first book, *Japanese Candlestick Charting Techniques* (Prentice Hall Press), back in 1991 BC (Before Candles).

Japanese candlestick (also called candle) charts, so-named because the lines look like candles with their wicks, in addition to being Japan's oldest methodology, are also Japan's most popular form of technical analysis. Candle charts are more than one hundred years old and, as such, are older than Western bar charts and point-and-figure charts. These trading techniques now have become one of the most discussed forms of technical analysis around the world.

Almost every technical analysis software package and Internet charting service now features candle charts, which would surely attest to their popularity and usefulness.

This is a very basic introduction to candle charting techniques, with a special focus on combining Eastern and Western technical analysis. With the primary candle signals discussed, you will discover how candles open avenues of analysis not available anywhere else. Our goal here is to provide a sense of the potential of what candles can offer.

The Benefits of Using Candle Charts

Candle charts are easy to understand. Anyone from the first-time chartist to the seasoned professional can easily harness the power of candle charts. This is because, as will be shown later, the data that is required to draw the candlestick chart is the same as that needed for the bar chart (the high, low, open, and close).

Candlestick charting tools will give you a jump on the competition. Candle charts not only show the trend of the move, as does a bar chart, but, unlike bar charts, candle charts also show the force underpinning the move. In addition, many of the candle signals are given in a few sessions, rather than the weeks often needed for a bar chart signal. Thus, candle charts will help you enter and exit the market with better timing.

Candlestick charting tools will help preserve capital. In this volatile environment capital preservation is just as important as capital accumulation. You will discover that candles shine in helping you preserve capital, since they often send out indications that a new high or low may not be sustained.

Candle charting techniques are easily joined with Western charting tools. Because candle charts use the same data as a bar chart it means that any of the technical analyses used with bar charts (such as moving averages, trendlines, retracements, Bollinger bands, etc.) can be employed with candle charts. However, candle charts can send signals not available with bar charts. Combining candle charts with Western technical analysis will be discussed in greater detail later in this chapter.

Candlestick charts can be used in stocks, futures, forex, and any market that has an open, high, low and close. And they can be used in all time frames—from intra-day to monthly.

Constructing the Lines

The broad part of the candlestick line in *Figure 1* is called the real body. The real body represents the range between the session's open and close. If the close of the session is above the open, then the real body is white. If the real body is black, the close of the session is lower than the open.

The thin lines above and below the real body are the shadows. These are the session's price extremes. The shadow above the real body is called the upper shadow, and the peak of the upper shadow is the high of the session. The shadow under the real body is the lower shadow, and the bottom of the lower shadow is the session's low.

Candle lines can be drawn for all time frames, from intra-day to monthly charts. For example, a 60-minute candle line uses the open, high, low, and close of that 60-minute period; for a daily chart it would be the open, high, low, and close for the day. On a weekly chart, the candle

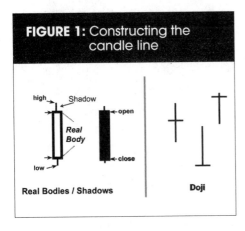

FIGURE 1: Constructing the candle line

high Shadow
open
Real Body
close
low
Real Bodies / Shadows

Doji

would be based on Monday's open, the high and low of the week, and Friday's close.

Notice that the candles to the right in *Figure 1* have no real bodies. These are examples of doji (pronounced doegee). A doji is a candle in which the opening and close are the same. Doji represent a market that is in balance between the forces of supply and demand. We will look more at the doji in one of the chart examples below.

While the candlestick line uses the same data as a bar chart, the color of the candlestick's real body and the length of the candle line's real body and shadows convey an instant x-ray into who's winning the battle between the bulls and the bears. For instance, when the real body is black, that means the stock closed below its opening price. This gives you an instant picture that the bears are in control. Those of us who stare at charts for hours at a time find candlesticks are not only easy on the eyes, they convey strong visual signals sometimes missed on bar charts.

Our firm's tagline is "Helping clients spot the market turns *before* the competition." This is because one of the most powerful aspects of candle charts is that they will often provide reversal signals not available with traditional bar charting techniques. Let's take a look at this aspect with a spinning top (see *Figure 2*).

As mentioned previously, one of the more powerful aspects of candle charts is the quick visual information they relay about the market's health. For example, a small real body (white or black) indicates a period in which the bulls and bears are more in a tug of war. The Japanese have a nickname for small real bodies—"spinning tops"—because of their resemblance to the tops we had as children. Such small real bodies give a warning that the market's trend may be losing momentum. As the Japanese phrase it, the "market is losing its breath."

Let's look at an example of how candle charts will often help you preserve capital, a benefit so important in today's volatile environment. In this scenario I will illustrate how a candle chart can help you avoid a potentially losing trade from the long side.

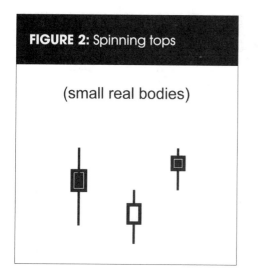

FIGURE 2: Spinning tops

(small real bodies)

If you take a look at *Figures 3* and *4*, one can see how a bar chart and a candle chart can tell a different story. On *Figure 3*, in the area circled, the stock looks strong since it is making consecutively higher closes. It looks like a stock to buy.

Using the same data as on the bar chart, we now make a candle chart (*Figure 4*). Note the different perspective we get with the candle chart than with the bar chart. On the candle chart, in the same circled area, there are a series of small real bodies or spinning tops. Small real bodies hint that the prior trend (i.e., the rally) could be losing its breath.

As such, while the bar chart makes it look attractive to buy, the candle chart shows there is, indeed, a reason for caution about going long—the small real bodies illustrate that the bulls are losing force. Thus, by using the candle chart, a trader would likely not buy in the circled area and, thus, help avoid a losing trade.

This is but one example of how candles shine at helping you preserve capital. Warren Buffet has two rules: Rule 1. Don't lose money. Rule 2. Don't forget Rule 1. Candles shine at helping you preserve capital.

As the real body shrinks, we ultimately wind up with what is called a doji. As shown on the right side of *Figure 1*, a doji is when the open and close are the same. The doji indicates a market in complete balance between supply and demand. Since a doji session represents a market at a juncture of indecision, it often can be an early warning that a preceding rally could be losing steam. Indeed, with a doji the Japanese would say that "the market is tired."

Properly used, candle charts may not only help improve profits, but also will assist in preserving capital. They can do this by helping traders avoid a potential losing trade or exiting a profitable trade early. *Figure 5* shows an example of the latter.

The horizontal line in *Figure 5* shows a resistance area near 135. A tall white candle pierces this resistance in early March. But observe

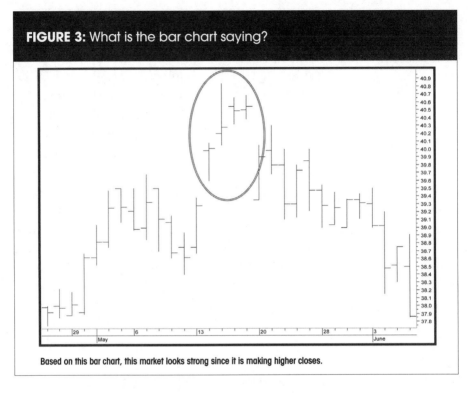

FIGURE 3: What is the bar chart saying?

Based on this bar chart, this market looks strong since it is making higher closes.

what unfolded during the next session—the doji. This doji line hinted that the bulls had lost power over the market (note: this does not mean that the bears have taken control). This is a classic example of the power of candle charting techniques. Specifically, within one session, we were able to see a visual clue via the doji that while the market was maintaining its highs, the doji shouted that the bulls were not in complete control. So while the market looked healthy from the outside, the internals (as shown by the doji) were relaying the fact that this stock was not as healthy as one might think.

We now look at a specific type of candle line that has a very long lower shadow called a hammer (*Figure 6*), so-called because the market is trying to "hammer out" a base. The criteria for the hammer are:

1. The real body is at the upper end of the trading range;
2. The color of the real body can be black or white
3. A bullish long lower shadow that is at least twice the height of the real body;
4. It should have no, or a very short, upper shadow.

FIGURE 4: What is this candle chart saying?

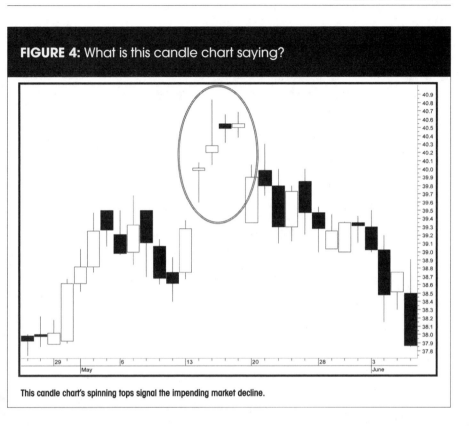

This candle chart's spinning tops signal the impending market decline.

The hammer reflects the market insights obtained from a candle chart—specifically the hammer's extended lower shadow shows that the market rejected lower price levels to close at, or near, the highs of the session. From our experience, most times when there is a hammer the market may not immediately move up, but may rally slightly, or trade laterally, and then, after expanding on a base, rally. If the market closes under the lows of the hammer, longs should be reconsidered.

There are two back-to-back hammers (denoted by the arrow) on the intra-day chart (*Figure 7*). These dual hammers took on extra significance since they confirmed a support level shown by the dashed line. This is a classic example of the power and the ease with which one can combine the insights of candle charts (the hammers) with classic western trading signals (the support line) to increase the likelihood of a market turn. This synergy of candle charts and western technical tools, if understood, should provide a powerful weapon in your trading arsenal.

An engulfing pattern is a two-candle pattern. A bearish engulfing pattern (shown on *Figure 8*) is formed when, during a rally, a black real

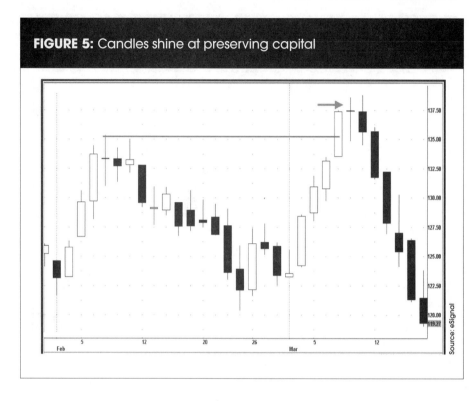

FIGURE 5: Candles shine at preserving capital

body wraps around a white real body. A bullish engulfing pattern (on *Figure 8*) is completed when, during a descent, a white real body envelops the prior black real body.

The engulfing pattern is illustrative of how the candles can help provide greater understanding into the behavior of the markets. For example, a bullish engulfing pattern reflects how the bulls have wrested control of the market from the bears. A bearish engulfing pattern shows how a superior force of supply has overwhelmed the bulls. The Japanese will say, for instance, that with a bearish engulfing pattern that "the bulls are immobilized." *Figure 9* shows how a bullish engulfing pattern in early October called a reversal at IBM's lows. This bullish engulfing pattern was especially potent because it reinforced a support area set by a hammer.

As already noted, candlestick charts are most effective when merged with Western technical analysis. The following examples illustrate how Eastern and Western technical analysis comes together to give traders a tremendous advantage over those simply using Western charting techniques along with a bar chart.

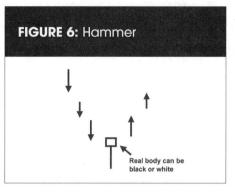

FIGURE 6: Hammer

Real body can be
black or white

Figure 10 is a daily chart of Amazon (AMZN). The stochastics oscillator had been in a downward trend from early through mid-October before making a bullish crossover from within oversold territory on October 21. Using Western technical analysis in isolation then would have generated a buy signal just ahead of the sharp decline on October 22.

Had candlestick chart analysis also been applied on the day of the bullish stochastics crossover, the trader would have noted that the

The History of Candles

While candlestick charts were first used in Japan in the 1870s, their foundation goes back hundreds of years—to the development of one of the world's first futures contracts—rice futures. In Japan the trading of "empty rice" coupons (that is, rice that was not in physical possession) began in the mid-1600s.

The rice market that originally developed was institutionalized when the Dojima Rice Exchange was set up in the late 17th century in Osaka, Japan. The merchants at the exchange graded the rice and bargained to set its price. Up until 1710 it dealt in actual rice. After 1710, the Rice Exchange began to issue and accept rice warehouse receipts, called rice coupons. These became among the first futures contracts ever traded.

Rice brokerage became the foundation of Osaka's prosperity. Because there was no currency standard (the prior attempts at hard currency failed due to the debasing of the coins), rice became the de facto medium of exchange.

In Osaka, life was permeated by the desire for profit (as opposed to other cities in which money-making was despised). And it was the trading of rice futures that actually engendered the beginnings of technical analysis in Japan. It was from these foundations that candle charts evolved. Interestingly, the striving for profit in Osaka was so important that, to this day, the traditional greeting in Osaka is "Mokarimakka," which means, "Are you making a profit?"

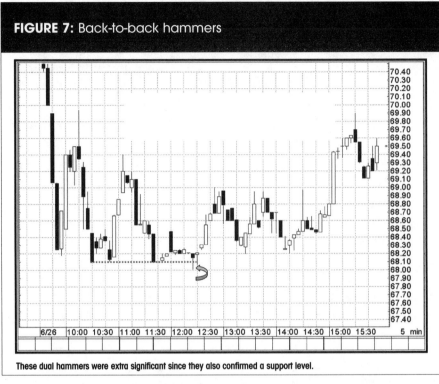

FIGURE 7: Back-to-back hammers

These dual hammers were extra significant since they also confirmed a support level.

candles offered up no bullish reversal signals. Indeed, the small real body of the October 21 candle line hinted that the market was tired, and this lack of bullish confirmation from the candles would have turned one away from entering a long position. As such, the trader would have avoided the loss that would have been incurred as a result of the October 22 market action.

Bullish Engulfing Formation
Soon after the October 22 decline, a bullish candle signal known as a bullish engulfing pattern emerged (noted with gray semi-circle in *Figure 10*). This pattern was previously discussed. With the emergence of the bullish engulfing pattern, one could have considered nibbling on the long side, placing an exit stop below the low of the bullish engulfing pattern. Added bullish confirmation, giving traders the opportunity to add to long positions, then occurred a few sessions later in the form of another bullish crossover by stochastics.

Not only did the combination of Eastern and Western technical analysis uncover a buying opportunity, but the use of the candle-

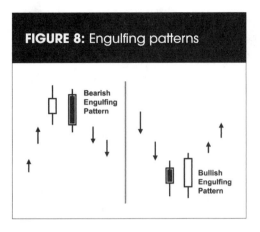

FIGURE 8: Engulfing patterns

stick chart also provided an earlier reversal signal than the stochastics oscillator. This is one of the advantages of candlesticks— getting in on the early reversal signals.

Those who rode Amazon higher into mid-November realized a respectable profit. But at what turned out to be the mid-November peak, we have an example of the potential danger of using candlestick charts in isolation. In mid-November, the candles did not give us any classic top reversal signals to warn that the bulls were running out of steam. However, stochastic was overbought and on November 18 made a bearish crossover. This would have been the trader's cue to take profits on the long position.

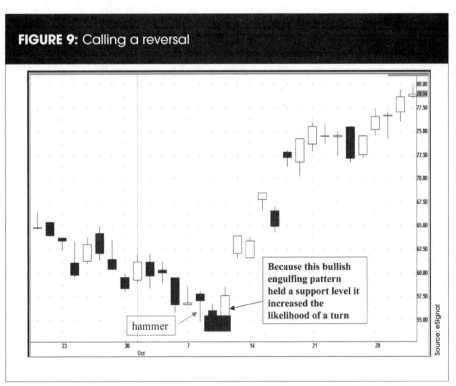

FIGURE 9: Calling a reversal

Because this bullish engulfing pattern held a support level it increased the likelihood of a turn

hammer

Source: eSignal

FIGURE 10: Amazon.com, Inc. (AMZN), daily chart

Morning Star Pattern

The live cattle futures contract chart action offers another example of the benefits of combining East and West (see *Figure 11*). This contract was in the midst of a rather steady decline until mid-June when a candlestick pattern known as a morning star developed (see semi-circle). A morning star consists of three candle lines. The first candle is characterized by a long black real body, the second candle has a small real body, and the third candle is a tall white real body, which closes deeply within the black real body of the first candle. This pattern must occur after a down-trend. The psychology behind the morning star pattern is as follows: the first black candle illustrates that heavy supply is still a factor; the second candle line's small real body warns of a decline of a bearish force; and the subsequent tall white real body proves the bulls have gained the upper hand.

This morning star formation occurred as cattle was still hugging support defined by the lower Bollinger band. A bullish cross by stochastics from within oversold territory added to the bullish evidence. When a reversal sign from the candles is accompanied by supporting evidence from Western technicals (e.g., a test of support at the lower Bollinger band and the crossover by stochastics), the chances of a reversal occurring are increased greatly. This confluence of signals as of the June 20 close screamed, "exit shorts and enter longs."

Using the low of the morning star as an exit stop would have kept the trader on the long side into early July, at which point the warning bells would have sounded. The July 6 candle represented a spinning top. As already noted, spinning tops warn that momentum is declining and are especially useful when they occur during a rally. Bearish confirmation then occurred during the subsequent session, which re-

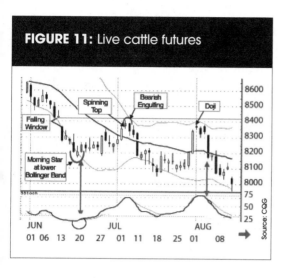

FIGURE 11: Live cattle futures

sulted in the formation of a bearish engulfing pattern (see black semi-circle on *Figure 11*).

Look for Support and Resistance

As already noted, the formation of a candle-stick reversal pattern is more likely to accurately forecast a market turn when the pattern occurs at a support or resis-tance level. This is where Western technical analysis comes into play. In this case, the bearish engulfing pattern formed against the upper Bollinger band. Furthermore, important resistance defined by a falling window, the Eastern equivalent of a gap in Western terminology, also was in play. Space does not allow us to delve any deeper into the interpretation of windows, but suffice it to say that windows are an extremely important aspect of candlestick chart analysis.

Waiting for the bearish crossover by stochastics, which did not occur until July 8, would have shaved off a portion of the trader's potential profit. There surely was enough evidence to take profits on long positions and perhaps enter the short side as of the July 7 close. This example illustrates how the combination of Eastern and Western technical analysis can help a trader spot early reversal signals.

Cattle then experienced a run to the downside, stabilized in mid-July, then made another run up to resistance late in the month. Following the strong rally on July 29, a doji appeared. The fact that this doji occurred against the upper Bollinger band as well as the resistance defined by the falling window—a level which already had proven itself in early July—gave the potential reversal signal added clout. The lower close the session following the doji offered a bearish confirmation and, with that lower close, the bulls should have stepped to the sidelines.

Another downside crossover by stochastics provided bearish confirmation, but that confirmation did not occur until August 4, after the contract already had corrected deeply from the August 1 high. Those using a bar chart along with the oscillator would have given back a good portion of their long position's profit, while those using a candlestick chart combined with the Western technical tools of Bollinger bands and resistance analysis would have had the opportunity to exit near the peak of the rally. In addition, using the twice-tested resistance near the 84.00-level as a stop, the savvy trader could have entered a relatively low-risk short position, aiming for a reward of a decline back to the mid-July low. Indeed, this also would have been a very successful trade.

This provides a brief introduction to candle charting techniques and illustrates how the combined use of Eastern and Western technical analysis can give the trader an important edge over those who are trading with bar charts and Western technical analysis alone. Bar charts simply do not offer visual clues regarding a market's internal strength. Candlestick charts, on the other hand, clearly depict whether the bulls or the bears—or perhaps neither of them—are in control.

As a closing note, there are many nuances to candlestick chart analysis that a trader must learn. Misuse of the candles can doom a trader's profits just as quickly as avoiding the candles all together. The Japanese proverb goes, "If you wish to know the road, inquire of those who have traveled it." Become proficient in candlestick chart analysis prior to adding the candles to your analysis toolkit. By doing so, the candles surely will light your way to greater profits.

Steve Nison, CMT, is president of Candlecharts.com, which provides educational products and advisory services to institutions and private traders. Nison is acknowledged as the Western world's leading authority on candlesticks.

Tracy Knudsen, CMT, is senior market strategist at Candlecharts.com. She is co-author of *Illuminations*, a daily market commentary that combines the insights of both Eastern and Western technical analysis.

Visit www.candlecharts.com for free educational video clips, educational articles, and free trials to daily market commentaries, candle scanning software, and much more. Versions of this article appeared in *SFO* in February 2003 and November 2005.

SECTION THREE
Interpreting Trends and Patterns

Developing confidence in your skills identifying trends and chart patterns is a critical piece of becoming a winning trader. Price development forms recognizable patterns on which technical analysts base trades. Trend is commonly held to be the most important consideration in technical analysis, because it determines which direction prices are moving: up, down, or sideways. A trend line, therefore, is one of the technician's primary tools for defining price trends and one of the simplest concepts to master. Literally connecting the dots can open your eyes to key trading opportunities. Peter Kaplan shows you the basics of drawing trend lines on a variety of charts, including pointers on finding the strongest areas of support and resistance found anywhere on a chart.

Trend following—placing trades based on identifying the direction of price movement—has proven to be one of the most effective systems of trading. We'll give you the pros and cons of chart reading and moving-average crossovers, two of the most common methods of trend following, and help you develop tactics to minimize risk and maximize profits. We'll also show you how to reduce drawdowns by incorporating trend following into your buy-and-hold strategies.

Understanding basic chart patterns, including common retracements and gaps, can help you make better sense of bar charts and use them to your trading advantage. Ken Shaleen will show you the difference between the four basic types of gaps and how they can help you plot your next market move. We'll also show you how to identify retracement patterns and what they mean for forecasting price movement.

The final chapter in this section is a primer on the top ten bearish chart patterns to watch for—from the least common triple top to the most common bearish three falling peaks. Master these and you'll be on your way to trading with the bears.

77

CONNECT THE DOTS:
Making Sense of Trend Lines

BY PETER KAPLAN

Each night while creating my newsletter for clients, the task that takes me the most time is drawing trend lines on the charts. The task that looks easiest is actually the most challenging and time-consuming aspect of what I do. Why? This is where most of the true analysis takes place. Those lines are the future—or at least the potential future—and every time I draw one I am making a statement about the chart and designating a potential inflection point. Additionally, it is during this process that I receive the purest insights about what is likely to happen next.

In the course of doing this over the years, I have come to some interesting conclusions about the proper use of trend lines. Here are a few little rules that I have found useful in my own trading.

What Are Trend Lines?

First, let's do a quick refresher course on trend lines. A traditional trend line is an angled line that helps delineate directional price movement on a chart. In the case of an up-trend, the line will slant diagonally from the lower left of the chart to the upper right, connecting the sequence of rising lows. In the case of a down-trend, the line will run from the upper left to the lower right, connecting the descending highs. They can be utilized with bar, line, or candlestick charts. When using candlestick charts, however, there often is a debate as to whether the lines should be drawn from the tails or the bodies of the candlesticks (see *Figure 1*). As it turns out, technicians

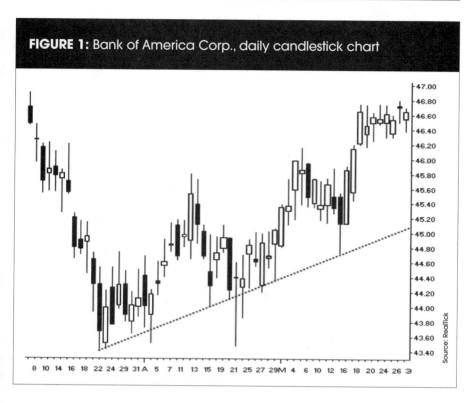

FIGURE 1: Bank of America Corp., daily candlestick chart

are divided on this issue, though the majority tends to favor the for-mer approach. Here is the best way to handle this dilemma: "ask" the chart itself the approach that it favors. By simply looking at the past data, it usually becomes quite clear which lines the market has been favoring. After all, it's the action of the market that matters most, not some dry technical debate between textbook authors. When it comes down to making money in the financial markets, our only interest in the left side of the chart is in predicting what will happen to the right. Technical correctness is utterly useless if it doesn't yield results.

Horizontal trend lines, usually referred to as support and re-sistance lines, tend to inspire much less debate. See *Figure 2* for an example of what these look like. Basically, any price zone that has more than two opens, closes, highs, and lows lining up laterally is a legitimate candidate and has the potential to offer support or resis-tance. After all, even the slightest area of congestion off to the left of a chart—where prices move within a confined range for an extended period—is a potential point of inflection. Consequently, when choos-ing to draw lateral lines, one wants to be thinking in terms of degrees.

FIGURE 2: Ford Motor Co. (F) and Barr Pharmaceuticals, Inc. (BRL), daily charts

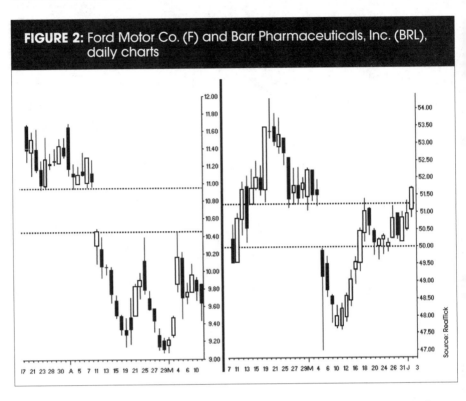

Source: RealTick

Mark the most relevant areas, and leave the lesser ones alone so that the picture doesn't become overly complicated.

How do we determine relevance? Like most things in trading, there's a mixture of science and art involved. The science part is simply a matter of arithmetic: the more opens, closes, highs, and lows on a particular line, the more relevant it is. The art aspect of this process involves the same technique previously mentioned: listen to what the traders themselves have said. Those who have bought and sold the security in the past provide the best clues about what they are likely to do in the future.

For example, a big gap down from a long, tight area of congestion is going to offer a lot of resistance on the way back up because some very traumatized emotions will have been generated by the event (see *Figure 2*). Even if the line isn't perfectly clean, the spot must be given special attention. After all, most of the people who bought up there will have been so badly surprised by the gap that they had absolutely no time to unload. A large number of them will be looking to get out the second they come anywhere close to breaking even. The art in this case might come down to deciding whether the heaviest resistance is on the near side or the far side of the gap—something that has a lot to do with the trading action since the gap. For instance, are the bars in the ensuing bounce closing near their highs, or are they closing well off of their highs? Are buyers able to string together several strong bars in a row, or is every display of strength quickly undermined by poor follow through. The former may well lead to a closing of the gap, while the latter probably won't.

Don't Be Fooled

One of the biggest misconceptions out there about trend lines has to do with placing too much emphasis on trend line breaks. These lines are pierced, altered and downright broken all the time in trading, and this doesn't mean that the trend itself has died—not yet at least. Sometimes the angle of ascent or descent is simply shifting. Other times the breach is a mere fake-out, and soon thereafter the security will pop right back inside the trend line, no doubt ejecting a whole hoard of literalist technicians in the process.

If the above is true, then what use are these silly technical tools?! If we can't count on the line to contain price movement, and if a break often doesn't provide us reliable information, why bother to draw the lines at all? Because, like all tools in technical analysis, when used correctly, trend lines provide clues, not hard facts. A good technician will combine them with other tools and other clues. When the entire combination is mixed together, hopefully one outcome seems a little more likely than another.

Look for Converging Points

While it's beyond the scope of this chapter, another useful technique is to combine trend lines with other technical tools. Within the realm of trend lines themselves, there is a combination called trend line convergences. Specifically, these are points on a chart where a horizontal line intersects a diagonal (see *Figure 3*). When price is headed toward one of these spots, a trader can count on a great deal of holding power at that level. No charting barrier is ever invincible, but these confluences are some of the strongest points of support or resistance in the market. Consequently, when scanning charts for potential trend lines, one ought to be aware of both angles: the horizontal

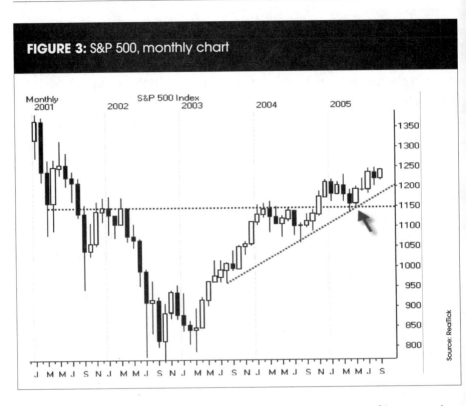

FIGURE 3: S&P 500, monthly chart

and the diagonal. If these lines can be drawn to a point of intersection and the intersection occurs anywhere near the price of the security being traded, expect a reaction upon contact. Price may eventually get through, but rarely will it do so without a fight. More often than not, at least a short-term reversal will occur at the intersection.

Putting Trend Lines into Action

This chapter has touched on just a few basics surrounding the use of trend lines. As with any technical tool, it takes time to develop the appropriate expertise to use them correctly. To recap, here are a few general guidelines about trend lines that traders may want to incorprate into their analysis:

- When drawing a trend line on a candlestick chart, don't make a hard and fast choice ahead of time about whether to use the real bodies or tails. Make that judgment on a chart-by-chart basis, and do so in accordance with the lines that the traders have obviously respected in the past. It's their opinions that matter most of all.

• Horizontal trend lines (otherwise known as support and resistance lines) demand less of an initial choice between tails and bodies. However, one should not go scrawling them all over their charts. Prioritization is key here and must be based on a) the sheer quantity of opens, closes, highs, and lows that line up at that level, and b) the potential psychological implications of the line. Quality technicians are always thinking in terms of the emotional baggage that lies at certain chart levels, and they seek to anticipate the inflection points where the crowd will react most aggressively upon contact.

• Above all else, seek out points on the charts where diagonal and horizontal trend lines converge. These end up being some of the strongest areas of support and resistance found anywhere in a chart and deserve an inordinate amount of attention. A technical trader should forever be scouring the charting landscape, looking for places where these intersections occur.

In closing, I'd like to encourage aspiring chartists out there to get into the habit of drawing on their charts. You will be amazed at how much clearer the picture becomes when you interact with your charts in this manner. Draw a few lines, erase them, and then try others until you get a real feel for the technical landscape. Be demanding as you seek out the correct lines and shapes. Great technicians, after all, are talented artists at their core.

Peter Kaplan began trading securities in the early 1990s, following an extensive education in technical analysis at New York University. He specializes in intermediate and longer-term trading, which he has melded into a comprehensive approach to the equities market. He is the co-founder of Nexus Capital Management, LLC, and can be reached at peter@nexuscapitalmanagement.com. This article originally appeared in *SFO* in November 2005.

DON'T REINVENT THE WHEEL: Just Follow the Trend!

BY MARK PANKIN & STEVEN LANDIS

Technical market analysts and traders widely agree that three types of indicators exist: trend, momentum, and sentiment. In very basic terms, here is how these three styles are defined:

• Trend determines the direction prices are moving, whether up, down, or sideways (also known as congestion).
• Momentum measures price movement in terms of velocity or rate of change.
• Sentiment quantifies the emotional components of trader activity, looking to profit from emotional overreaction.

In this chapter, we will be focusing solely on the use of trend-following indicators. Why? Between trend, momentum, and sentiment indicators, trend is the primary consideration in technical analysis, according to Robert W. Colby in *The Encyclopedia of Technical Market Indicators* (McGraw-Hill, 2003). Besides, trend following is one of the most effective, simple-to-monitor, and low-maintenance systems that exists! Unless you really enjoy making lots of trades, trend-following systems have the potential to make a ton of money with substantially less trading activity. Traders do what they do for either or both of two objectives relative to buy-and-hold investing: they are looking either to outperform buy-and-hold investing or to reduce the risk associated with buy-and-hold.

Many styles of trading exist and are used successfully to produce enviable returns or manage market risk. Not all methodologies, however, are successful at accomplishing both. Of all the trading styles, trend following has been described as the one of the most successful and profitable, according to Michael Covel in his book, *Trend Following: How Great Traders Make Millions in Up or Down Markets* (Financial Times Prentice Hall, 2004). A good trend follower can trade for excellent profits at reasonable risk levels.

At least on the face of it, trend following is one of the simplest trading techniques. The basic premise involves identifying a change in the direction of a stock, bond, and market index or, for that matter, any tradable security, and trading in the direction of the trend. The secret lies in identifying when a trend either has developed or has ceased to exist.

When the trader identifies an up-trend, he places a long trade in the direction of that trend and holds the position until the up-trend ceases and prices begin to reverse. The trader has a number of alternatives:

- Close the long trade and wait for another up-trend to develop at a later date;
- Take an opposing trade by going short in the same security; or
- Search for a different security that is developing a new up-trend.

Take a look at *Figure 1*. Let's assume that Kinder Morgan Partners (KMP) began a new up-trend in August 2002. A trader would enter a long position in the stock at about $32 and hold it until the trend has been exhausted, in this case in February 2004. At that time, the trade would be closed at about $46, giving the investor a gain of 43 percent.

After closing that successful trade, the investor could either short KMP, search for another security that is developing an up-trend or wait for KMP to develop a new up-trend in which to go long. An example of this last alternative is illustrated, again in *Figure 1*. In July, after falling about 8 percent, KMP begins another up-trend at $42. The trader enters the trade and (ideally) holds his position until November 2004, exiting the trade at $46 for a gain of 9 percent.

A Reactionary Method

The reality is that a trend trader will always leave some money on the table, as he will never get out at the exact top or buy at the exact bottom. The reason is because the trend trader is looking to detect a change in

FIGURE 1: Kinder Morgan Energy Partners (KMP), 2002-2006

direction of the current, dominant trend. Trend following is a reactionary rather than a forward-looking methodology, which eliminates the difficult task of trying to predict major changes. Typically, active trading methods are compared with buy and hold, the strategy that is proffered by most financial professionals. So let's compare trend following with buy and hold:

- Trend following will incur more activity than buy and hold which, by definition, will have no trading activity;
- Trend following will experience fewer and smaller drawdowns;
- The equity growth line for buy and hold will illustrate greater volatility than that for trend following (unless leverage is used by the trader);
- Trend following allows the investor to exit a losing position. Subsequently, the position can be re-entered at a later time when profit potential has increased. On the other hand, buy and hold will ride the roller coaster, hoping that the next big ride up is just ahead.

It might be said that buy and hold is the lazy man's way to riches. Eventually, with little or no effort, most quality stocks will increase in value. The question at hand is whether the investor could have improved his situation by becoming actively involved, participating in up markets, and avoiding down markets. We contend that over time, an average trend-following program will provide, at minimum, market-average returns with significantly lower risk. If you're not yet convinced about using a trend-following system, consider the following:

- Trend-following programs do not necessarily involve frequent trading because the period between trades may be several months;
- Long traders incur market-equal volatility while invested, yet do not incur equal drawdowns during bear markets when they will be on the sidelines;
- Winning trades may occur less frequently than losing trades, yet the profitability of the system can be competitive with broad market averages due to avoidance of down markets;
- Because trend followers often use stop-loss orders, they incorporate an additional element of loss prevention.

So exactly how is the trend of the market or an index determined? To paraphrase an old adage, "trend is in the eye of the beholder." Numerous methods exist, but two of the more common methods are explained in the following sections.

Method #1 Chart Reading: Higher Highs, Lower Lows

Using this well-known method, an up-trend is declared when the market or security exhibits a sequence of higher highs and higher lows and conversely (lower highs, lower lows) for downtrends. Though it is a good method of determining market trend, the approach is subjective; consequently, the observer must determine which highs and lows to incorporate and which to ignore. This method and others based on chart reading have the disadvantages of requiring development of chart-reading skills and being difficult to backtest or evaluate.

Method #2 Moving-Average Crossovers

This approach is best illustrated by the classic moving-average crossover method. For example, an up-trend is declared when the price (e.g., closing price) of the market or security moves above its 200-day simple moving average (MA), and a downtrend is declared when the price moves below its 200-day MA. An advantage of this system, compared with chart reading, is that it is objective. There is no question about when the price moves above or below the moving average. Another advantage is that this quantitative method allows for backtesting, which can provide useful evaluation of potential profitability and risk levels.

Moving averages are among the most popular tools for trend followers and for good reason. The technique is very effective at identifying trends and enabling traders to maintain their positions until the trend is over. Moreover, by varying the lengths over which the MA is calculated, the sensitivity to smaller price changes can be adjusted to suit traders' preferences. Shorter MAs involving a smaller number of days or weeks are more sensitive and provide quicker and more numerous signals than longer moving averages. No method of investing or trading is without its drawbacks and weaknesses. Short moving averages are subject to whipsaws in congested markets, and while longer MAs are less so, they will generate signals farther away from lows and highs than do shorter MAs. Because of their popularity among so many traders and investors, we will provide some examples of moving averages. However, the subject is rich, with a number of books, articles, and research papers in publication. We are just going to scratch the surface.

Understanding Moving Averages

It's worth pointing out that there are two types of moving averages: simple and exponential. The simple type is literally an average of prices over a fixed period, most commonly daily or weekly. The exponential variety computes a weighted average of the most recent price and the average's prior value. Giving a larger weight to the recent price relative to the prior average effectively shortens the period and makes the calculation more sensitive to recent market activity. Exponential has some advantages, but in practice the two are about equally effective. We use simple MAs in our examples.

Moving averages can be applied to any price or data series to generate buy and sell signals for both long and short positions. Both authors trade primarily stocks or mutual funds, so we will use those instruments in our examples and take the typical long-only position. Because we strongly believe the most important aspect of successful investing and trading is risk control, we will show how trend-following MA techniques work in that regard, in addition to their profitability. For illustration we use the S&P 500 index, as it has a long history and is representative of the broad U.S. stock market.

Putting the Method into Action

We start with a simple and popular method for the S&P 500 or a mutual fund/ETF, such as the exchange traded SPDRs, that closely track the index. Go long when the index is above its 40-week simple MA, and sell into a money market fund when the index falls below its 40-week MA. In terms of complete years, the last full secular bear market extended from 1966 to 1981, the period between 1982 and 1999 saw an incredible secular bull, and the current secular bear market started in 2000. We will look at performance over the 40-year, 1966-2005 period and for the periods of the secular bears and bull.

For the entire period, buying and holding the S&P total return index, which includes reinvested dividends, would have realized a compounded annual rate of return of +10.3 percent, while the 40-week MA method would have trailed slightly at +9.8 percent. Looking at the 1966-81, 1982-99 and 2000-05 periods shows the advantage of the trend-following method in reducing risk. Respectively, those returns are +5.9 percent buy and hold the S&P versus +8.0 percent trend following in 1966-1981, +18.5 percent versus +14.5 percent in 1981-99, and -1.2 percent versus +1.3 percent since 2000. Trend following performed better during weak markets but could not quite keep up with what might have been the best bull market ever.

Drawdowns, which are the most commonly cited risk measure, were much lower for the MA method. However, consider a risk measure that better captures the overall experience: the percent of months that incur losses. Buy-and-hold investors saw negative returns in 40 percent of the months, but the trend-following trader would have seen negative numbers in only 29 percent of the same months. There were similar reductions during each of the three secular market periods.

Figure 2 shows how the 40-week MA crossover method would have worked in 1999-2005, including the end of the secular bull market. There would have been some small, inconsequential whipsaws (when the S&P crossed below the 40-week MA and moved back above the MA soon thereafter) as the bull market ran its course. The fall of the index below the 40-week MA at the end of September 2000 proved to be an extremely effective sell. It illustrates how trend following works. That sell signal came after the high as trend-following methods will, about six percent below the highest point in this case, and it avoided the subsequent plunge in stock prices.

There were a couple of minor whipsaws along the way before. In April 2003 the crossover above the MA provided a nice buy signal for the cycli-

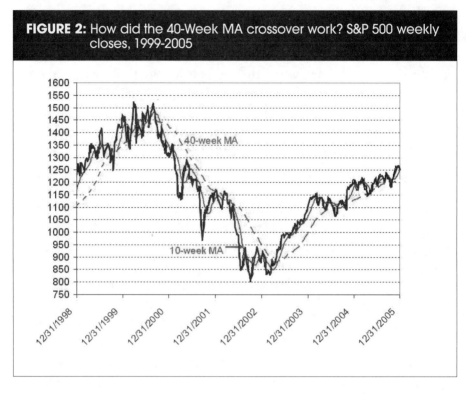

FIGURE 2: How did the 40-Week MA crossover work? S&P 500 weekly closes, 1999-2005

cal bull market that lasted into early 2004. We then see another couple of whipsaws and participation in the strong market beginning in late October 2004. This type of behavior, which shows their great value, is quite typical of trend-following methods in general and MA techniques in particular. One way to reduce whipsaws is to generate signals from crossovers of a shorter moving average rather than the index itself. Doing so with a 10-week MA crossing the 40-week MA improves the trading of the S&P 500.

Figure 3 illustrates that these trend-following methods reduce risk levels in all periods and improve returns during periods with weak markets, although they trail buy and hold in stronger markets. That chart has four groups of bars: for the entire 1966-2005 period, for the 1966-81 secular bear market, for the 1982-99 secular bull market, and from 2000 on. Each group has six bars. The three bars to the left show the annualized returns for the S&P 500 with dividends, and the three down bars show the percent of negative months. Buy and hold is shown by the leftmost solid bars, the 40-week moving average crossover results by the middle dotted bars, and the 10-week crossing over 40-week method by the rightmost bars with vertical stripes.

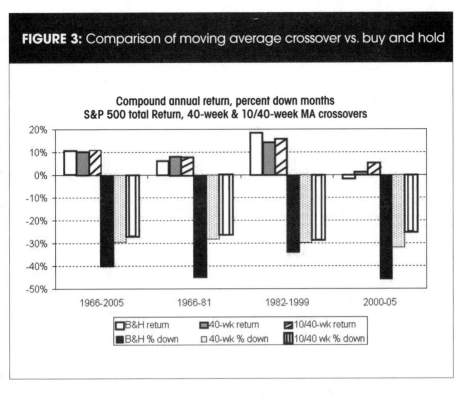

FIGURE 3: Comparison of moving average crossover vs. buy and hold

Over the 40-year period, the returns are close, but the risk levels for the moving average methods are considerably less, proving that trend following has a definite advantage over buy and hold. It should be noted that we selected popular values for the moving averages and did not attempt to optimize the system.

The Tip of the Iceberg

There are many additional technical analysis tools beyond the scope of this book that can be used in conjunction with moving averages. Most trend-following methods are based solely on the price of the instrument to be traded. Many trend followers would argue that considering anything but the security's price reduces the effectiveness because the current price is the only thing that matters.

In summary, though, it is safe to say that there are more methods for trend following than for any other trading method. While trend following is not for everyone, particularly those who will be frustrated and discouraged by a series of fairly small losses, it probably is the easiest way to become an excellent trader or investor. Stock investors and many others will find the risk reduction to be even more important than the trading profits. Just about any reasonable trend-following method would have enabled stock investors to avoid most of the horrible two-year-long drop in stock prices that began in late 2000, and avoiding severe drawdowns is a critical element of profitable investing. What more can one ask for?

Steven Landis is the founder of Landis Financial & Investment Services and has been a past president and chairman of the National Association of Active Investment Managers (NAAIM), an organization for professional, active investment managers. A registered investment advisor and Certified Financial Planner®, Landis has, in the past, been ranked among the top group of Select Advisors out of more than 250 traders monitored on the website SelectAdvisors.com money management platform. He can be contacted at steven@stevendlandis.com or at sdlandis@yahoo.com.

Mark Pankin, who has a PhD in mathematics, is the founder and owner of MDP Associates LLC, and has been the secretary and a member of the board of directors of NAAIM. Before becoming a registered investment advisor in 1994, he taught math at the university level and worked as an operations research analyst. In 2000, his Rydex sector fund-trading program ranked in Select Advisors' top five for the year. Pankin can be reached at mdp2@pankin.com. This article originally appeared in *SFO* in May 2005.

MAKING SENSE OF JUMPS IN CHARTING:
A Basic Analysis of Gap Theory

BY KEN SHALEEN

An estimated eighty percent of traders use technical analysis in one form or another. Studying technical analysis can be exhausting and intense, but understanding just the basic principles can enlighten even the most novice trader. The underlying notion of this type of analysis is that it is possible to determine price moves by studying past patterns or trends. When these patterns are foreseen, a trader may determine when his next opportunity could materialize.

In a perfect world, of course, all trends would maintain a consistent interpretable pattern without interruption or chaotic activity. However, what happens when there is a break, or gap, in the trend on the price chart? Is there really a significant change brewing? Or is it just a slight interruption in the pattern? To help determine what these gaps signify, a study of gap theory is necessary. This article unveils the basic principles of that theory, as related to technical analysis. Those who are more familiar with the concept may find this a bit elementary; however, it is valuable information that any up and coming technical trader will find beneficial. And, there's no better way to identify gaps than by showing numerous charts. After a while identification becomes a much simpler task than at the beginning.

Gap theory is a pillar of classical bar charting. Basically, there are four types of gaps that form on a bar chart and are useful to a technical trader to identify:

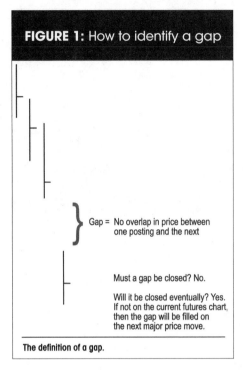

FIGURE 1: How to identify a gap

Gap = No overlap in price between one posting and the next

Must a gap be closed? No.

Will it be closed eventually? Yes. If not on the current futures chart, then the gap will be filled on the next major price move.

The definition of a gap.

- A market in a sideways price consolidation;
- The start of a new price trend;
- The continuation of an existing, dynamic price trend; and
- The likely termination of a price trend.

Figuratively, a gap is a void that may or may not be filled, noting that something is obviously missing. To a technical trader, a gap is present on a bar chart when there is no overlap in price from one trading session to another (see *Figure 1*).

The first problem is identifying when one trading session ends and the next one begins. The world as a whole can be considered a 24-hour market. If so, there would never be a gap on a 24-hour chart because after one "day" ended, a nanosecond later a new "day" would begin; a gap on such a daily bar chart would never form, except over a weekend. A gap between the Friday price bar and the Monday price bar could exist. This analysis of gap theory will focus on the still-important use of gaps in a major world time zone (a subset of the 24-hour day)—regular trading hours in North America.

The Four Legs on the Gap Stool

The four basic types of gaps can be classified as pattern gaps, breakaway gaps, measuring gaps, or exhaustion gaps. Identifying which type of gap is present depends on where it occurs in a price move or trading range. Each gap classification has traits unique to itself. Once the type of gap is determined, it is then easier to figure out what the next move will be. An example of each is shown in *Figure 3*.

Pattern Gap: The pattern gap occurs within a trading range or congestion area (sideways activity). It is quickly closed. Often, quickly means before the current trading session is finished, as noted in *Figure 2*. And

FIGURE 2: Pattern gaps

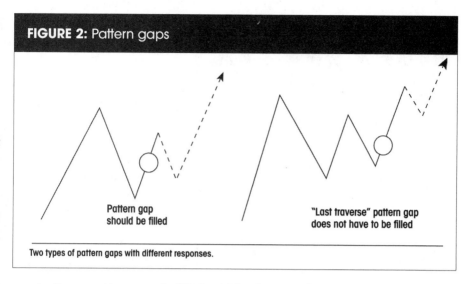

Pattern gap
should be filled

"Last traverse" pattern gap
does not have to be filled

Two types of pattern gaps with different responses.

most often a pattern gap is filled within the next four trading sessions. This gap has no measuring implication for a classical bar chartist. It simply alerts the technician that the entity being charted (stock, future, index) should experience additional net sideways price consolidation.

The gap might exist within a classical bar charting price pattern, but this is not necessary. The bible of price pattern recognition, *Technical Analysis of Stock Trends*, 9th ed. by Edwards, Magee, and Bassetti (Auerbach, 2007), says a better name for this pattern would be a "common" or "area" gap.

The Last Traverse Pattern Gap: This is an exception to the notion that all pattern gaps are quickly filled. If the gap occurs on the last traverse across the congestion area prior to the breakout and then the price exits (breaks out) from the trading range, the pattern gap does not have to be closed. What this really means is that a day trader must examine the next longer-term (for them) timeframe chart—the daily chart. It is extremely important to determine whether a market is close to the boundary of a potential breakout. Why? Because it could lead to a much more dynamic form of gap—the breakaway.

Breakaway Gap: This type of gap occurs at the beginning of a new price move. A breakaway gap is most often associated with the penetration of a trend line on a bar chart. The trend line may represent the boundary line of a classical bar charting price pattern. A break-

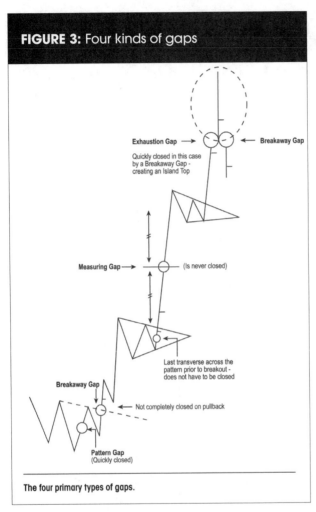

FIGURE 3: Four kinds of gaps

Exhaustion Gap →
Quickly closed in this case
by a Breakaway Gap -
creating an Island Top

← Breakaway Gap

Measuring Gap → (Is never closed)

Last transverse across the
pattern prior to breakout -
does not have to be closed

Breakaway Gap

← Not completely closed on pullback

Pattern Gap
(Quickly closed)

The four primary types of gaps.

away gap can also form on a price move into new high or low ground on a chart. A breakaway gap does not have to be closed. Volume is the key—the higher the volume on the day that created the gap, the less likely the gap will be closed. The breakaway price move is confirmation that the trend line penetrated was, indeed, significant.

Measuring Gap: A relatively rare type of gap, a measuring gap is found during a rapid, straight-line price move. The term "measuring" is used because this type of gap produces a distinct measuring objective. The gap represents the mid-point of a dynamic price trend. A chartist measures the distance from the prior breakout to the center of the gap and extends that distance to obtain a price target.

Exhaustion Gap: An exhaustion gap develops at the end of a price move. It is quickly closed. This type of gap only forms after the price has moved a considerable distance in one direction. An exhaustion gap should not form in a congestion area.

Obviously, a trader does not want to confuse the exhaustion gap with any of the others, especially the measuring gap. Exhaustion gaps tend to be relatively wide gaps—not just a few minimum price increments. And volume often virtually explodes to blow off proportion in a market in the process of exhausting itself. The tick mark for the close in relation to the range for the price bar can be an aid. Was the close strong or weak in relation to its distance from the high or low of the trading session? This means that a trader has to wait until very late in the trading session to make the determination of whether or not to exit from an existing position.

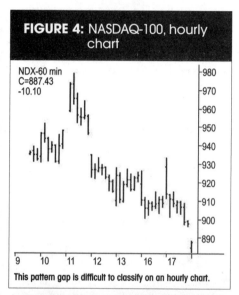

FIGURE 4: NASDAQ-100, hourly chart

NDX-60 min
C=887.43
-10.10

This pattern gap is difficult to classify on an hourly chart.

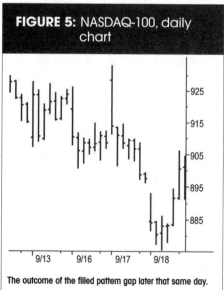

FIGURE 5: NASDAQ-100, daily chart

The outcome of the filled pattern gap later that same day.

The schematic diagram in *Figure 3* shows where the four types of gaps would normally occur. Note that the combination of an exhaustion gap and a breakaway gap produces an island formation on a bar chart, showing a definite reversal pattern.

While examining the four basic types of gaps, it should be noted that two additional types of gaps might form. For individual equity trades in the U.S., an ex-dividend gap is possible. The New York Stock Exchange lowers the closing price by the amount of the dividend paid on the ex-dividend date. But this type of gap is not significant. It does mean, however, that even technical traders must be attuned to the fundamental statistic of dividend payment dates.

New under the technical sun for U.S.-based futures traders is the possibility of a gap within a 24-hour bar chart—in between the electronic dealing and open outcry trading sessions. If a gap is present, it is labeled as a suspension gap. But, by itself, a

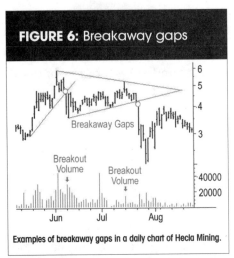

FIGURE 6: Breakaway gaps

Examples of breakaway gaps in a daily chart of Hecla Mining.

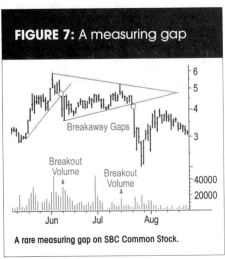

FIGURE 7: A measuring gap

A rare measuring gap on SBC Common Stock.

suspension gap has no meaning. It must be classified into one of the four basic types.

Gaps and Indexes

A trading arena that is prime for the application of gap theory involves the daily charts of the various U.S. equity indexes. Index futures are open prior to the start of regular trading hours for the cash market. If the index future is trading substantially higher or lower (above or below the previous day's cash market range), a gap on the chart of the cash index would be expected on the open. A problem exists, however. The gap on the cash market chart will only appear if the data vendor or exchange reports the opening of the cash index correctly. Rarely does a gap on the chart of the cash Dow Jones industrial average appear on a chart. The open is most often at the same price level as the previous day's close. Obviously, it is impossible to buy or sell the cash index at an unchanged open if the futures are trading substantially higher or lower.

The daily NASDAQ-100 cash chart is excellent for showing gap openings. NASDAQ-100 day traders during regular trading hours often have the opportunity to initiate a trade based on their interpretation of the gap.

Figure 4 shows the technical state of the cash NASDAQ-100 thirteen minutes after the open on September 18, 2002. The index was trading 10.10 points lower, and a gap existed overhead. It is impossible to classify the gap on this hourly chart. A daily chart was necessary to infer that the NASDAQ-100 was within a congestion area. Thus, the gap would be classified as a pattern gap. As such, a technical trader would figure that the gap would be filled if an excellent chance existed—leading to a speculative long position.

Figure 5 shows the outcome. The gap was filled but not without some trauma for the speculative long. The price moved lower in the next two hours after the opening hour, and the outside range hour started the rally to fill the gap. So even when gap theory works, it is not easy!

Breakaway and Measuring Gaps

Two examples of breakaway gaps (through a trend line) can be seen in *Figure 6*, a daily chart of Hecla Mining. Note the increase in volume on the day that created the gap.

The rare measuring gap occurred on SBC Common Stock, as seen in *Figure 7*. SBC broke out of a symmetrical triangle to the downside. Before reaching the standard vertical height-measuring objective of the triangle, a gap at half-way was posted.

Gap theory is a general technical tool that all market techies can deploy to develop their innate sense of price discovery. By having an awareness of the basic types of gaps we've covered, it's possible to make greater sense of bar charting and how these charts can be used in determining future price moves. Gap theory gives insight into what may be happening in a trending market. Technical traders can use the theory to help determine the continuation or termination of a price trend, the start of a new price trend, or a market in a sideways price consolidation. By first identifying the type of gap, it is possible to reveal how the market may develop. Even the novice trader can begin to hone his skills to turn these basic principles into potentially profitable moves.

Ken Shaleen has been teaching technical analysis for the Chicago Mercantile Exchange since 1974. His students are still required to submit a hand-constructed chart in lieu of a final exam. Shaleen is the founder of Chartwatch (www.chartwatch.com), a company that produces weekly technical research reports and daily telephone market updates covering selected financial instruments and grain futures. He is the author of technical analysis classics *Volume and Open Interest* (Probus, 1991, 1997) and *Technical Analysis and Options Strategies* (Probus, 1992). This article originally appeared in *SFO* in November 2002.

FIND HIGH-PROBABILITY ENTRIES WITH FLAGS

BY ADAM GRIMES

One of the first hard lessons a new trader learns is that markets do not move in straight lines. A trade is initiated, the market moves a little in favor of the trade, then dips back against the position. This back and forth movement continues until the trader gives up and dumps the trade at a loss. Of course, the market then immediately takes off like a rocket, and the trade would have ended up being very profitable "if only it had been held a few more days." Some new traders repeat this process many times before giving up in exasperation.

The reason this happens is that the trader does not understand the fundamental structure of the market, which is that markets alternate between periods of trending activity and trading ranges. This is why when a trade is initiated in a hot, fast-moving market, the market often goes flat and dead as soon as the trade is put on. Traders must learn to see this underlying structure in the market so that they may make trades that take advantage of it. What was formerly a source of frustration to the novice trader becomes the basis for a high-probability trading methodology that can offer a high percentage of winning trades, excellent win-loss ratio and clearly defined risk management points.

Retracement patterns in trends are a fundamental, enduring element of market structure. These patterns worked a hundred years ago, they worked through the dot.com bubble and subsequent crash, and they continue to work in today's contracting volatile environment. They appear and are tradable in all active markets and all time-

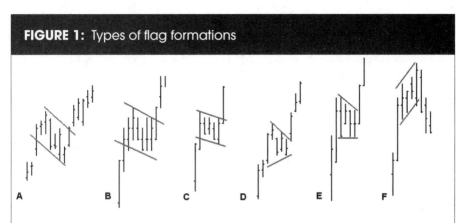

FIGURE 1: Types of flag formations

A   B   C   D   E   F

Examples A, B, and C show ideal retracement patterns in bull markets. These identical patterns appear inverted in bear markets. Important structures to note are the parallel trendlines that contain the formation, which slant back against the trend. Examples D and E also slant against the trend, but they have converging trendlines. These structures are traditionally called triangles, wedges, or pennants. Example F shows a pattern to avoid. Notice that this pattern slants with the direction of the trend. More often than not, these types of patterns lead to reversals rather than continuation.

frames. These principles could be applied equally well to intraday futures, daily forex, or even to monthly stock charts.

Continuation Patterns: The Trend Will Continue

Traditionally, authors have used a variety of terms to describe the chart formations that result from the market's tendency to pause between impulse moves: flags, pennants, rectangles, wedges, diamonds, boxes, corrective waves, and x-y-z retracements. These patterns, which form on bar charts in any timeframe, are technically known as retracement patterns or continuation patterns and are visual representations of the market's tendency to pause and to consolidate between impulse moves. To simplify matters a bit and to keep terminology consistent, we will refer to all of these chart formations under the broad term "flag." It is often difficult to explain in words what may be seen very easily on a chart, so *Figure 1* shows schematic representations of several types of flag formations.

The Pole

All of these patterns are preceded by a fairly sharp impulse move that forms a pole on the chart. This pole is a pattern of several bars that is a visual representation of the strength of the trend. If the pole is too short or too shallow, or if it is made up of only one large bar, it

TABLE 1: Retracement Win Percent

MARKET	TIMEFRAME	DATES	WIN%	# TRADES
S&P	daily	4/1/93-4/1/03	65%	54
T-Bonds	daily	4/1/93-4/1/03	74%	49
Crude Oil	daily	4/1/93-4/1/03	77%	83
Gold	daily	4/1/93-4/1/03	65%	60
Sugar	daily	4/1/93-4/1/03	70%	63
Live Cattle	daily	4/1/93-4/1/03	70%	50
Wheat	daily	4/1/93-4/1/03	65%	48
MMM	daily	4/1/93-4/1/03	59%	44
MER	daily	4/1/93-4/1/03	75%	55
GM	daily	4/1/93-4/1/03	69%	58
IBM	daily	4/1/93-4/1/03	73%	62
ES	5 min	6/5/99-4/1/03	67%	7342
US	5 min	2/11/2-4/1/03	70%	1240

This table shows the results of applying a simple retracement system to many years of market data in various timeframes. This is not intended to be a representation of a complete trading system, but merely empirical proof that there is an edge to entering retracements in trending markets.

may be an indication that the trend is not strong enough to generate high-probability flags. The best retracement patterns will occur in strongly trending markets, and these will set up poles that contain more than one bar.

Eventually, the move that formed the pole will expend itself and the market will go quiet. The market starts to trade within a fairly narrow range, and this range usually slants against the direction of the pole. In other words, if the pole was going up, the flag will tend to float back down. Bull flags usually have a downward bias, and the expectation is that price will break out of the flag and continue the uptrend. Bear flags occur in down-trending markets and usually slant upward.

Flags that slant in the direction of the trend often lead to poor trades (see *Figure 1*, Example F). It is almost as if the energy in the flag pattern is being expended in a slow trickle; these types of patterns often lead to significant reversals. These are not good trading formations—avoid trading flags that slant the "wrong" way.

Most of the time, there will be a sharp break out of the flag formation. About two-thirds of the time, flags will resolve in the direction of the prevailing trend. Bull flags tend to be followed by a move up, and bear flags tend to break downward. No trading methodology is without its losses, and there are certainly times when the market comes out of the "wrong" side of the flag. A consistent stop loss is needed to exit losing trades before they become large losses.

Retracement patterns have a verifiable, statistically valid edge. Trading every flag that forms in a trending market will result in a win ratio of about 69 percent (see *Table 1*), but it is possible to increase this win ratio to about 80 percent by taking certain elements of market structure into account. The first and most important rule: do not look for flags in trading ranges. Flags result from the natural alternation of impulse and consolidation that occurs in trending markets. Though chart formations which resemble flags may form in trading ranges, they are not true flags and do not have the same probability of continuation as true flags. It is necessary to be sure the market is actually trending before looking for retracement patterns.

Know When to Get Out

When looking for the best patterns to trade, the shape and appearance of the flag also can be used as a filter. The best flags will be fairly tightly contained patterns. Beware of flags that have a lot of back and forth spikes and of flags that take too long to form. Continuation patterns tend to end fairly quickly—if a pattern takes a long time to form, there is actually a higher probability of reversal than of continuation. Again, this is something that will vary a bit from market to market, but twenty bars on any timeframe is a very long time to wait for a flag to resolve itself. If you have entered such a pattern and the flag does not kick out within the expected timeframe, exit the trade.

Being aware of the overall technical structure of the market is also important. The best retracement trades will come at significant turning points. For instance, imagine that the market has been in a down-trend, makes a basing pattern, and then gives signs of a up-side reversal...or that a market has been locked in a small, tight trading range and breaks out to the up-side. The first retracement after either of these scenarios would be an exceptionally high-probability trade.

Once the flag pattern is visually identified, it is time to start considering entry criteria, profit targets, and stop loss levels. Buying a bull flag as it sets up (or the reverse, selling a bear flag as the market is rising) is, in essence, initiating a countertrend trade against the short-term trend of the market. If this entry technique is used, the trader needs to be aware that the market often will continue to work against the position for a short time, and the trade certainly may fail outright. An initial stop must be used to limit the loss if the flag never turns back up.

It is also possible to wait for the market to turn and enter once the primary trend has already resumed. One way to do this is to use a very short-term breakout system, like buying above the high of the previous bar while a bull flag is forming. This entry technique sacrifices initial trade location in return for some added confidence that the trend has turned and the market is moving in the right direction. Either of these entry styles can be profitable—the choice will depend on the individual trader. Most traders find one entry style suits their personality and feels much more natural to them than the other.

It is also possible to enter at Fibonacci retracement levels, or to set mechanical entry levels based on an average true range (ATR) or percentage function. For example, a trader could decide always to buy once a bull flag retraces a fixed percentage from the swing high. Each market develops its own characteristics and tends to pull back more or less the same amount each time. If you become familiar with a specific market and examine its recent retracements, you will easily gain a sense of how big the average pullbacks in that market tend to be.

Stops Are Necessary

Though trading retracement patterns is a high-probability trading methodology, there are still losses, and stops must be used to limit these losses. As a general rule with any trading system, larger stops will work better than very tight stops. It is possible to set stops based on visual chart inspection (good retracements usually respect recent swing points) or on Fibonacci levels (if the trade is entered at the 50-percent retracement level, perhaps the stop could go just beyond the 62-percent retracement level).

With a high-probability trading strategy, the highest win ratio will be achieved if the initial stop is somewhat larger than the anticipated profit. This goes against much of the conventional wisdom that says

What is Average True Range?

Range means the high of the bar minus the low of the bar. True range accounts for price gaps (when the low of the current bar is above the high of the previous bar, or when the high of the current bar is below the low of the previous bar) and adds the range of the gap to the calculation.

True range is averaged over a time window to produce average true range. The length of time window is not extremely important—smaller values (5 and under) will respond more quickly to changing market conditions, and larger values (20 and over) will smooth out all but the most significant fluctuations. Ranges of 10 to 30 work well in most markets and timeframes.

True range is a useful concept because it more accurately represents the area that price covered. Simple range calculations ignore gaps in markets. However, the market usually did trade through those prices (for instance, in overnight or overseas markets), and a trader holding a position through the gap would certainly have been exposed to a price change. For these reasons, system developers and programmers almost always favor true range over range, for any market or time period.

However, applying true range to intraday data may cause some distortions. For instance, if the S&P market gaps 20 points on the open, the true range of the first five-minute bar of the day will be at least 20 points (from the previous day's close to the current day's open), even though the market may cover a much smaller range in the first few minutes. This can create distortions in those calculations that depend on true range, and some calculations will carry this error through many hours of the trading day. Intraday traders should consider whether simple range may or may not be a more accurate way to evaluate intraday data.

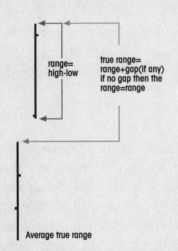

range=
high-low

true range=
range+gap(if any)
if no gap then the
range=range

Average true range

profit targets should be several times the size of the risk, but tests out well in real-time trading. A stop loss twice the size of the anticipated profit is acceptable if you can achieve a win-loss ratio over 75 percent. Note that this refers only to initial stop placement—as the trade works, the stop should be pulled in to reduce risk.

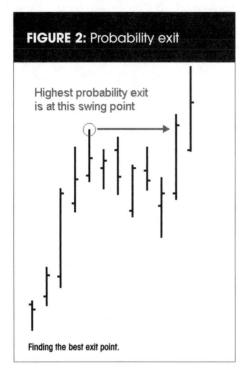

FIGURE 2: Probability exit

Highest probability exit is at this swing point

Finding the best exit point.

A reasonable profit objective is the swing point that ended the pole (see *Figure 2*). When used to predict the near-term direction of the market, flags are very high-probability patterns. Be careful of trying to predict too far into the future with these patterns; accuracy (and profitability) fall off the farther into the future one looks. Highest win ratios will be achieved by playing for the smaller target, but this technique may also be used to establish positions in trending markets and to play for a larger win.

Whatever exit technique is used, the trader should be aware that flags usually give rise to one push out of the formation. If this push falls short of the profit objective or does not extend as far as anticipated, the trade should be exited or stops ratcheted up to lock in profits. Never let a winning trade turn into a loser when trading these patterns.

A Trade Example

Figure 3 illustrates how these concepts can be applied to real market data. This figure shows a flag that set up on April 22, 2003, on a five-minute E-mini S&P 500 chart. The market opened with a small gap down and traded higher, then began a strong push at 10:30 EDT. This move extended over the next 25 minutes and began to pull back after reaching a high of 901. At 11:15, I judged that the market had pulled back about enough and went long on a limit order at 896. My initial stop was established at 892, which was just under the 50-percent retracement level for the push up. Over the next five bars, the market moved a little against the position but was never more than two points under water. This was an aggressive entry technique, as I essentially bought a falling market. However, the price structure showed a clear

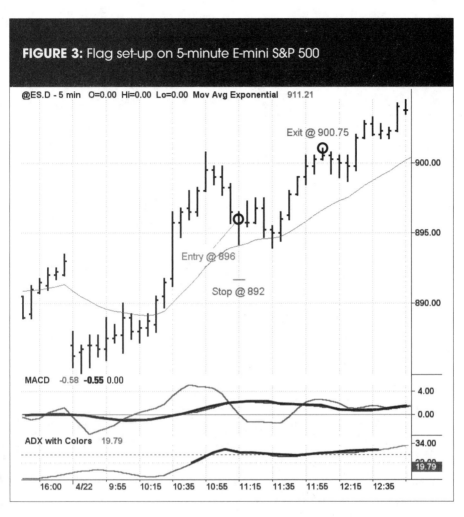

FIGURE 3: Flag set-up on 5-minute E-mini S&P 500

flag, the trend preceding the flag was strong, and the flag pattern itself looked good, so I judged there was a high-probability expectation of a continued push to the up-side.

At 11:33, the market seemed to have made a short-term low, and I moved the stop up just below that swing low. This reduced the risk on the trade to $150 per contract. From that point, the market worked higher, reaching the price objective of 900.75 (the previous swing high that ended the pole formation) at 12:01, about 45 minutes after the trade was initiated. This example illustrates the most aggressive entry technique and shows that the market may move against the position for some time if this kind of entry is used. A reasonable stop must be established and the trade must be

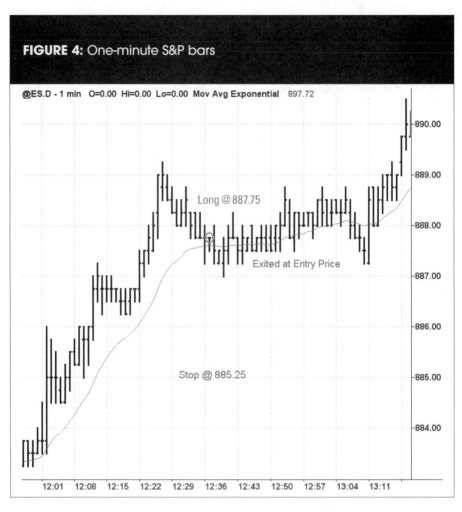

FIGURE 4: One-minute S&P bars

@ES.D - 1 min   O=0.00 Hi=0.00 Lo=0.00 Mov Avg Exponential   897.72

Long @ 887.75

Exited at Entry Price

Stop @ 885.25

exited if the market goes flat after entry, but the trade must also be given enough time to work. It is impossible to always buy the exact low point of a retracement (or to sell the high point). Rather, this technique gives an approximate zone within which a trade may be initiated. A wide enough stop must be used to allow for some inaccuracy on the entry.

One last example will suffice to illustrate the worst-case scenario. *Figure 4* shows a trade that was initiated based on a bull flag on one-minute S&P bars. There were ample warning signs not to take this trade: there were multiple divergences on several timeframes, and the chart pattern suggested a short-term reversal point had been reached. In addition, continuation patterns that form at lunchtime in the stock index futures tend to have less follow through than trades made in the morning or afternoon. This trade had nearly everything going against it. Nonetheless, I was frustrated at having missed the move up that morning and entered long at 887.75 at 12:37, establishing an initial stop 2.5 points under the entry price at 885.25.

As the market traded sideways over the next few minutes, I realized the error of my ways, and I was able to scratch the trade by exiting at the entry price. This trade is an excellent example of spectacularly poor judgment and illustrates a clear error in even entering this trade in the first place. However, in this case, the market gods took pity on me and let me out without a scratch.

This example, embarrassing as it may be, illustrates several important points. Even the bad trades tend to give a grace period for exit by trading sideways. The times when the market spikes hard against the position are very, very rare, but they do occur. This is why I suggest using an actual resting stop order in the market instead of a mental stop. (They are called mental stops because they make you "mental" if you use them!) Once a mistake is realized, it must be quickly corrected. No one is ever immune to errors and mistakes.

Flags Should Pay Off Quickly

Also notice that this trade did eventually (forty-five bars later) reach the profit objective. This is far too long to have held the trade, even though it never came close to the stop loss level. Continuation patterns should work quickly, as the other trade examples have shown. This particular trade was initiated based on one-minute bars. To have held it 45 minutes hoping for a profit would have immeasurably compounded the initial error, even though the trade would have been a winner. Consistent profits can be achieved only by consistently following trading rules.

The flag is a basic chart pattern that it is often overlooked in favor of much more complicated and flashy tools. Traders, especially newer traders, love complex indicators requiring many lines of computer code, trading strategies that analyze more than a dozen factors before entering a trade, and chart patterns that have lots of complicated elements. The more obscure and complex the mathematics involved, the better. This sort of thing sells lots of books and software, but it often fails to produce winning trades.

In trading, simple is often better. Retracements are simple patterns that work. Certainly there is more to profitable trading than knowing when to enter a market, but if you do not know how to identify low-risk entry points, chances are you will not be profitable in the long run. Retracement patterns offer excellent trading opportunities. In fact, it is possible to build a profitable trading program based on these patterns alone. These are enduring and robust patterns that offer insight into the deep, true structure of trends and provide a consistent, low-risk entry methodology.

Adam Grimes is an active trader with twelve years experience in futures, equities and options markets. He is an expert in technical analysis and statistical market analysis. Grimes is currently the head trader and system designer at Level Partners, LLC, a hedge fund in Columbus, Ohio. This article originally appeared in *SFO* in August-September 2003.

WHEN THE BULLS TIRE...
TOP 10 CHART SIGNAL PATTERNS

BY THOMAS BULKOWSKI

It was one of those days, an unremarkable day by most measures except for one thing: my discovery of a fundamental truth. I realized that traders do not trade chart patterns. Instead, they trade the buy and sell signals issued by those patterns. So, I did some research and found the top ten sell signals that appear most often in today's stocks.

The Countdown

This is not exactly a David Letterman's Top 10, but here they are, including identification tips and performance numbers. We'll start by looking at the pattern that appears least often and conclude with the most widely seen bearish chart pattern, just as Dave would do if he had any idea at all about these patterns.

#10. Triple tops

The left half of *Figure 1* reveals a triple-top pattern. Of the ten chart patterns, this one appears least often in the stocks I examined. Look for three large, distinct minor highs with peaks near the same price. Volume usually trends downward from left to right, as shown. A three-bump pattern becomes a valid triple top when price closes below the confirmation line. That is the sell signal. After the breakout, a pullback (when price returns to the confirmation line) occurs about half the time.

Triple tops can be wide (a year or more) or narrow, but the average length is four months. Half the triple tops will decline 17 percent

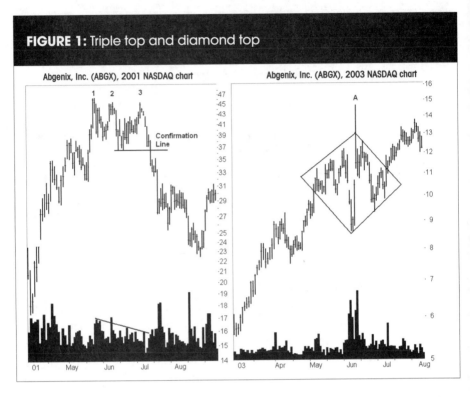

FIGURE 1: Triple top and diamond top

Abgenix, Inc. (ABGX), 2001 NASDAQ chart

Abgenix, Inc. (ABGX), 2003 NASDAQ chart

in a bull market, measured from the breakout to the lowest low, before price rises at least 20 percent.

#9. Diamond tops

The right half of *Figure 1* shows a diamond top. I did not include the long price spike at the top (point A) because I wanted to show a classic example of a diamond. Draw a diamond pattern by connecting the minor highs and lows on each side. Two or more touches of each trend line are required for a properly selected diamond.

Diamonds rarely look as good as the one pictured. Most often, the diamond shape appears pushed to one side, perhaps with uneven trend line lengths. For diamond tops, price enters the pattern from the bottom, but the breakout can be in any direction. A breakout occurs when price closes outside of the trend line boundary. Volume usually trends downward, unlike that shown in the example.

After the breakout, the average decline is 22 percent in a bull market, but half the patterns decline less than 21 percent. Some diamonds have a quick rise leading to the pattern (a rise of several points

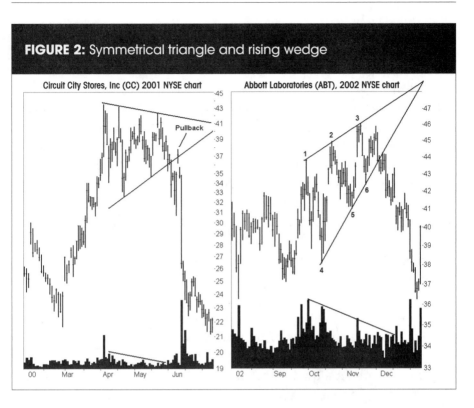

FIGURE 2: Symmetrical triangle and rising wedge

Circuit City Stores, Inc (CC) 2001 NYSE chart

Abbott Laboratories (ABT), 2002 NYSE chart

in just a few days). After the downward breakout, price often returns to the launch point (just before the quick rise began). Jump ahead to *Figure 3* for an example of a quick rise leading to a broadening top. Notice how price almost returns to where it started.

#8. Symmetrical triangle tops

For the uninitiated, the left side of *Figure 2* shows what a symmetrical triangle top looks like. Price enters the pattern from the bottom but can exit in any direction. Draw two trend lines along the minor highs and lows, joining declining highs and rising lows. There should be at least two touches of each trend line. The breakout occurs when price closes outside the trend line boundary, usually about 80 percent of the way to the triangle apex. Volume trends downward during formation of the pattern and can be very low a day or two before the breakout. The average pattern length is two months.

When a downward breakout occurs, price declines 20 percent on average. Half of the patterns will decline less than 18 percent in a bull market. Upward breakouts show rises averaging 35 percent, with the median rise being 28 percent. Pullbacks (or throwbacks if the break-out is upward), occur 51 percent of the time.

#7. Rising wedges

A rising wedge appears on the right of *Figure 2*. Look for higher highs and higher lows bounded by two up-sloping trend lines that eventually intersect. Be skeptical of wedges that have less than five touches total (two on one trend line and three on the other). For example, the example shows six touches. A touch is a minor high or low, and it should come close to or actually intersect the trend line. The breakout does not count as a touch unless it occurs at a minor low. Volume usually trends downward. The average wedge length is 1.5 months long and rarely longer than three or four months. The minimum length is about three weeks. Chart patterns shorter than that are referred to as pennants.

A breakout occurs when price closes outside the pattern boundary. The average decline is 19 percent, with half of the patterns declining less than 15 percent in a bull market. Price is supposed to drop to the pattern's low, at a minimum, but that measure only works 63 percent of the time.

#6. Broadening tops

The left side of *Figure 3* shows a broadening top after a quick rise. Notice how price almost returns to where it started. In a broadening top, look for higher minor highs and lower minor lows bounded by two sloping trend lines. The megaphone shape should have at least two touches of each trend line. Volume is usually irregular but tends to rise as price climbs and recede as price declines. The breakout—a close outside the trend line boundary—can occur in any direction.

The average decline is 16 percent after a downward breakout, and for upward breakouts, the average rise is 34 percent. Both numbers are from bull markets. Half the patterns will have prices drop less than 14 percent or rise less than 25 percent.

#5. One-day reversals, tops

One-day reversals, or ODRs, go by many names. Some call them a selling climax, climax day, or tail. The right side of *Figure 3* shows an example. The ODR is that one-day spike near the top of the example.

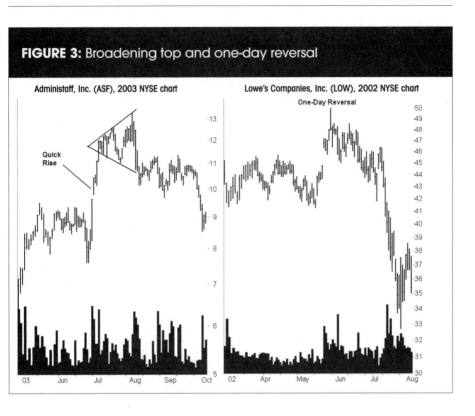

FIGURE 3: Broadening top and one-day reversal

Administaff, Inc. (ASF), 2003 NYSE chart

Lowe's Companies, Inc. (LOW), 2002 NYSE chart

In a typical ODR pattern, price closes within a third of the intraday low, but has a large intraday trading range. ODRs generally appear after a price up-trend. The decline after an ODR is usually not as large as that shown in the example. The average decline is 19 percent, with half the patterns showing price drops of less than 10 percent. The one-day volume is usually quite high, towering above the surrounding landscape. That, however, is not the case in *Figure 3*, as the ODR occurs in the middle of high volume.

#4. Descending triangles

The left half of *Figure 4* shows one of the triangle family's patterns, called a descending triangle. The top trend line slopes downward, but the bottom trend line is flat. Look for at least two minor high and two minor low touches of each trend line. Traders must resist the temptation to cut off a rounding turn and call it a descending triangle. Price must cross the triangle several times, filling the white space like that shown in this example. In a rounding turn cut-off, the middle of the

115

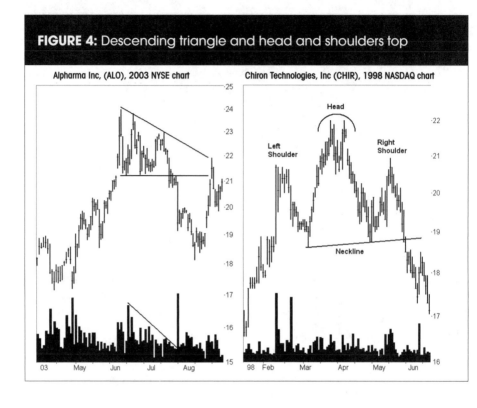

FIGURE 4: Descending triangle and head and shoulders top

Alpharma Inc, (ALO), 2003 NYSE chart

Chiron Technologies, Inc (CHIR), 1998 NASDAQ chart

triangle will be white space and price will tend to crawl along the top trend line.

Traders should be aware that volume usually recedes like that shown in the example. A day or two before the breakout, volume tends to be quite low and then shoot upward during the breakout. The breakout occurs when price closes outside the trend line boundary, and it can be either up or down. The average distance of the breakout to the triangle apex is about 70 percent regardless of breakout direction.

After a downward breakout, price drops 18 percent on average. For upward breakouts, price rises 42 percent in a bull market. Half of the time, the drop will be less than 17 percent and the rise less than 34 percent.

#3. Head and shoulders tops

The right half of *Figure 4* shows a head and shoulders top. Those versed in chart patterns will recognize the dual head of a complex head and shoulders top, but ignore that for a moment. Look for a three-peak pattern with the middle peak towering above the others.

The shoulders should top out near the same price level and be about the same distance from the head. The pattern should look symmetrical about the head—the shape of the left shoulder should mirror the shape of the right. Volume typically is highest on the left shoulder, diminished on the head and the lowest on the right shoulder. This example shows the head having the lowest volume. Thus, traders can expect variations in both the volume trend and the appearance of the shoulders.

Get ready—the average decline is 21 percent in a bull market. Half of the patterns will decline less than 18 percent. Patterns with up-sloping necklines tend to perform slightly better than do those with down-sloping necklines. The neckline, by the way, is a trend line drawn connecting the shoulder lows—the armpits, if you will.

#2. Double tops

Figure 5 shows a double top. More experienced traders that know their chart patterns will recognize an Eve & Eve double top, the classic double-top pattern. Price trends up and forms two peaks that top out near the same price. The decline between the two peaks is usually 10 to 20 percent, but allow exceptions—especially on the high end. The time between the two peaks ranges from a few weeks to a year or more. Volume is heavier on the left peak than the right—most of the time.

The twin peak pattern becomes a valid double top once price closes below the confirmation line that marks the lowest low between the two peaks. A pullback, where price returns to the confirmation line, occurs between 51 percent and 59 percent of the time, depending on a bear market or bull market, respectively. The average decline measures 18 percent in a bull market, with half of the patterns dropping less than 14 percent after the breakout.

And finally, #1, the most widely seen bearish chart pattern: three falling peaks.

The right half of *Figure 5* shows a three-falling-peaks chart pattern. They occur more often than most any other bearish chart pattern. How does one recognize this important and frequently occur-

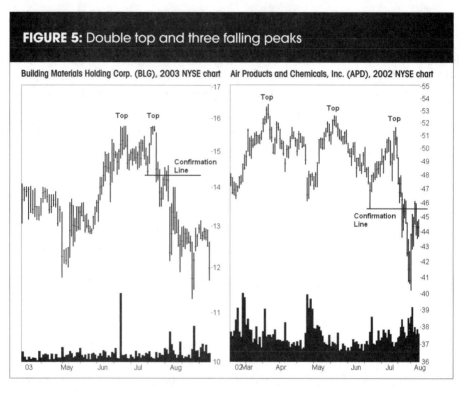

FIGURE 5: Double top and three falling peaks

Building Materials Holding Corp. (BLG), 2003 NYSE chart

Air Products and Chemicals, Inc. (APD), 2002 NYSE chart

ring pattern? Look for three peaks, each lower than the previous one, beginning with the highest high on the chart. These occur in downward price trends and at major bearish turning points. Each peak should look similar, that is, do not mix wide minor highs with small and narrow ones. The three-falling-peaks pattern confirms as a valid pattern once price closes below the lowest low between the three peaks.

After the breakout, price declines 18 percent in a bull market. Almost half (47 percent) will fail to drop more than 15 percent below the confirmation line. That may not sound like much, but because price was declining from the first peak, the complete drop is higher.

Looking for the Target?

For all chart patterns mentioned here except the rising wedge, use the pattern height (highest high minus the lowest low) projected downward (from the lowest low) to get a target price. Price reaches the target between 50 and 80 percent of the time, so it performs about as well as a nearsighted sharp shooter without his glasses.

When trading stocks, it does not matter where the signal comes from. Whether it is an indicator or a chart pattern yelling "sell," obeying the signal may be the smartest move a trader could make. Traders will see these ten chart patterns in the stocks they follow. If the pattern confirms, then price is going down—guaranteed. It may not drop far, but it won't matter because they sold the stock when they got the sell signal.

The ability to sell, you see, is what separates professional traders from the amateurs.

Thomas N. Bulkowski is a private investor and author of several books: *Getting Started in Chart Patterns* (Wiley 2005), *Encyclopedia of Chart Patterns*, 2nd Edition (Wiley Trading, 2005), and *Trading Classic Chart Patterns* (Wiley, 2002). Before earning enough from his investments to retire at age 36, he was a hardware design engineer at Raytheon and a senior software engineer for Tandy Corporation. Bulkowski can be reached at tbut@hotmail.com. This article originally appeared in *SFO* in November 2004.

SECTION FOUR
Technical Indicators

Understanding the basic technical indicators well and incorporating them into your trading practice will undeniably improve your results. We'll explore common technical indicators such as volume, moving averages, momentum, Fibonacci clusters, and oscillators. This section features some of the most knowledgeable names in the industry talking about the indicators they invented: Bollinger on Bollinger bands and Appel on the moving average convergence divergence (MACD), as well as many other experts in the field.

Most indicators are a function of price and are plotted alongside price on the same chart. Moving averages are simple and versatile price-based tools that can help identify a trend and signal when it may be turning. We'll tell you how you can use moving average channels to decipher shorter and longer-term signals. Momentum indicators are price-based tools commonly used to catch precision turns, but they don't catch every turn. We'll clear up some of the mechanical issues to help you use them effectively to properly identify divergence.

Nina Cooper writes about the valuable information that can be derived from stochastics. Thinking about stochastics as merely overbought and oversold signals is an oversimplification that ignores the wealth of timing information that these oscillators offer.

Volume is one of the few indicators unrelated to price, which makes it a valuable confirming or contradicting signal. Volume frequently demonstrates the conviction behind price moves.

To the uninitiated, wave analysis can sound confusing. Combining the Elliott wave principle with traditional technical analysis can increase your probability of a successful trade. Jeffrey Kennedy demystifies wave analysis and tells you how to use it to identify entry and exit points, as well as to place protective stops. He shares the three cardinal rules of the wave principle to help you minimize risk and maximize profits.

TRADING THE INDICATORS: Understanding Volume

BY KIRA MCCAFFREY BRECHT

Many technical traders will tell you that price is king. Everything comes down to price, and price is the most important indicator in and of itself. Experienced traders know that many technical indicators are simply price massaged, oiled, and spit out into a fancy blue or red line at the bottom of one's chart. But volume is a completely different animal. While you'd have to travel far and wide before you'd chance upon a trader who would say that volume readings are more important than price, they are useful and significant raw data readings that measure the amount of action and psychology of the market players.

Volume, of course, is simply the measure of the number of shares of Intel or Qualcomm or any stock traded during a day. In the futures arena, volume measures how many corn contracts or S&P E-minis changed hands that session. For those who are trading on an intraday basis, 5-minute volume bars can be found, or for traders more comfortable with a longer-term view, weekly or monthly volume data can be called up just as easily.

Remember back to high school physics: Newton's first law of motion reflects the concept underlying volume analysis in the financial markets. This law says that an object in motion will stay in motion unless acted upon by an unbalanced force.

Thus, many technical traders call volume the fuel behind a market move. Is the gas tank full and providing powerful momentum for that Porsche speeding down the Autobahn? Or is the gas tank nearing empty, which means the engine is likely sputtering, and the driving machine is slowing and limping toward the shoulder of the road? For a trader who is looking to put on a stock trade from the long side, knowing how much gas is likely left in the tank is an important variable. After all, how many smart drivers set off for a long trip with only a gallon of gas left in the tank?

Joe Granville, editor of the *Granville Market Letter* and developer of the popular volume tool called on balance volume (OBV) [we'll get to this later...], puts it another way and says that volume "is the steam in the boiler that makes the choo choo go down the tracks."

Use It to Confirm

"Generally speaking, volume has to confirm price," explains John Murphy, author and chief technician at Stockcharts.com. "When price breaks out to the upside [or downside], we normally like to see a nice pickup in volume to confirm that."

One of the basic rules of thumb for traditional volume analysis is that a healthy up-trend would see expanding volume on up days and contracting volume on down days. Just the opposite would be true for a down-trend. "When you get an exception to that, it can be a sign that trend is changing," says Phil Roth, chief technical analyst at Miller Tabak + Co. Daily volume data is easy to find and can even be tracked via the *Wall Street Journal*, and most charting software packages offer an option for volume bars across the bottom of the chart.

"A market rallying on light volume is a sign there isn't as much bullishness. It is a hesitant market," says Murphy. "When we don't get volume, we get more suspicious."

Or another subtlety for which to be on the lookout is "big volume in an up-trend, but no price progress. That could be a signal that you've hit resistance," adds Roth. The idea is that an unusual change in a volume pattern could signify a possible reversal.

Some other basic rules of thumb in relation to volume are that bull markets tend to have bigger volume, while bear markets tend to have lighter volume. "Markets must be pushed up but can sink on their own weight," notes Roth. In a down-trend, traders would like to see increasing volume on down days and decreasing volume on up days.

Brian Shannon, director of research at Marketwise, uses volume in his trading and analysis. He says "volume is second only to price. Price is what pays, and volume lets us know about the emotional condition of the buyers and sellers."

Shannon highlights a couple of his favorite reflections on volume:

• Big volume without further upside equals distribution;
• Big volume without further downside equals accumulation;
• Volume tends to peak at turning points;
• Volume often precedes price movement;
• Volume is a relative study.

Shannon outlines an example for a stock that is rallying. "You'd like to see that stock advancing on increasing volume each day, say 600,000 the first day, a million the second day and a million-five the third day. Price pullbacks should see successively lower volume, such as 900,000, 600,000, then 450,000" to reflect a healthy advance.

One of the old market adages says that once a trend is established, it is more likely to continue than to reverse. "That is even more likely to be true if pullbacks are on declining volume," says Shannon. For traders who may have missed an entry opportunity on a breakout, if a stock posts a retreat on declining volume, that may offer a second entry opportunity for a trend move.

Divergence
Themes that come up over and over again in the field of technical analysis are the concepts of confirmation and divergence. Divergence often is used in the world of oscillator readings with such tools as stochastics or the relative strength index. Simply, the idea with those tools is that with a bullish trend, one should see rising oscillator readings. When that doesn't occur, a divergence occurs, and that is an important red flag warning signal that trend could be about to change. Example? If a price made a new high in an up-trend, but stochastics failed to make a new oscillator high and actually turned lower, it would represent a bearish divergence.

Take that concept and apply the same principle to volume. For example, in a bull trend, does a stock or a commodity price hit a new high for the rally move, but declining volume is seen for that session? Red flag time.

Blow-Off and Climax

Now for the exciting stuff: blow-offs and climaxes. Blow-offs tend to occur at major market peaks, while climaxes emerge at market bottoms. These terms simply reflect a huge amount of volume that emerges late in a market rally (or decline) with a sudden peak. Prices then abruptly reverse.

"Volume tells me where the action is. It shows me the collective psychology of the participants if they are fearful or overly optimistic," says Shannon. However, "it's tough to say what a climax or blow-off is until after it is over."

Confirm Pattern Breakouts

Another use of volume analysis is to incorporate volume readings along with pattern breakouts. For those schooled in traditional pattern analysis, volume can be a helpful confirming indicator for double bottom or top, flag, triangle, or any type of pattern breakout. How does it work? Jordan Kotick, global head of technical analysis at Barclay's Capital says that for him, "Volume shows conviction. Is there conviction in a move?"

Combining a price breakout with a volume confirmation simply helps a trader to see if there is conviction behind that price breakout. Let's say that corn futures have been in a down-trend. But because markets don't ever simply go straight up or down, the bear trend takes a pause, prices consolidate for several weeks, and a continuation triangle develops on the daily chart. Then one day, traders wake up and corn breaks out to the downside of that triangle, blasting below the lower triangle line at the final bell. On that day, traders could look for a high-volume day, a large and long volume bar relative to the recent sessions. A high-volume day would be viewed as confirmation to the downside breakout of that pattern.

For those wanting to take volume analysis to the next step, traders could study what is called upside volume, versus downside volume, when analyzing the major U.S. stock averages. Just as it sounds, the upside-downside ratio simply reveals the relationship between the total volume of advancing shares, versus the total volume of declining issues.

On-Balance Volume (OBV)

There are a variety of tools and ratios based on volume, but one of the early volume indicators, developed by Joe Granville in the early 1960s, is known as OBV. This tool can help traders avoid the subjective nature of eyeballing those volume bars streaming across the bottom of the chart. (Is that one slightly bigger or smaller?) The OBV indicator turns the volume data into a line graph, which can be displayed across the bottom of one's chart. Traders actually can draw trendlines on the OBV indicator just like a price chart. When the OBV turns and breaks that trendline, it can signal a potential turning point in price. It also can be used like an oscillator to help pinpoint divergences between price highs and volume peaks or price lows and volume troughs.

"If price is moving up, OBV should be moving up, too," explains Murphy. He also notes that OBV could actually be a leading indicator. "OBV can break out before the stock does," Murphy says.

The calculation behind the OBV is extremely easy to understand even for those who are as math-challenged as this author. The total volume for a session is given a plus or minus value depending on whether prices closed higher or lower that day. A higher close would result in the volume to be counted as a plus, while a lower close would result in a minus value. Thus, a running total is achieved by simply adding or subtracting volume, depending on direction of the market close.

For those who are just beginning to use volume as part of their analysis and trading, Granville advises students to "pick a stock, preferably a well-known stock. Follow it every day in the newspaper. Keep a running total of volume. If it closes up, add all the volume of the stock traded that day. If it closes down, subtract the volume of that day from the previous figure. You'll see a running commentary on the action of the stock. You'll see the evidence that volume precedes the price trend."

Equivolume Charts

Volume analysis has spawned a range of indicators and even a new type of charting technique, called equivolume bars. This type of chart actually combines price and volume into one bar or box. For those familiar with Japanese candlestick charts, the concept is somewhat similar. Basically, the top of the equivolume box represents the day's price high, while the low is seen at the bottom of the box. The width of the box represents the day's volume. The wider the box, the heavier the volume during that session. "By just glancing at the bars, you can tell which days have heavier volume," explains Murphy.

Traditionally, some technical analysts have combined volume with the study of open interest, which simply refers to the number of outstanding contracts still open at the end of the trading day in the futures markets. With the advent of 24-hour markets and the rise in popularity of foreign-exchange trading among individual traders, the study of open interest appears to have waned somewhat. But for those wanting to understand the basic rules of thumb, they still apply.

Traditional Open Interest and Volume Guidelines:

- If prices are rising and volume and open interest are increasing, it represents a strong market;
- If prices are rising while volume and open interest are falling, it reveals a weakening market;
- If prices are falling while volume and open interest are increasing, it represents a weak market;
- If prices are falling while volume and open interest are falling, it represents a strong market.

According to Marketwise's Shannon, one of the biggest misuses of volume is an interpretation when a stock is declining. Let's say a trader is long a stock and price begins to pull back. "People convince themselves to hold on because it [the pullback] is on light volume," Shannon says. But that may not be the best way to manage a trade. "Would you rather lose ten percent of your money on light volume or big volume?" asks Shannon. He instead advises traders to exit a position "based on price action."

Another common mistake is that many traders could point to a heavy volume day and be convinced that it is a climax or blow-off day. "Most people end up misreading big volume," says Shannon. "Just because it is the biggest volume in three days, doesn't mean the move is over. Volume could be even bigger the next day."

Timing Is Everything

Typically, trading in the stock market (and the futures market on the major stock indexes) sees the heaviest volume during the first hour-and-a-half of the day and then the last hour-and-a-half of the day. Traders can use this generality to help them in their intraday trading. "The midday doldrums occur because institutional traders are waiting you out," warns Shannon. Often times, major institutional players will execute large portions of orders in the morning and then wait for heavy volume and renewed trending action late in the day to finish orders.

This can be helpful information for those who are trading very short term on an intraday basis. "If you are a hyperactive trader and have to take your profits, take them during the first move in the morning," says Shannon. There may be another opportunity during the second late-day wave of action. Otherwise a trader who bought, say, the S&P E-mini early in the day and saw some profits in that trade may slowly watch that profit erode during the lunchtime doldrums as prices simply tick slowly lower. For those who get spooked on pullbacks or don't have the patience to wait for the afternoon move, it may be wise to simply book the profits early on.

Here are a few more tidbits on incorporating volume into your trading and analysis.

- Use volume simply as a screening tool. For those who are scanning thousands of stocks looking for a good trading opportunity, volume can help distinguish between those that are in an up-trend or down-trend (depending on whether one is looking for long or short trades). How? Those stocks with the best volume profile or pattern can help weed out the stocks most likely to continue with that trend.
- Barclay's Kotick closes with another tip for beginning volume followers. "It's not the level of volume that is key, it is the trend of volume. Look at it over a range of time." One day of volume can't be viewed in a vacuum. Volume analysis is most useful when compared to previous sessions. Some like to say volume is simply a reflection of supply and demand. A high-volume day simply reflects more demand in the marketplace. But overall, traders and analysts note that volume should be used as a confirming indicator. Most

still agree that price remains the most important factor to consider while trading. Volume may offer up warning signals, red flags, or generate trading ideas. But use it as a supplementary tool.

- If you've haven't incorporated volume readings or analysis into your trading, it may be worth exploring. "Volume is very useful and important. You can't do good technical analysis without looking at volume," concludes Murphy.

Kira McCaffrey Brecht is senior editor at *SFO* magazine. She has been writing about the financial markets for sixteen years. Posts during her career include Chicago bureau chief at *Futures World News*, market analyst at *Bridge News*, and technical analyst at MMS International. McCaffrey Brecht holds a political science degree from Brown University. This article originally appeared in *SFO* in August 2005.

FIBONACCI CLUSTERS AND THE POWER OF CONFLUENCE

BY BERNARD MITCHELL

Leonardo Pisano, better known by his nickname Fibonacci, published Liber Abaci in 1202, in which he posed the following problem:

> A certain man puts a pair of rabbits in a place surrounded on all sides by a wall. How many pairs of rabbits can be produced from that pair in a year if it is supposed that every month each pair begets a new pair, which from the second month on becomes productive?
>
> The resulting sequence is 1, 1, 2, 3, 5, 8, 13, 21, 34, 55, ... each number in the series is the sum of the two numbers preceding it. He also discovered that each number in the sequence is 1.618 times the preceding number and .618 of the next number.

Many technicians use Fibonacci numbers when trying to determine support and resistance, frequently using .382, .50, and .618 retracements. It is commonly believed that a .382 retracement from a trend move will tend to imply a continuation of the trend. A .618 retracement implies that a trend change may be in the making. Technicians have adopted many such rules. My approach is different in that I do not use Fibonacci retracement numbers to determine the trend. My long-term trend is determined by a simple 89-period moving average. It is effective from a one-minute chart to a monthly chart. This moving average is the literal battleground between the bulls and bears.

My use of Fibonacci clusters will determine support and resistance in the direction of the main trend (which is always determined by prices either above or below the long-term moving average). It is what I call my "main 89 line." Most charting packages will enable you to create a simple

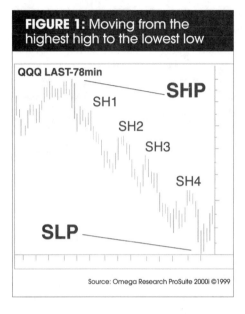

FIGURE 1: Moving from the highest high to the lowest low

QQQ LAST-78min

SHP

SH1

SH2

SH3

SH4

SLP

Source: Omega Research ProSuite 2000i ©1999

89-period moving average. I encourage you to look at the market this way.

What are Fibonacci clusters and how are they different in calculating support and resistance from the standard ratios with which most traders are familiar? Simply put, Fibonacci clusters are more accurate because they use more data points and the Fibonacci ratios are calculated differently. I include as many as seven swing highs and swing lows in addition to the significant high and low points in the calculations.

Let's review the approach I use to calculate support and resistance levels. The first thing I need to identify is a trend move, i.e., a significant high point to a significant low point or vice versa. These points are the extreme boundaries of the trend.

Within these extreme points are contra-trend swing highs within an overall down-trend and swing lows within an overall up-trend. In other words, I look to capture the high and low points of a contra-trend move within the longer trend. These contra-trend high and low points are swing points and are critical to my calculation of Fibonacci clusters.

The normal retracement levels of .382, .50, and .618 of the main trend are simply not accurate enough when the pinpointing of support and resistance becomes crucial to pulling money out of the markets. First, it is important to understand the concept of support and resistance. In this writer's opinion, unless you can determine precise support and resistance, most traders will achieve mediocre results at best. Simply put, support means there is sufficient buying pressure (volume) at a given price level to halt a down-trend, and resistance means there is sufficient selling pressure (volume) at a given price level to halt an up-trend. Support places a floor under the market, and resistance places a ceiling above the market.

The higher the volume, relative to the range of the price bar, the more significance is given to the price level as support and resistance. I measure this in terms of ticks in a price bar. A greater number of transactions (ticks) within a given timeframe (when divided into the range of the bar and compared with the previous two price bars, with the mathematical result being lower) will produce a robust squat with high predictive power for market reversals. The squat bar is my trigger to enter a trade. The only thing I now need to know is where support and resistance will likely take place.

This is where my calculation of Fibonacci clusters comes in. The resulting output is four levels of support and four levels of resistance. They are:

- lower resistance
- stopping point resistance
- upper resistance
- maximum resistance

- upper support
- stopping point support
- lower support
- maximum support

Each of the first three levels of resistance and the first three levels of support are tradeable levels, as long as a squat is generated on the entry bar. The maximum resistance and support levels are normally not used for entries unless they are a confluence number from a larger or smaller trend. There will be more on this later. Prior to the development of computer software, it was time consuming to create these levels of support and resistance, except on daily and weekly data. We can now produce reliable, tradeable numbers on intra-day data, even when highs and lows are constantly changing.

Find Resistance and Support

Resistance is demonstrated when the market has made a significant high point (SHP). Now the market proceeds to correct, contrary to the main trend and puts in a series of swing highs (SH), finally registering a significant low point (SLP).

Observing *Figure 1*, you can easily identify the highest high (SHP) and the lowest low (SLP) in the trend and a series of swing highs (SH) that fall between the two extreme points. The selection of swing highs is straightforward. There needs to be a minimum of three bar highs.

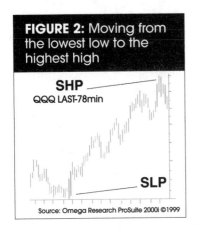

FIGURE 2: Moving from the lowest low to the highest high

SHP

QQQ LAST-78min

SLP

Source: Omega Research ProSuite 2000i ©1999

Support is demonstrated when the market has made a significant low point (SLP). Now the market proceeds to rally, contrary to the main trend, and puts in a series of swing lows (SL), finally registering a significant high point (SHP).

Observing the chart, you can easily identify the highest high (SHP) and the lowest low (SLP) in the trend and a series of swing lows (SL) that fall between the two extreme points. The selection of swing lows is straightforward. There needs to be a minimum of three bar lows.

We will now look at some examples of Fibonacci clusters and apply the calculations to different time frames (i.e., weekly, daily, and intra-day).

Weekly Charts

Atmel Corporation (ATML) had a huge bull run and peaked on March 24, 2000, at 30.688 (see *Figure 3*). It then proceeded to correct, making several important lows, down to its recent low of 7.625 registered on April 6, 2001. Prior to that, a low was made on December 1, 2000, at 9.375. To project resistance from that point, I selected a series of three strength weekly highs starting from 24.406, 21.938, and 16.625. Using SHP 30.688 and SLP 9.375, along with the three swing highs, the result was:

- lower resistance: 16.26
- stopping point: 18.62

- upper resistance: 21.51
- maximum resistance: 25.75

Note that the market then proceeded to stage a choppy rally over ten weeks, peaking at 18.438, just shy of our stopping point, 18.62. Over the next ten weeks a new low was made at 7.625. Using the new low as my new SLP, and using the 18.438 rally high as my new SH3, a new series of resistance numbers have now been projected. Since this is in the future, we need to wait and see how these numbers eventually work out.

Observing the output from the two trends, each with a different SLP, i.e., 9.375 and 7.625, a series of confluence-resistant points have been established. They are:

132

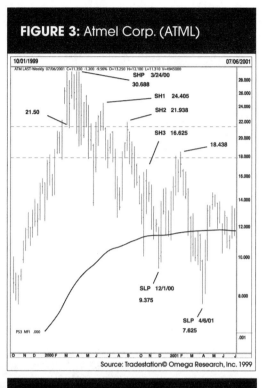

FIGURE 3: Atmel Corp. (ATML)

Source: Tradestation© Omega Research, Inc. 1999

FIGURE 4: Texas Instruments, Inc. (TXN)

Source: Tradestation© Omega Research, Inc. 1999

- 16.26 and 16.65: lower resistance
- 18.62 and 18.64: stopping point
- 21.51 and 21.07: upper resistance

At these three levels, shorts or exits to previously held long positions can be taken, provided a squat bar is generated on the daily charts.

Daily Charts

After rallying off a low, Texas Instruments (TXN) peaked at our daily 89-period moving average at 42.91 on May 22, 2001 (see *Figure 4*). It then broke sharply to 28.25 where it created a SLP. Between the two extremes we find SH1 at 39.39 and SH2 at 32.95. Thus, using the four inputs the result is:

- lower resistance: 32.94
- stopping point: 34.22
- upper resistance: 35.76
- maximum resistance: 39.77

Going one step further in attempting to find confluence, I used the SH1 as my SHP. The result:

- lower resistance: 31.55
- stopping point: 32.49

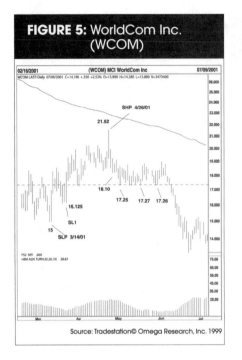

FIGURE 5: WorldCom Inc. (WCOM)

Source: Tradestation© Omega Research, Inc. 1999

FIGURE 6: S&P 500 index (SP U1)

Source: Tradestation© Omega Research, Inc. 1999

- upper resistance: 33.54

- maximum resistance: 37.01

You will note that the lower resistance (32.94) on the longest trend comes close to the stopping point (32.49) on the shorter trend, and the stopping point on the longer comes fairly close (not perfect) to upper resistance on the shorter trend. Observing the chart, the high point of 34.01 falls between these two numbers before the market started a significant sell off.

Starting from a SLP on March 14, 2001 at 15, WorldCom (WCOM) rallied, establishing an SHP on April 26 at 21.52 (see *Figure 5*). The market then proceeded to correct off the highs, creating a 15-day low at 18.10, penetrating our stopping point by just 13 points (18.23 - 18.10 = 13).

To find confluence, I used the SLP of 16.125 with the same SHP. This produced important support between 17.37 to 17.28. As you can see, the market spent twenty-six days trying to hold this support level, before finally succumbing in a waterfall decline to 13.

Intra-day Charts

Looking at the September 2001 S&P Futures 135-minute chart (see *Figure 6*), the SLP was established on June 26 at 1211. The SHP was established

FIGURE 7: E-mini S&P 500 (ES U1)

Source: Tradestation© Omega Research, Inc. 1999

on June 5 at 1297.80. Using the SH1 at 1289.50, SH2 at 1272, SH3 at 1249.30, and SH4 at 1240, the calculations are as follows:

- lower resistance: 1244.84
- stopping point: 1254.03
- upper resistance: 1265.42
- maximum resistance: 1279.23

From the SLP low, the market rallied to 1244.90 eight bars later, just shy of lower resistance. A series of squat bars showed up as the market spent nine more bars before finally tanking. Confluence numbers were also created showing important resistance around 1244. On July 6, with new lows being made, a new series of resistance levels can be calculated.

610 Ticks

Fibonacci clusters are most advantageous for day traders looking to scalp profits on small moves using the benefits of electronic execution. I have created resistance levels from the huge down-trend that started with the SHP at 1247.25 on July 3 at 6:00 a.m. EDT, culminating in a SLP at 1189 on July 9 at 10:04 a.m. EDT (see *Figure 7*).

Using seven swing highs as my inputs along with SHP and SLP, the resistance levels are as follows:

- lower resistance: 1214.04
- stopping point: 1219.81

- upper resistance: 1226.45
- maximum resistance: 1234.79

In addition, I have attempted to find confluence numbers by using two different SHPs, thus calculating from smaller trends. Those resistance levels come in at:

- lower resistance: 1209.43
- upper resistance: 1220.03

- stopping point: 1214.44
- maximum resistance: 1229.87

and:

- lower resistance: 1205.13
- stopping point: 1209.52

- upper resistance: 1214.35
- maximum resistance: 1222.60

The very first thing to notice is numbers that are confluencing around 1214.04 (lower resistance on the largest trend). They are 1214.44 (stopping point next largest trend) and 1214.35 (upper resistance smallest trend). Average these three numbers and arrive at 1214.27. The series of confluence numbers on the big trend come in around 1220.75. They are 1219.81 (stopping point largest trend). Those numbers average out to 1220.82.

The third series of confluence numbers on the big trend come in around 1228.25. They are 1226.45 (upper resistance largest trend) and 1229.87 (maximum resistance smaller trend). They average 1228.16. Shorts can be taken at all three levels as long the entry bars are accompanied by squats. The point to remember: this resistance will be constantly updated in real time as new lows are made.

After more than twenty years of working with the natural numbers that make up the Fibonacci sequence, Fibonacci clusters with the power of confluence come closest to pinpointing support and resistance.

Bernard Mitchell is the president of PBSP, LLC. He is a systems developer with designation as an Omega Research Solutions Provider under PBSP, LLC, which provides online trading advice and educational programs. Mitchell has trained more than 800 traders in his trading methodologies. He can be reached at pbsp@feargreed.com. This article originally appeared in *SFO* in March 2002.

TRADING THE INDICATORS: Understanding Moving Averages

BY KIRA MCCAFFREY BRECHT

Within the field of technical analysis, which includes some very subjective forms of looking at the market (such as pattern identification, Elliott wave counts, etc.), moving averages offer an objective manner to view price and trend.

"The first job of a technician is to identify trend," says Ralph Acampora, well-known technical guru and head of technical research at Prudential. "The simplest way to do that is to identify higher highs and higher lows and draw a trend line." And he adds, "The problem with that is that my trends might be a little different from your trends because we might draw the line a little differently. A moving average, by definition, is a mathematical trend line."

The basic concept is that if price is above the 10-day moving average, then the short-term trend is up (just flip that example on its head for a downtrend). Remember that there are three basic timeframes to which technical traders refer: the short-, medium-, and long-term trend. And unless one is doing very short-term intraday trading, it is worth knowing where all three trends stand (and all actually can be different).

Moving on, if price is above the 50-day moving average, then the medium-term trend is generally considered to be up. Finally, the big mama of all moving averages is the 200-day moving average. Most technical traders and analysts consider this moving average to be a proxy for the long-term trend—it's the key line in the sand. Are prices above the 200-day moving average? Then the dominant, major trend is up. If prices are below the 200-day moving average, it would signal that the longer-term trend is down.

Just a little note on timeframes—traders can adjust moving averages to any period, which could be a 10-, 20- or 50-period moving average. It's called a period because if one is looking at an hourly chart, it would be a 10-hour moving average, or on a weekly chart, a 10-week moving average. It all depends on the timeframe of your chart. Also good to know, moving averages are a universal tool, which can be used on any market, including foreign exchange, individual stocks, crude oil futures, or the S&P E-mini contract.

Moving averages can signal when a new trend has started or when a trend is completed. However, because of the way they are constructed, moving average signals are lagging, not leading, indicators.

So how are they formed? Actually, they are very simple to compute. Let's say one is trying to calculate the 20-day moving average of closing prices. Add up the last 20 days and divide the total by 20 to determine the moving average. The average moves because every day the oldest day is dropped off as the current day's information is added. And don't worry—you don't have to do the math yourself. This technical tool is widely available in all standard charting software packages. Simply click on the moving average option and voilà!—it appears. There will be a function to change the parameter of periods, such as a 20-day or 10-hour (depending on chart timeframe) for the moving average.

When to Pull This Trick out of the Bag?

Technical traders generally rely on a number of technical tools in their trading arsenals. The more one learns about technical analysis, the better they will understand the concept of confirmation. For example, the more technical tools that are flashing the same signal at the same time, the better the odds that a trading idea would be successful.

But traders also need to know how and when to apply different technical tools to maximize their usefulness, and moving averages are most useful in trending market environments. Says Acampora, "When the market is going sideways, you can get many false signals."

Avoid whiplash! If a market has shifted into a well-defined sideways consolidation band, the best advice is don't use moving averages. However, there is a caveat. For extremely short-term swing traders, moving averages can help pinpoint turning points in sideways markets. If there is a well-defined price ceiling and price floor for the sideways band, traders could use "shorter lengths of moving averages to pick off short-term swings in the longer-term context of going sideways," according to John Bollinger, president of Bollinger Capital Management.

While traders have heard over and over again that there is no Holy Grail, in the world of technical analysis, where do moving averages fit in? They are not the answer within the crystal ball, but the big and widely watched moving averages do attract some media hype and perhaps, at least to some extent, can become a self-fulfilling prophecy, at least for the short-term. CNBC may proclaim, "XYZ stock has been trading above its 50-day moving average for months now, but today fell to that level. Will it hold?" A media buzz is created around the 50-day or 200-day moving averages. And for the most part, those are the averages flashing on many individual and institutional traders' screens every day. When "prices fail to hold a certain moving average, it can have a pronounced psychological impact on the community," Bollinger notes. And by now, readers must be well aware how much psychology plays into price movement!

Build Your Own System

For those who don't understand the basics of a moving average crossover system, it's actually very simple. One could easily construct a moving-average system that issues buy and sell signals. If a trader is using just one moving average, a buy signal is triggered when the closing price moves above the moving average. Conversely, a sell signal is flashed when the closing price moves below the moving average.

Many technical traders will rely on the crossover method as an attempt to reduce false signals and noise. Using the crossover strategy, a trader might pick the 20-day and the 50-day moving average. When the shorter average (in this case the 20-day) crosses above the longer average, a buy signal is seen. Sell signals are produced in the opposite fashion. Fewer whipsaws are seen when traders rely on this type of methodology. See *Figure 1* for an example. A circle signals a buy signal when the 10-day crossed over the 20-day moving average in late January. Cocoa prices rallied substantially from that signal,

FIGURE 1: Daily New York Board of Trade May cocoa

The 10-day moving average, as seen in the dashed line, and the 20-day moving average in the gray line.

Source: FutureSource Xtra

roughly from the $1,580 dollars per metric ton level to the mid-March peak at $1,850.

While moving averages can be helpful, traders need to do their homework when using them. If it were as simple as this example, everybody would be using this system to make millions, and I'd be sitting at the floor-to-ceiling windows of my mansion overlooking Lake Michigan, with French champagne in one hand and hors d'oeuvres in the other.

Some of the drawbacks that traders need to consider are that the buy signal isn't formally issued until after the close, which means the entry point is the next day. Also, as evidenced by this example, moving-average signals don't get you in at the bottom of the trend. Nor do they get you out at the top. But you may be able to catch a good part of the middle of the trend (which should be enough to be profitable, if proper discipline and money management techniques are firmly in place).

In late March, as seen in *Figure 1*, cocoa prices plunged sharply in an apparent bull trap failure. But as of this writing, a sell signal has not yet been seen. A trader who faithfully follows buy and sell signals would still be sitting in this trade watching his profits erode. Despite this, however, there is value in moving averages. They can be used as part of a discretionary methodology or as part of a mechanical trading system.

"When people first come to technical analysis and look at moving averages, they seem to offer great buy signals," says Bollinger. "But when traders do a little work, the reality turns out not as rosy as they had hoped it would be." Yet he admits that moving averages can be "good in a carefully constructed trading system, provided one tests carefully with extensive out-of-sample testing and avoids optimization. With proper system testing and proper system construction, such systems can work."

Other Uses of Moving Averages

Linda Bradford Raschke, CTA and president of LBR Group, says moving averages can pinpoint good buying spots during a trend. For shorter-term discretionary traders, who are trading a trending market, pullbacks to the moving average can be good buy spots, she explains. Markets don't go straight up or down. For example, let's say the S&P contract is rallying, but intraday price stages a pullback to the 20-period moving average on the hourly chart. That level could offer a good buy spot. However, warns Raschke, "Buying on the first or second retracement is OK. But be careful as the trend matures. If you see a buy or sell climax, don't buy the pullback."

Looking at a basic technical analysis book, you'll notice different types of moving averages: simple, exponential, and linearly weighted. While they are slightly different, experienced traders suggest not getting bogged down in the details, as they all basically work the same and offer the same type of signals. For the record, however, the simple moving average is the one we defined above.

A criticism to the simple moving average concept is that each day's action carries equal weight. The linearly weighted moving average gives greater weight to more recent closes, as the calculation would multiply the closing price on the 20th day (for a 20-day moving average) by 20 and the 19th day by 19, and so on. The total then is divided by the sum of the multipliers. The exponential moving average also assigns greater weight to more recent data but also includes in its formula all of the data in the history of that instrument (in order to take into account the importance of data that may have occurred before the specified period). Traders also actually can define what percentage weighting to be given to the last day's price.

Many traders seem to use either the simple or the exponential, but it's worth trying the various indicators to see which fits best for you. "Personally, I like exponential moving averages," says Raschke. "They give more weight to the data on the front end. But you can start splitting hairs on this stuff. It comes down to what tickles your eye." The crux of the matter is that traders need to experiment or test on their own to determine which moving average and what type fits best with their trading style and timeframe.

Many technical tools, such as moving average convergence divergence (MACD), moving average envelopes, and Bollinger bands are more advanced indicators, which in some way borrow from the moving-average concept.

Understanding the basics of moving averages, however, will allow one to delve further into the technical arena. Moving averages can be a useful tool for those looking to identify what type of trend the market is in and when a turning point has occurred. Again, traders will never catch exact tops or bottoms with moving averages, as they are lagging indicators, but they can catch a lion's share of a major market move.

Kira McCaffrey Brecht is senior editor at *SFO magazine*. She has been writing about the financial markets for sixteen years. Posts during her career include Chicago bureau chief at *Futures World News*, market analyst at *Bridge News*, and technical analyst at MMS International. McCaffrey Brecht has passed Level I and Level II of the MTA's MCT exams. She holds a degree in political science from Brown University. This article originally appeared in *SFO* in May 2005.

THE TWO FACES OF MOMENTUM

I like to say that trades are like relationships—a lot easier to get into than to get out of. I believe in the adage that maintains that if you have a good exit system, entries hardly matter.

Our approach to entries is very simple. Using a bar length that is one-fifth to one-third the length of the bar upon which we wish to focus, we take second signals in the direction of the trend. We use simple momentum crossover signals and wait for a crossover, a pull-back, and a new crossover, at which time we consider the entry signal valid. Once a similar signal is generated on the main or monitor bar chart, we monitor the trade on that chart. Once in, our goal is to get out on the next bar following the maximum profit bar, or to cut our losses when necessary as soon as called for.

The two components of a good exit system are momentum divergence signals that identify market turns accurately and stops that are set in such a way as to minimize losses, but also allow profits to run.

We view using momentum divergence exits as soft landings and hope always to exit right after the maximum profit bar (the bar at which point the trade was the most profitable) through the use of such exits. Remember that stops are only useful if a market turns without warning, or if the trade has never become profitable to begin with. Using a stop is the hard landing.

Toward this end, the focus of this chapter is on the use of momentum indicators for exits, and it covers two issues. The first issue

143

relates to the mechanics of how to use momentum indicators. The second issue relates to the question of how well momentum indicators work.

A Quick Review

Popular momentum indicators include the stochastic, relative strength index (RSI), and MACD histogram. In our practice, not surprisingly, we also make use of the Kase PeakOscillator and KasecD (KCD).

The stochastic evaluates the placement of the close relative to a high-low price range over a certain time period. The idea behind the stochastic is that in a market with good momentum, the closes will be moving in the direction of the trend. For example, the closes will rise relative to the high-low range in a rising market.

The RSI looks at the ratio of up-closes and down-closes to the total number of close-to-close fluctuations over a certain period. If the market is moving with good momentum the rate of change of the closing prices will keep up with the rate at which the market is making new highs, in a bull market, or lows, in a bear market.

All standard oscillators are calculated as the difference between two moving averages. The MACD histogram is the difference between an exponential moving-average oscillator and its own average. So, the MACD is an oscillator of an oscillator. If an oscillator is a rate of change or velocity indicator, the MACD histogram is then an acceleration indicator. Markets with good momentum will be accelerating, not decelerating. Thus the MACD gives a clue as to the strength of the trend.

Momentum divergence signals are generated in the same manner for all momentum indicators. One looks for a higher or equal high in price to be matched by a lower or equal high in the momentum indicator for bearish divergence and the opposite for bullish divergence. Once a divergence signal is generated, traders should begin to take profit.

Let's look at *Figure 1* to identify proper divergence comparisons (solid line) and incorrect comparisons (dotted line). Making the distinction between the two will undoubtedly factor into a trader's success in the market. The following illustrates both correct and incorrect comparisons between price and momentum:

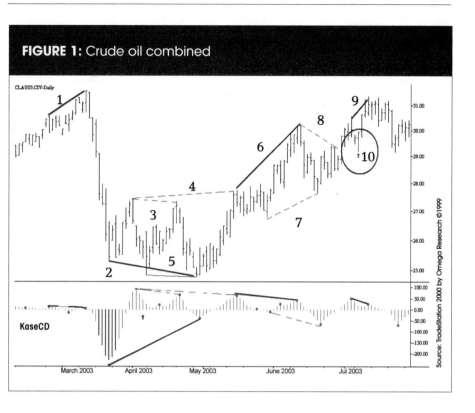

FIGURE 1: Crude oil combined

1. The first divergence, labeled "1," is correct because it compares two highs in price with two highs on the momentum indicator in a rising market.

2. Divergence 2 is correct as it compares two lows in price with two lows on the momentum indicator in a falling market.

3. In a falling market, one does not compare highs, only lows, so comparison 3 is wrong. Also, even if the market was rising, the second high is lower than the first high. A comparison must be between rising highs or falling lows.

4. Along the same lines, one does not compare a high from a falling market to a high in a rising market, so 4 is also wrong.

5. There must be both a peak in price and a peak in the histogram. In this case, the price comparison is correct—two lows are compared

in a falling market—but there is no downward peak relating to the first price low to be compared. The arrow labeled "5" illustrates this point.

6. Divergence 6 is correct because it compares two highs in price with two highs on the momentum indicator in a rising market.

7. In a rising market, one only compares highs, not lows, so comparison 7 is wrong.

8. In rising markets one compares rising highs, and in falling markets one compares falling lows. In this case, the second high is lower than the first high, so the highs are not rising but falling.

9. Finally, 8 is correct, similar to 6.

Avoid Mistakes in Identifying Divergence

In addition to these issues, there are two common errors traders make in identifying divergence: failing to properly identify peaks and not matching price to indicator peaks.

For a peak in price to actually be considered a peak or for a peak in the momentum indicator to actually be considered a peak, a bar following the peak must take place. In a rising market in which bearish divergence is taking place, a price bar that has a lower high than the peak must be generated.

On the histogram, an indicator value with a lower value than the peak must be generated. The inverse is true for a bullish divergence in a bear market. A low peak is circled and labeled "10" on the chart, with an arrow pointing to the low. There is a higher low before and after the peak, which confirms the bar labeled as the low. It is fine to have a plateau made up of multiple bars with equal prices or indicator values, as long as the plateau is preceded by and followed by bars with less extreme values.

Next, the peak in price and the peak in the histogram do not have to take place on the same bar, but they should be close to each other. Our guideline is to have the peaks within two bars of each other on daily charts, and within no more than four of each other on intra-day charts.

Another rule of thumb to keep in mind—if prices continue with the trend before the divergences confirm, it is not a valid divergence. Let's get more specific. Say there was a peak in price followed by a peak on the momentum indicator. However, by the time that the momentum indicator confirmed its peak, prices had begun to rise again. In such cases, we would not consider the divergence to be valid.

Now, relative to the second issue, let's evaluate the performance of the Kase indicators, the PeakOscillator and KCD against the traditional indicators. The Kase indicators, rather than using a fixed number of periods, use a loop built into the code that chooses the best cycle length. Also, when volatility increases, traditional indicators often overreact. Kase's indicators account for changes in volatility and, thus, avoid such overreactions.

Both indicators are based on the Kase serial dependency index where $\ln(H[N-1]/L[0])/V$ is used for up moves and $\ln(L[N-1]/H[0])/V$ for down moves, where:

$H[N-1]$ = high N bars ago
$H[0]$ = this bar's high
$L[N-1]$ = low N bars ago
$L[0]$ = this bar's low
V = historical volatility over N bars
N = a number from N1 to N2 that gives the highest resultant value for the index

For those of you not into formulas, here's the written explanation of the above. Volatility is a measure of the standard deviation of the logarithmic rate of change of the market. Standard deviation is related to probability, for example a two-standard-deviation move has a 2.5-percent probability of occurrence, relative to a normal bell curve, which is based on random activity. Thus, the further the market moves in relationship to volatility, the less likely the movement is to be classified as random, and the more likely it is trending. Instead of using moving averages like old-fashioned oscillators do, Kase indicators use trend-indices based how far the market has moved relative to volatility. This is not to be confused with standard deviations of price, commonly called Bollinger bands, which use only price and not volatility as their basis.

The PeakOscillator is the difference between two trend measurements, one for rising markets and the other for falling markets, and the KCD is the PeakOscillator minus its own average. So, the PeakOscillator takes the place of a traditional oscillator, and the KCD takes the place of the traditional MACD.

So, What's a Successful Indicator?

To measure how well the momentum indicators work, we first must define what constitutes a successful indicator. For purposes of this study, we measured an indicator's success rate in two ways. First, an indicator's success was measured in terms of how often the market turned sufficiently to hit stops following a momentum divergence signal. Second, success was measured by how often market turns that were of sufficient magnitude to hit stops were preceded by a divergence signal. So, we can classify our performance measures in terms of what follows, (e.g., does a turn follow the signal?), and what leads, (e.g., did the signal take place before the turn?).

For the stops, we employed the Kase DevStops, a system that uses the reversals based on true range to set stops. True range is the maximum of the high minus the low, the previous close minus the high, or the low minus the previous close. The warning line is set at the average two-bar reversal, and the three additional stops, dev1, dev2, and dev3, are set around levels which represent one, two, and three standard-deviation reversals.

On *Figure 2*, July 2003 high grade copper, the four stops just noted are labeled in the circle marked 10. One can see that minor reversals test dev1 or dev2, while the major reversals tend to break dev3, and the stops follow the market moves well.

In order to evaluate the performance of the indicators discussed, we set up daily data charts over a range of futures contracts data, including cattle, coffee, corn, cotton, crude oil, gold, natural gas, and the S&P 500 index. Altogether, our test was performed on 47,000 days of data, about 185 years in total.

Divergence signals were programmed on the traditional indicators and on the Kase indicators using the rules and guidelines outlined above relative to the proper mechanics of identification. For the first part of the momentum performance study, we looked at which stops were hit following divergence.

TABLE 1: Do turns follow signals?		
Stop Hit	Stochastic & MACD	Kase Peak Oscillator & KCD
Warning %	89	90
Dev1 %	74	76
Dev2 %	54	57
Dev3 %	32	34

TABLE 2: Are turns preceded by signals?		
Stop Hit	Stochastic & MACD	Kase Peak Oscillator & KCD
Warning %	51	76
Dev1 %	50	77
Dev2 %	48	78
Dev3 %	43	78

Because two Kase indicators, the PeakOscillator and KCD, are always used together, we show their results along with the results of two traditional indicators—the stochastic and MACD— which, when used in conjunction with one another, give the best results.

As *Table 1* illustrates, we found that relative to what follows, the indicators work about the same. The Kase indicators result in an average improvement of about 4 percent, with the level of improvement increasing with the size of the reversal.

However, a huge difference is seen between the traditional indicators and the Kase indicators when we evaluate the data in the opposite direction, as to what leads. The traditional indicators catch less than half of the market turns, and the Kase indicators catch more than three-quarters of them (see *Table 2*). There is an overall improvement of more than 60 percent, and the larger the reversal, the greater the level of improvement.

If one were to use all three traditional indicators, the performance would be marginally better. The results would increase from an average of 48 percent of the turns caught to about 57 percent. The Kase performance level of 78 percent is so high over the statistically significant sample of 47,000 days of test data used that even if one had managed to follow all three traditional indicators in addition to the Kase indicators, only a marginal improvement in performance, around 10 percent, would have resulted.

Figure 2 illustrates this point. The turns caught by both indicators are solid lines, while those only caught by the KCD are dotted lines.

10. Divergence 11 was caught by the KCD when prices made a lower low and the indicator made a higher low. The MACD failed to

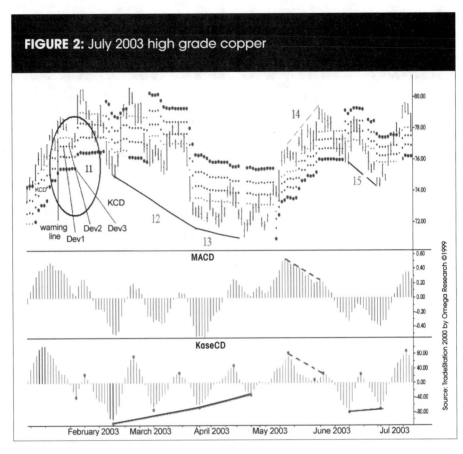

FIGURE 2: July 2003 high grade copper

Source: TradeStation 2000 by Omega Research ©1999

catch it because it made a lower low. In this case, dev1 was broken, and prices stalled right below dev2.

11. The same is true of 12 as 11, and the market reversed well beyond dev3 following that turn.

12. Both indicators exhibited a lower high when prices made a higher high and dev3 was definitively broken thereafter.

13. After the decline that followed 13, the market turned back up, and that turn was caught by a higher low on the KCD that matched a lower low in price. The MACD failed to catch this turn that broke dev3.

Kase and Company's research has shown that all of the momentum indicators studied are great at predicting turns, but of these, only the Kase indicators have worked well as a reliable exit system. Traditional indicators miss over half the turns, but Kase's catch more than three-quarters of them, illustrating the superiority of a momentum approach that is self-optimizing for the number of periods in the indicator and which adjusts for volatility.

Nevertheless, regardless of which set of momentum indicators traders choose to work with for exits, they can custom-tailor their exit system to their particular risk appetite, based on the odds of hitting a stop once divergence takes place, per *Table 1*. If a trader were only willing to suffer a loss equivalent to the average two-bar reversal, he would exit a large portion of his trade, based on the warning line's hit-rate of 90 percent. Those willing to hold a trade through a larger loss—say a two standard deviation move of the two-bar reversal dev2 on Kase's stop system—could take 57 percent of profit when a divergence took place.

Cynthia A. Kase, CMT, became an oil trader for Chevron in 1983 after ten years in chemical engineering. She was Chemical Bank's first commodity derivatives trader and later consulted with the Saudi oil ministry. In 1992 she launched Kase and Company, Inc.,which offers the indicators discussed in the article, StatWare, and provides energy hedging and trading solutions. Log on to www.kasestatware.com for more information. Kase can be contacted at kase@kaseco.com. This article originally appeared in *SFO* in October 2003.

CHANNEL YOUR FOCUS:
The Moving Average Band

BY GERALD APPEL

The moving-average trading channel, widely available on computer programs that track technical market indicators, provides a variety of benefits to both active short-term traders and longer-term investors. Interpreted properly, moving-average trading channels help traders determine whether the stock market is showing increasing strength or losing upside momentum. They also can help traders identify where forthcoming support and resistance levels are likely to develop and whether initial attempts to break through those support or resistance levels may offer good follow through. Finally, traders can use moving average channels to determine when it is safe to buy market weakness or pinpoint when and where market retracements are likely to occur and whether the odds favor subsequent recovery.

Constructing a Channel

Moving-average trading channels are fairly simple to create and can be used across a variety of timeframes from intraday to monthly. With this flexibility, they can be used across many markets, including the various stock market indexes, individual equities, commodities, and the bond market, among others.

To use them, simple—not weighted or exponential—moving averages for the markets that one is tracking must be created, charted, and maintained on an ongoing basis. And, quite obviously, the moving average lengths should reflect the timeframe in which one is trading or investing. I have found that the 21-day moving average reflects intermediate stock market trends well and provides useful indications for longer-term trends. However, other moving average lengths may be appropriate, too, depending on the markets tracked, patterns of recent price movement, and the timeframe in which one is trading. The exact length of the moving average probably is not crucial, so readers will see that the charts used in this chapter` illustrate a number of different possibilities.

Let's begin by putting one of these channels together. First, simply create upper and lower boundary lines above and below the moving average by employing percentage offsets above and below the moving average. For example, for a 21-day moving average of the Nasdaq Composite Index, a trader could plot lines 4 percent above and 4 percent below the 21-day moving average of closing prices of this index (see *Figure 1*). Although the moving average and channel widths are based on closing prices, intraday price movements are significant as well in the interpretation of these moving average channel patterns.

Again, the precise lengths of moving averages probably are not significant, nor are the exact amounts of offset employed to create moving-average trading channels—these vary by the markets being tracked, some of which are likely to show greater or lesser price fluctuation than others. Traders should use offset parameters so that approximately 90 percent of price movement takes place within the moving average channels they are creating. Only about 10 percent, give or take, should be seen outside of the channels.

Channel Reflects Volatility

The more volatile the market being tracked, the wider the channel will be that encompasses its price movement. For example, in August 2005 I tracked the Nasdaq Composite Index with a 21-day moving average using 4-percent bands above and below the moving average. The less-volatile Standard & Poor's 500 Index tracks well with a 21-day moving average, too, but with bands 2½ percent above and below the moving average.

The length of the timeframe of the moving average also will affect the amount of offset employed in a trader's moving average channel charts. Longer-term moving averages reflect longer-term timeframes, providing more opportunity for fluctuation and requiring wider channel offsets than shorter-term moving averages.

My own approach, by and large, is to maintain constant bandwidths of moving averages for relatively long periods of time. But these periodically do have to be adjusted to reflect changing volatility patterns in the various markets. For example, the volatility of the Nasdaq Composite Index declined considerably from mid-2000 to mid-2005, so adjustments have been made in moving average channels of this index over the years.

Though I use a fairly consistent width for moving-average trading channels, other technicians prefer to employ moving average trading bands with boundaries that rapidly compress and expand along with the shorter-term volatility changes that inevitably take place in all investments. Readers may want to check out John Bollinger's website (www.bollingerbands.com) or read his book, *Bollinger on Bollinger Bands* (McGraw-Hill, 2002) for another perspective on this issue.

Bollinger Bands: A Different Approach

In technical parlance moving average channels are also known as percentage envelopes. The key element regarding percentage envelope channels, as highlighted in this chapter, is that the lines will stay a constant percentage width apart. Traders can set the percentage at 2, 4, or whatever percent seems to match their criteria. But the lines will always stay constant around the moving average. Some technical traders, however, prefer an alternative approach.

Well-known trader and author John Bollinger has developed the widely used Bollinger band technique. This is similar to moving average channels or envelopes in that two trading bands are utilized around a moving average. However, a key difference is that Bollinger bands are placed two standard deviations above and below the moving average. Generally, traders choose the 20-day moving average when using Bollinger bands. The construction of Bollinger bands simply means that these lines will widen and narrow based on the last 20 days of market volatility. For example, during times of extreme market volatility (i.e., wide price swings), the distance between the bands will expand. Conversely, during quiet, consolidative market periods the distance between the bands will contract.

Technicians often read the width of the bands for technical clues. For example, an extreme widening of the bands may suggest that a current trend is nearing an end. Or, a very narrow distance between the bands may suggest that a new trend or breakout is about to occur. Traders need to experiment with fixed or constant percentage envelopes, versus expanding and contracting bands, to see which works best for them.

Reading the Channel

Clearly, trading in the stock market and other markets is not based on any certainties, except for the certainty that no timing model or trading approach is profitable for each and every trade. Trading success can be based more reasonably on probabilities. This is the spirit in which the following observations regarding trading bands should be approached.

Penetrations above and below the moving average channel are usually followed by fairly rapid retracements in price movement to back within the channel. As a general rule, it usually is possible—at least in the short term—to profitably trade by buying on downside repenetrations below the channel's lower boundary, or on the flip side, to sell on upside penetrations above the upper boundary of the trading channel. Additionally, a trader can await repenetrations back into the channel before adding to new long positions.

Again, though, these general guidelines are for very short-term price swings only. Why? Penetrations below and above trading band channels often suggest further movement ahead in the direction of the penetration—especially if the penetration is the first in a series. Areas A and F on *Figure 1* illustrate these points. As seen, all downside penetrations of the channel in area A and at C provided opportunity for at least short-term scalping potential on the long side; at F the upside penetration provided an opportunity for short-term profit taking.

As a general rule, the first penetration below or to the lower boundary of a moving-average trading channel suggests strong downside momentum, unlikely to be immediately reversed. Expect the first recovery attempts to run into resistance at mid-channel, the moving average line. This point is illustrated on *Figure 1* at area B—the center line of the moving-average trading channel—where the first rally attempt from the lower boundary stalled.

The subsequent recovery from C had a much better chance of proving more durable because, first, it was a second rally attempt from the lower boundary, and second, the rally was supported by improvements in other technical indicators. In this case, the moving average convergence divergence (MACD) was producing favorable patterns in the flat double bottom formation. See the point marked X on *Figure 1*, which represents a positive divergence and non-confirmation of new lows in the Nasdaq Composite Index. If the center channel line of the moving-

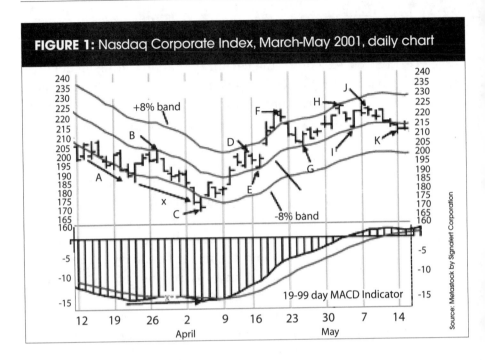

FIGURE 1: Nasdaq Corporate Index, March-May 2001, daily chart

Source: Metastock by Signalert Corporation

average trading channel is penetrated by an advance from or below the lower band of the moving-average trading channel, the advance is likely to continue until the upper band of the trading channel is reached. This concept is illustrated in *Figure 1* by the acceleration in market recovery that took place following the rise from the low point at C. Price movement accelerated as the moving average was crossed, the advance rapidly reaching the upper boundary of the trading channel at D.

If prices reach the upper boundary of the trading channel, support, especially during initial declines, is likely to develop at the mid-channel line (the area of the moving average). Strong market advances are likely to develop between or just above the upper boundaries of the trading channel and the moving-average line, which may be used as the area in which to accumulate new positions for further advances.

The decline following the advance to the upper-channel boundary at D did indeed find support at E, the center line of the trading channel. The subsequent rally to area F carried prices to above the upper boundary of the trading channel, suggesting improving market momentum and strength because the rally to D had not penetrated the upper boundary. MACD was still rising steadily at the time, further confirming a favorable technical picture. The odds strongly favored the Nasdaq

Composite Index finding support once again at the mid-channel line (G) where it did, as expected, do so.

If a market advance does not carry as far above or as close to the upper boundary as it did during the previous upswing, this is a sign of diminishing momentum and strength. The odds increase that the next decline will penetrate the mid-channel line and is likely to fall to below the level of the moving average. The rise from G to H developed at a lesser slope than the advance from E to F; prices moved more sluggishly from the middle band of the channel to the upper band. This indicated weakening upside momentum. As it turned out in this case, the retracement did find support at the center channel once again (I). However, the subsequent recovery to area J failed to even reach the upper boundary of the channel—a clear warning that the subsequent decline was likely to penetrate below the center line of the trading channel, which it did at K. So here's a rule to keep in mind: if a market advance fails to reach the upper boundary of the trading channel, the next decline probably will penetrate the support area provided by the center line of the moving average channel.

More Trading Strategies

Let's take a look at two additional strategies using trading channels to project future price movements based on past price action. When market reversal patterns from moving-average trading channels are confirmed by other technical indicators, the odds of these patterns being signifi-cant improves considerably. The moving-average trading channel, seen in *Figure 2*, provided a good indication of the bearish transition in stock market technical patterns that developed in the now-historic March of 2000. The failure of prices to reach the upper boundary of the trading channel at area E (compared to area C) was one warning. Also notice the confirmations of developing weakness that were provided by the 14-day relative strength index (RSI) indicator and the 19-39 day MACD indica-tor, both of which traced out declining top formations as price action traced out similar declining peaks.

This brings us to another general guideline for traders who are using channels: if a market peak fails to move as high as a previous market peak, the odds are high that the next decline will carry beneath the low area that separated the previous two peaks. If a market low is followed

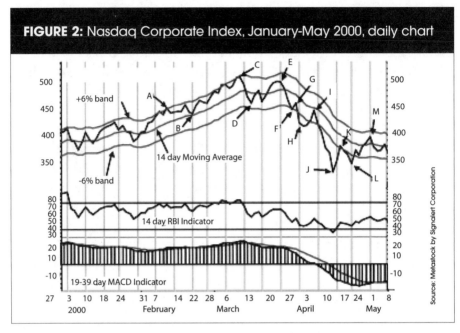

FIGURE 2: Nasdaq Corporate Index, January-May 2000, daily chart

by a lower market low, the odds are that the next advance will not immediately surpass the peak of the previous high.

This concept is well illustrated by the declining highs—C, E, G, I—and the intervening lows at D, F, H, and J in *Figure 2*. The failure of the market, at L, to decline to below J suggested that something more positive was developing. The recovery to K and the final retreat to L before prices turned up did illustrate the tendency for the outer bands of channels to act as support if advances clearly rise above the upper boundary—and as resistance if the lower boundary is clearly penetrated (the latter was seen in this example).

Another useful point to consider is that often the mid-channel line will act as support (see *Figure 3* for an example of this tendency). The mid-channel line held in downside price action during the bullish phase in area D. Market weakness was indicated as price traded below the moving-average trading channel during 2002. Market strength was demonstrated with the ability of prices to hold within the channel early in 2003 (area C). Traders also will notice confirmations by MACD of moving average trading band patterns.

Experiment for Success

As with all technical indicators, there are different schools of thought

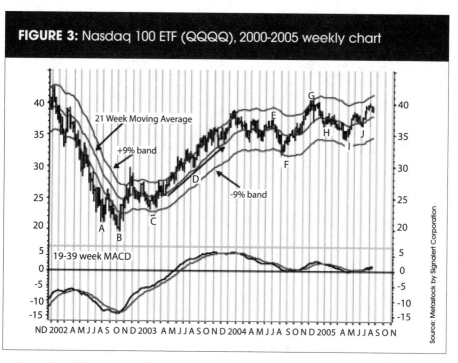

FIGURE 3: Nasdaq 100 ETF (QQQQ), 2000-2005 weekly chart

Source: Metastock by Signalert Corporation

on how best to use moving average trading bands. Doubtlessly, the last chapter is yet to be written as traders discover their own particular uses in addition to those that my staff and I employ on a daily basis in our trading activities. Experiment with moving averages of different lengths, with bands of varying widths, reflecting different time frames. It will be time well spent.

Gerald Appel, president of Signalert Corporation, has been publishing the technical newsletter, *Systems and Forecasts*, since 1973. Appel, the inventor of MACD, has published numerous books, articles and videotapes related to technical analysis. His most recent publications are *Technical Analysis: Power Tools for Active Investors* (Financial Times Prentice Hall, 2005) and *Opportunity Investing: How to Profit When Stocks Advance, Stocks Decline, Inflation Runs Rampant, Prices Fall, Oil Prices Hit the Roof...and Every Time In Between* (Financial Times Prentice Hall, 2006). This article originally appeared in *SFO* in November 2005.

BOLLINGER BANDS AND VOLUME OSCILLATOR: Pair Up For Range Trading Stock Strategy

BY JOHN BOLLINGER

In the 1970s and early 1980s, traders and investors faced a stock market very much like today's market. The stage had been set by the magnificent post-World War II economic expansion that carried stock prices to a peak in 1966, while delivering more economic growth than anyone thought possible. From 1966 onward, the stock market was confined to a trading range, albeit a very large one, from which it did not break out until 1982. ("Giant sideways" is what one trader called it at the time.) Thus, it took 16 years to work off the excesses of the WWII expansion and set the stage for the next bull market.

This period was so long that it contained three speculative bubbles, each of which had to be worked off in turn. First there was technology; computer time-sharing was the name of the game in those days. That wave of speculation crashed against the shore in 1968. Then came the Nifty Fifty stocks, the "one-decision" stocks that could be bought and held forever. That paradigm's turn on the rocks came in 1973. Finally, there came a massive wave of speculation in energy shares, the resolution of which turned out to be the birth of the mightiest bull market ever—the massive run from 1982 to 1998.

Sideways Range Encouraged Swing Trading

Sixteen years showed no progress, but a great deal of ground was covered. Ignoring all the little wiggles and considering only swings of 20 percent or more, the S&P 500 covered 679 points from a peak of 96 in early 1966 to the trough of 100 in mid-1982, while racking

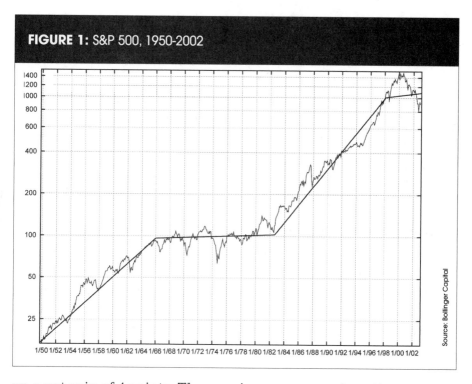

FIGURE 1: S&P 500, 1950-2002

Source: Bollinger Capital

up a net gain of 4 points. Those swings were very tempting oppor-tunities, and traders and frustrated investors-turned-traders found them and, at the time, pursued them aggressively. Those intrepid souls were called "swing traders," and they focused on the moves of 20, 30, and 40 percent or more in stocks that took weeks or months to accomplish. (There were no index products for traders at the time.) That's quite different from today's definition of swing trad-ing that rarely includes spans of more than just hours. (The only other discipline that I know of that made money during this period was relative strength.)

The post-WWII period can be seen as a sixteen-year expansion from 1950 to 1966; a sixteen-year consolidation from 1966 to 1982; and a sixteen-year expansion from 1982 to 1998, when the broad market peaked out. Given that timeline, we are four-and-a-half years into a consolidation that can be expected to run for quite a while, perhaps through the end of the decade (see *Figure 1*).

During the years of stagnation from 1966 to 1982, buy-and-hold investors earned little but the dividend yield of the stocks they held—cold comfort in a time of raging inflation and volatile markets. With today's reduced dividend payout ratios, matters are even worse—since the peak in 1998, buy-and-hold returns have been negative, including dividends. To wit, the total return for the S&P 500 for the five years ending September 30, 2002, is -1.63 percent.

Clearly, the strategy of choice from 1982 to 1998 was buy and hold, perhaps tempered with a bit of relative strength to juice things up. But just as buy and hold didn't work from 1966 to 1982, it is a complete failure in today's market. If the investor/speculator/trader is to be profitable in the current environment, the name of the game is trading—swing trading to be specific.

Equity Market Consolidation Could Continue for Some Time
We believe that the present consolidation may take as long as its 1966 to 1982 precursor, perhaps even longer. Valuations were much more extreme at the end of this expansion than they were in 1966 and may take longer to work off. The speculative bubble in the Internet stocks was the largest bubble ever in the U.S. stock market and may well be the greatest speculative bubble of all time. It could take a generation or more to heal that damage.

So, let's turn back the clock and examine what worked in the span from 1966 through 1982. Then we'll update those tools and put them to use in the present. In the mid-to-late '70s, trading systems based on trading bands were quite popular. There were two general approaches. Cyclical analysis based on the work of J. M. Hurst was one, and trading signals based on non-confirmations was the other.

Cycles analysis is beyond the scope of this article. For a look at Hurst's work, try his Prentice Hall book published in 1970, *The Profit Magic of Stock Transaction Timing*. Our focus here is on trading signals based on non-confirmations.

As the '80s dawned, a very popular trading approach consisted of fitting percentage bands around the price of a stock or a market average and comparing price action within the bands to indicator action. For the market, oscillators based on advancing and declining issues were popular and, for stocks, volume oscillators or momentum oscillators were the indicators of choice.

These systems were popular because they worked well in the trading range environment that prevailed from 1966 to 1982. They weren't suited to the roaring bull market of the '80s and '90s, just as they weren't suited for the 1950 to 1966 bull market, so they fell into disrepute and disuse. However, once again we find ourselves in a trading-range environment, so let's dust them off, spruce them up, and put them back to work.

Our focus here is on stocks. For more on market-timing techniques please visit our site, www.MarketTechnician.com. Now, the details for stocks. One of the reasons I developed Bollinger bands is that percentage bands are so problematic. By switching from percentage bands to Bollinger bands, we eliminate having to set the bandwidth for each issue, and we no longer have to change the bandwidth as market conditions change. The volatility measurement that drives Bollinger bands takes care of this for us. Bollinger bands are almost certainly included in your analytical software, so use the defaults of 20-periods and two standard deviations and let volatility do the work for you.

Volume Tool Works as Good Companion to Bands

Since our focus is on stocks, we'll need a volume-based oscillator. What could be a better choice in this institutionally dominated market than David Bostian's "intraday intensity," an indicator designed to track the action of institutional traders? (Intraday intensity, or II as we'll refer to it, masquerades under many names. On some systems, it is called Money Flow, on others Accumulation Distribution, or possibly something else. Check with your software vendor to make sure you are using the right formulation, regardless of the name they assign to it. Check the formulas to make sure.)

The idea behind II is that as institutions operate within the trading day, they drive price in the direction of their needs. If institutions are selling, stocks will close near the lows of their daily ranges. If they are buying, prices will close in the upper portion of the range. The price portion of the II formula evaluates to 1 if the stock closes at the high, -1 if we close at the low, or 0 if we close mid-range. In between the mid-point and the period's extremes, the calculation gradually increases as the close approaches the high or decreases as the close nears the low. Via this mechanism, II places more weight on days where price closes near the extremes than on days where price closes mid-range.

The next part of II involves multiplying the price portion of the calculation by volume, which is volume weighting. Thus, days on which volume is heavy get additional weight in the indicator, and days on which volume is weak contribute in a less important manner. It is this juncture of weighting price and volume that makes this indicator so effective.

For the mathematically inclined, the single-period formula for intraday intensity is (2*close-high-low)/(high-low)*volume. The single-day readings may be accumulated over time to form an open-ended indicator. To create an II oscillator, keep a running sum such as a 21-day sum to a closed-form indicator. To normalize this oscillator, divide each period's sum by the sum of volume for the same accumulation period. The normalized version is referred to as 21-day intraday intensity percent.

21-day Intraday-Intensity Percent Formula

$$\sum_{1}^{21} \left((2c - h - l)/(h - l) * v \right)/ \sum_{1}^{21} v_i * 100$$

Keep in mind that the purpose of trading bands is to define whether prices are high or low on a relative basis. Our two building blocks are price within Bollinger bands using the default values of 20 days and two standard deviations and 21-day II percent.

Trading Signals Based on Non-Confirmations

How can you trade this? Our approach is to look for non-confirmations. We will take a tag of the upper band—prices are relatively high—accompanied by a negative II percent reading as a sell alert and a tag of the lower band—prices are relatively low—accompanied by a positive II reading as a buy alert. Then, we'll use a subsequent down day as a sell confirmation and a subsequent up day as a buy confirmation.

Let's look at some charts and see how this works.

While using these tools together offers no guarantees to the trader, it is a viable approach that will alert you to potential trading opportunities in a stock market that is likely to deliver a good number of such opportunities over the next few years. This approach can be adapted for market timing—try using a market-breadth measure such as an advance-decline oscillator or an up-down volume oscillator and a market average with Bollinger bands. It also can be adapted

FIGURE 2: DuPont (DD)

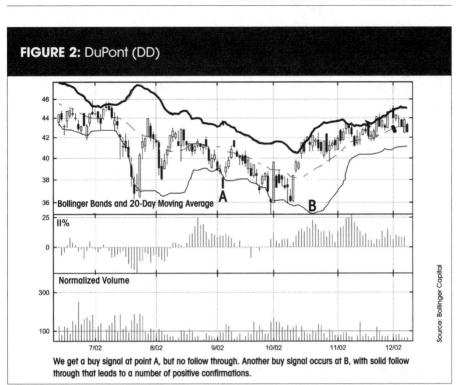

We get a buy signal at point A, but no follow through. Another buy signal occurs at B, with solid follow through that leads to a number of positive confirmations.

FIGURE 3: AT&T (T)

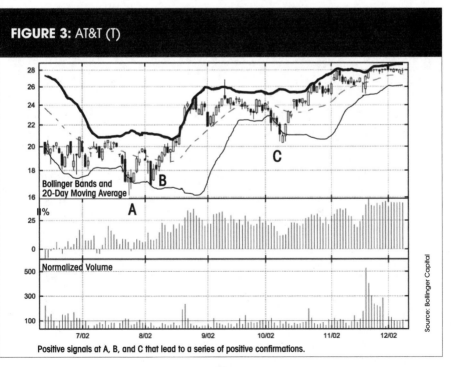

Positive signals at A, B, and C that lead to a series of positive confirmations.

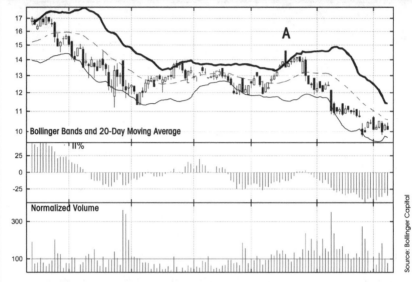

FIGURE 4: Humana (HUM)

Bollinger Bands and 20-Day Moving Average

Normalized Volume

Source: Bollinger Capital

An important sell signal at A that leads to a waterfall decline and a number of negative confirmations.

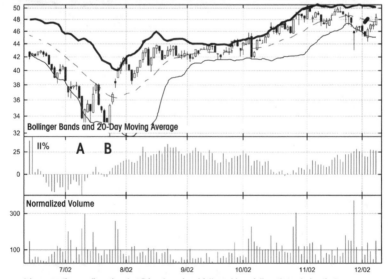

FIGURE 5: Varian Medical (VAR)

Bollinger Bands and 20-Day Moving Average

Normalized Volume

Source: Bollinger Capital

A is a negative confirmation, but B is a buy signal followed by a follow-through day that leads to a long series of positive confirmations.

166

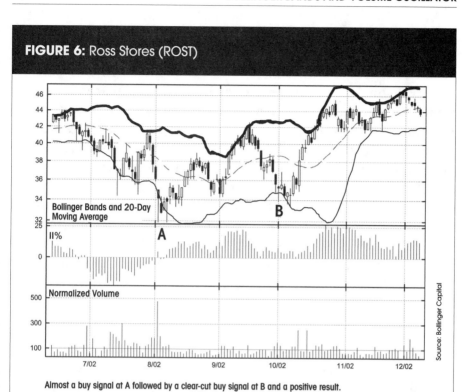

FIGURE 6: Ross Stores (ROST)

Almost a buy signal at A followed by a clear-cut buy signal at B and a positive result.

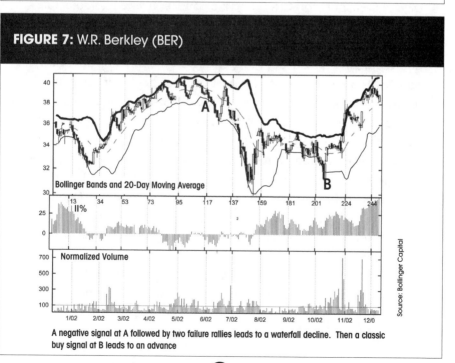

FIGURE 7: W.R. Berkley (BER)

A negative signal at A followed by two failure rallies leads to a waterfall decline. Then a classic buy signal at B leads to an advance

to groups and sectors using the multiplicity of exchange-traded funds (ETFs) available these days.

As market technicians have seen, price patterns, cycles and history do tend to repeat themselves in the financial arena. As a trader, the challenge is to identify what type of environment the markets are currently in and apply appropriate trading strategies to the current atmosphere. No longer are U.S. equities in the midst of a major bull market, in which buy and hold practically assured a profit. Now it appears as if U.S. equities have shifted into a cycle similar to the 1970s and early 1980s. If we are in more of a trading range environment, investors and traders need to appropriately shift their goals and strategies. Swing trading strategies have proved successful in past trading-range markets, and these tools offer the trader a potentially profitable strategy in today's environment.

John Bollinger is the president and founder of Bollinger Capital Management, Inc., an investment management company that provides technically driven money management services and develops proprietary research for institutions and individuals. He is a regular contributor on CNBC and is a speaker at financial seminars worldwide. Bollinger is probably best known for his Bollinger bands, which have been widely accepted and integrated into most of the analytical software currently in use. His book *Bollinger on Bollinger Bands* was published by McGraw Hill and has been translated into seven languages. His two-volume DVD set, *Bollinger on Bollinger Bands—The Seminar* features over nine hours of presentations. He has also developed several financial Web sites: www.EquityTrader.com, www.FundsTrader.com, www.BollingerBands.com, www.BollingerOn-BollingerBands.com, www.GroupPower.com, www.MarketTechnician.com, and www.PatternPower.com. He is a Chartered Financial Analyst (CFA), a Chartered Market Technician (CMT), and a former board member of the Market Technicians Association. Bollinger is the recipient of the Technical Securities Analysts Association of San Francisco Lifetime Award for outstanding achievement in technical analysis and the 2005 Market Technicians Association Annual Award for outstanding contribution to the field of technical analysis. This article originally appeared in *SFO* in February 2003.

SPOTLIGHT ON FACTS AND FICTION ABOUT STOCHASTICS

BY NINA COOPER

With literally hundreds of technical studies and tools available to traders these days, wouldn't it be nice to find a simple timing technique? As an "Elliottician," I realized long ago that having a tool to add confirmation at turning points would be a way to increase my confidence in my wave count and execute entries and exits more accurately. Stochastics are a basic technical tool that do just that.

In recent years, instead of counting waves I have shifted to a combination of approaches, each contributing an important type of information: fractal structure to get directional information and phi analysis to identify price objectives. (Phi analysis projects price targets based on the 1.618 relationship that seems to underlie market behavior.) For timing, I use stochastics. Taken together, these three techniques produce incredibly accurate signals. But whether or not you count waves, you still need to master timing techniques if you want to be successful. If you are having problems getting in or out of positions in a timely way, here are some tips on how to use stochastics to give you better signals.

Why Stochastics?

Stochastics are oscillators that register changes in momentum. When a trend is about to change, momentum in the current trend tends to subside. Being able to recognize that the trend is losing power before the (wave) pattern is complete gives me a heads up that a reversal is approaching. And that helps confirm my other analysis and gets me in and out of positions promptly.

Stochastics are offered in virtually all trading software and have been around since 1957, when they were developed by George Lane. Yet many traders overlook stochastics because they don't know how to use them effectively. Certainly they understand the overbought and oversold concept. And, too, most understand that stochastic signals inconsistent with the price action (divergences) are better signals for trend changes. But many are turned off by long periods of extreme readings that appear meaningless and without signals in a trending market. And traders are sometimes put off by the labeling—what do %K and %D actually mean anyway? The relative strength index (RSI) or moving average convergence divergence (MACD) may seem easier to understand. Yet, selecting tools for trading signals should be about accuracy. I've found stochastics to be an extremely helpful tool for timing—far more helpful than RSI or MACD. In fact, stochastics offer a lot more information than developer Lane ever imagined.

Stochastics are oscillators that react to changes in momentum. They reflect the tendency for prices to end near the highs during rallies and near the low during declines, regardless of the time interval selected. When the close is near the bottom of the range in a rally, or near the high in a decline, we have a signal that the momentum in the trend is changing.

Stochastics are calculated using various amounts of data to determine the stochastic values (the %K line). In addition, a moving average is plotted (the %D line) to help smooth away the minor fluctuations. ("Slow" stochastics use a moving average for the %K and a moving average of that for the %D line.)

Values are calculated as a percentage figure that moves from 0 to 100 and back. Readings above the 80-percent mark are said to be overbought, and those below 20 percent are oversold. When these two lines cross, we get a signal that something is changing. Of course, in the course of normal trading we get lots of crossovers. Deciding which crossover signal to take is the key to correctly using this technical tool. But, before tackling that issue, let's start at the beginning.

Debunking the Myths

There are common misconceptions about stochastics that prevent many traders from using this effective tool. Here's the real story:

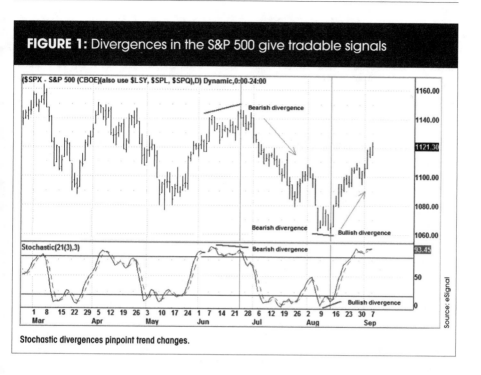

FIGURE 1: Divergences in the S&P 500 give tradable signals

Stochastic divergences pinpoint trend changes.

• %K and %D refer to some complex higher math. According to Lane, the inventor of stochastics, the labels were arbitrary names and simply used to identify specific mathematical calculations among many that were investigated. These names could as easily be "A" and "B" or "data" and "average." Nothing mysterious there.

• Overbought and oversold readings imply a trend reversal. In fact, an extreme reading implies a high degree of momentum that will continue the current move. While a brief correction could occur and allow the stochastic to subside a little, being overbought is bullish, and oversold is bearish.

Lane remarks that tradable signals come only when the %K reverses and crosses through the %D line and only when new extremes in price are not being confirmed (diverging) by the stochastic (see *Figure 1*). In order to have a divergence, price must make a second advance or decline before a divergence is possible. My work shows that sometimes three advances or declines are needed before the final extreme in price and a reliable trend change occurs. These three

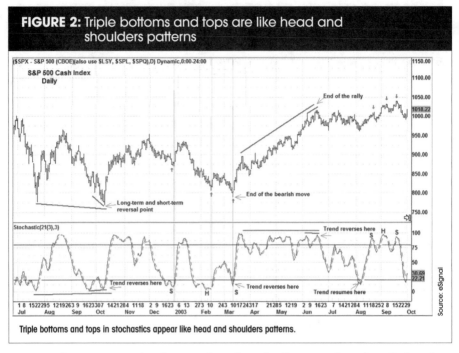

FIGURE 2: Triple bottoms and tops are like head and shoulders patterns

Triple bottoms and tops in stochastics appear like head and shoulders patterns.

moves often appear in the stochastics similar to a head and shoulders pattern. The third price extreme and the right shoulder in the stochastic is the signal for a turn—not the earlier overbought or oversold reading. Waiting for the stochastic pattern to be completed will keep a trader in the market until the ultimate price extreme is reached (see *Figure 2*).

• Stochastics are useless in trending markets because they go to an extreme and stay there. While this statement is true if one relies on the wrong value, using an appropriate value continues to give great signals no matter how directional the price action is. Stochastic readings that stay above 80 or below 20 for extended periods ("flutter," as Lane called that condition) mean that the market is trending. Minor corrections along the way don't last long enough to permit the stochastic to react unless you shorten the time interval. When the market flutters, try shifting to a smaller time value and see how well you get signals for the minor corrections. But, don't forget that these corrections will give renewed signals for the larger trend! Stochastic crossovers in the neutral zone mean that the original move is resuming.

Want to Be Stochastic Savvy?

Other important but little-discussed facts often are overlooked. Here are some tips to help derive better signals:

• Stochastic readings, whether overbought or oversold, make absolutely no promise about the level of prices. An extreme stochastic reading has no bearing on whether the price is near a high or a low. With stochastic readings at 100 or 0—very bullish or bearish respectively—the market can go much higher or lower. From an extreme stochastic reading, any crossover and break of 80 or 20 signals a correction, not the start of a new trend.

• Stochastics that cross over in overbought or oversold territory without a divergence signal that a correction is starting. While the initial crossover gives the most time-sensitive signal, those are less reliable than the signal that comes with the break at 80 or 20 following the crossover. If one waits for the stochastics to leave the extreme zones, a trader has a filter that will prevent entries on a brief, minor move.

• All stochastic %K -%D crossovers give valuable signals. Some are just shorter term than others. Those occurring between overbought territory and oversold territory are minor corrections in the trend. If you are looking for a place to enter a trade after the move has started, you can use one of these intermediate signals to get you in.

• Time is an important factor in corrections (see *Figure 3*). Prices can go sideways during rallies, giving stochastics the opportunity to pause and drop back from overbought levels to neutral or even oversold levels without any meaningful price decline. Likewise, prices can sit unchanged in a downtrend while stochastics become overbought. These conditions are set ups for the trend in progress to continue. Renewed %K-%D crossovers—whether from the middle of the neutral zone or from overbought or oversold levels—give renewed buy or sell signals as the current trend resumes. That is, renewed buy or sell signals following minor corrections often occur in the neutral zone without a divergence. These renewing trend signals are great places to build positions.

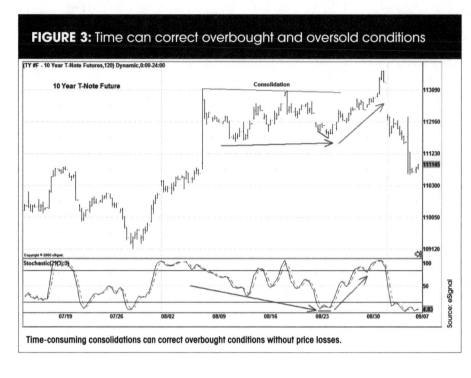

FIGURE 3: Time can correct overbought and oversold conditions

Time-consuming consolidations can correct overbought conditions without price losses.

Anticipating Divergences

Overbought, oversold, and divergences are the most obvious and best-known signals that stochastics produce. But understanding the behavior of the indicator and how it functions lets us use it in ways that Lane may not have considered.

For example, we know that the best signals come on divergences. That implies at least two moves in the direction of the trend. Often the first extreme stochastic reading looks like an Elliott wave three with the final wave five high producing the divergent stochastic reading. The same process occurs with corrective wave A's and wave C's. Sometimes in strong trending moves, wave one will produce explosive momentum, and the stochastic will easily reach the overbought or oversold zone. The following wave three will produce another extreme—sometimes with a divergence, but often without.

So how do we know if the trend is over? The secret is in the extent of the corrections. Stochastics that come back to neutral and then do not reach the same level on further corrections warn that the trend is not over. We can look for a third trending move before the final extreme is in place.

174

What's in a Wave?

Elliott wave theory is a technical approach to market analysis based on the work of Ralph Nelson Elliott, the founder of the Wave principle.

The most basic tenets of Elliott wave suggest that markets tend to move in well-defined five-wave moves, followed by a three-wave corrective move. According to Elliott, a five-wave move can only be seen in the direction of the trend. Within that first five-wave move, waves 1, 3, and 5 are in the direction of the trend, while waves 2 and 4 are corrective (or counter-trend). Once the fifth wave is complete, the three corrective waves will be seen and are called A-B-C. See also chapter 21, "Use the Wave Principle to Improve Your Success Rate."

Trending Signals

Want a quick way to determine what the long-term or short-term trend is? Stochastics can also be used to determine trend, quite a handy feature when the market is mired in consolidation.

Getting a reliable directional indication is as simple as changing the time value to a much slower (larger) number. For example, 21 (alternatively, some charting software asks for stochastic values as well as two moving average values, e.g., 21,3,3) units. This can be hours, days, weeks, or months depending on your timeframe. Twenty-one is generally slow enough to be able to smooth the noise of consolidations. If needed, the number can be higher, but keep in mind that the higher the number, the less sensitive the indicator to a trend change. At a reversal point, a very slow stochastic value will not react quickly enough to let a trader enter quickly. By the time the directional reading reverses, the trend will be well established, and one risks entering just as correction is about to begin. Using a combination of both short-term values for execution signals and longer-term values for directional signals is helpful.

Traders sometimes get frustrated with stochastics because they remain overbought or oversold for extended periods of time. Often traders fall into the trap of believing that the default values programmed into their stochastics studies are the correct ones. Only you know what is going to be appropriate for your trading timeframe.

If one assumes that the set-up on the trading software is automatically correct, the trader will end up using the default without a second thought. In many charting platforms, the default value is 14 (or 14, 3, 3). This value may be correct for a person who has a longer-term horizon. But, for most traders a 14 (or 14, 3, 3) interval stochastic is too slow to give good execution signals and too fast to give reliable trending information. So it is up to the individual trader to adjust the time sensitivity of his stochastic settings to fit his timeframe. A 5 (or 5, 3, 3) interval may be a better fit to give timely signals for those with shorter time horizons; 21 (or 21, 3, 3) works well for slower, directional information.

Tweaking Timing

Adjusting the time interval of your stochastic can improve your timing signals. Understanding what the crossovers mean can help you distinguish between corrections and trend changes.

Now let's look at using a multi-timeframe to refine timing even more. Time is a factor in market analysis that many people tend to ignore. Sure, we're all looking for perfect entry and exit timing. But, by looking at the signals at various levels of time, we can get a jump on a developing signal.

We have discussed sensitive stochastic time intervals to give timely entry and exit signals. But, changing the timeframe of the chart itself is another way to make the signals more or less sensitive. If you are making decisions about trend based on your daily chart, slower value stochastics will tell you a good deal about direction and help keep you with the trend once you are in a trade. But, getting into the trade using daily signals often means that you are late—even if you downshift to use a 5, 3, 3, stochastic.

Instead, try using a 5, 3, 3 stochastic on an hourly chart as your entry or exit reversal is approaching. Traders will find the necessary divergence signal will occur much sooner on the more sensitive chart, giving one plenty of warning for the coming trend change, long before the same signal appears on the daily chart.

By the way, the logic that allows divergences to appear on the shorter-term chart is that each price swing, no matter how limited, is a component in the larger structure (this is fractal theory). If you can tell where one of the internal segments will end, there will be a better chance of being correct about the reversal on the slower, longer-term timeframe, too.

I've shared some stochastic techniques that you can use to help you sharpen your timing. Thinking of stochastics as merely over-bought or oversold is an over-simplified view that ignores the wealth of timing information stochastics offer. Adjusting stochastic time values, understanding how divergences work and when they are expected, and what simple crossover signals mean can help you get in and out more profitably. Stochastics are a flexible technical tool that gives a savvy user the timing edge.

Nina Cooper is the president and principal of Pendragon Research Inc., where she has been working with traders and investors since 1995 (www.pendragonresearch.com). Cooper has been working in the capital markets in the U.S. and London since the 1980s, and her experience includes stints in the institutional bond markets and in global portfolio management. She is an instructor at the Chicago Mercantile Exchange, where she teaches advanced stochastics, phi analysis, and Elliott wave theory. Cooper is a founding member and past president of the American Association of Professional Technical Analysts. She can be reached at ngcooper@pendragonresearch.com. This article originally appeared in SFO in November 2004.

USE THE WAVE PRINCIPLE TO IMPROVE YOUR SUCCESS RATE

BY JEFFREY KENNEDY

Every trader, analyst, and technician uses favorite techniques when trading. When these traditional technical studies fall short, though, the wave principle can provide a lens to view price action accurately. Although the Elliott wave principle gets high marks for market analysis, I hear a common complaint along these lines: "You can't use it to help you to trade in real time, because it doesn't provide the defined rules and guidelines of a typical trading system." But not so fast. I plan to show in this chapter how you can use the wave principle to trade in three ways:

1. Finding high-probability price targets;
2. Distinguishing high-probability trade set-ups from the ones that traders should ignore;
3. Using its built-in rules to place protective stops in a real-time trading environment, even though the wave principle isn't a trading system in and of itself.

Price Patterns and Crowd Psychology

But first, what is the wave principle? The wave principle recognizes that price patterns originate from crowd psychology. Ralph Nelson Elliott first discovered this relationship in the 1930s after spending many years analyzing stock market data. Finding that stock prices trend and reverse in recognizable patterns, he then named, defined, and illustrated thirteen such patterns and described how they form

FIGURE 1: Cornerstone of the wave principle

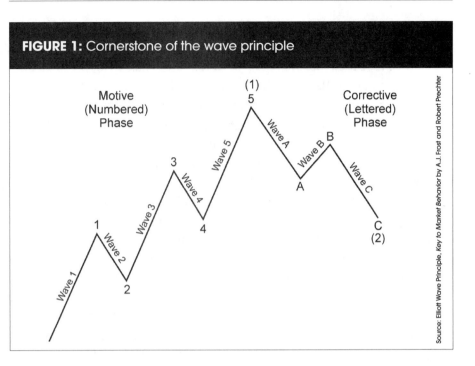

larger and smaller versions of themselves. He called this discovery the wave principle.

Figure 1 illustrates the basic building block of the wave principle. Elliott observed that when prices rally in a bull market, they do so in five distinct waves, which he called impulse waves. Once a five-wave move is complete, prices decline in three waves, correcting a portion of the preceding advance. Once the sequence finishes, the pattern repeats in larger and smaller versions of this same basic pattern. The same holds true for bear markets, in which case this pattern is inverted—five-wave declines precede three-wave rallies.

Where Technical Studies Fall Short

Looking at the broad field of technical analysis, there are three main categories of technical studies: trend-following indicators, oscillators, and sentiment indicators. Trend-following indicators include moving averages, the moving average convergence-divergence (MACD), and the directional movement index. A few of the more popular oscillators many traders use today are stochastics, rate of change, and the commodity channel index (CCI). Sentiment indicators include put-call ratios and Commitment of Traders report data.

These technical studies do a good job of illuminating the way for traders, yet each falls short for one major reason: they limit the scope of a trader's understanding of current price action and how it relates to the overall picture of a market. For example, let's say the MACD reading in XYZ stock is positive, indicating the trend is up. That's useful information, but wouldn't it be more useful if it could also help to answer these two questions: Is this a new trend or an old trend? If the trend is up, how far will it go? Most technical studies simply don't reveal pertinent information such as the maturity of a trend and a definable price target—but the wave principle does.

As a second example, stochastics is an excellent tool for identifying overbought and oversold conditions in price. An overbought reading typically occurs when the stochastic is above 80 percent. Oversold conditions exist when the stochastic reads less than 20 percent. But the question is, how long do these periods actually last? Overbought and oversold conditions can be brief or last a long time. Moreover, if the stochastic is overbought and, therefore, warning of a pullback in price, it raises the question of whether the expected decline is a minor correction within a larger uptrending market or the beginning of a new downtrend in price. If traders misinterpret this oscillator when prices are overbought or oversold, they often enter or exit a trade too soon. Sentiment indicators present the same problem by generating signals well in advance of an actual reversal in price.

Does the wave principle answer the questions that traditional studies leave behind? Yes, and then some. Although technical studies do have their place in every trader's toolbox (I use a few myself), it is important to view them in context with the overall picture of market activity. So how exactly does the wave principle provide that overall picture to improve trading? Here are five ways:

1. The wave principle identifies the direction of the dominant trend. A five-wave advance identifies the overall trend as up. Conversely, a five-wave decline determines that the larger trend is down. So why is this information so important? Because it is easier to trade in the direction of the overriding trend—it is the path of least resistance and undoubtedly explains the saying, "the trend is your friend."

FIGURE 2: The fractal nature of the wave principle

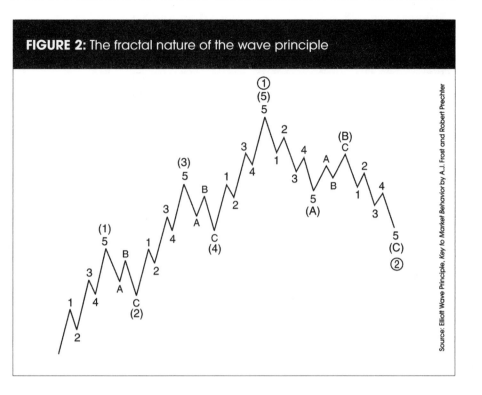

Source: Elliott Wave Principle, *Key to Market Behavior* by A.J. Frost and Robert Prechter

The probability of a successful stock trade is much greater if a trader is long a stock when the major indexes are rallying.

2. It identifies countertrend moves. The three-wave pattern is a corrective response to the preceding impulse wave. Knowing that a recent move in price is merely a correction within a larger trending market is especially important for traders, because corrections are opportunities for traders to position themselves in the direction of the larger trend of a market.

3. It can help by determining the maturity of a trend. As Elliott observed, wave patterns form larger and smaller versions of themselves. This repetition in form means that price activity is fractal, as illustrated in *Figure 2*. Wave 1 subdivides into five small waves yet is part of a larger five-wave pattern. How is this information useful? It helps traders recognize the maturity of a trend. If prices are advancing in wave 5 of a five-wave advance, for example, and wave 5 has already completed three or four smaller

FIGURE 3: Fibonacci analysis and the wave principle

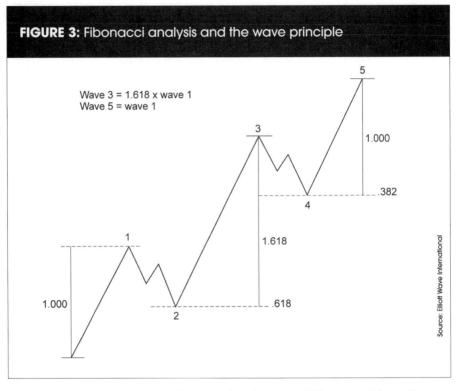

Wave 3 = 1.618 x wave 1
Wave 5 = wave 1

Source: Elliott Wave International

waves, a trader knows this is not the time to add long positions. Instead, it may be time to take profits or at least to raise protective stops.

Because the wave principle identifies trend, countertrend, and the maturity of a trend, it's no surprise that it also signals the return of the dominant trend. Once a countertrend move unfolds in three waves (A-B-C), this structure can confirm the point where the dominant trend has resumed— namely, once price action exceeds the extreme of wave B. Knowing precisely when a trend has resumed brings an added benefit: it increases the probability of a successful trade, which is further enhanced when accompanied by traditional technical studies.

4. It provides high-probability price targets. That's something that traditional technical studies simply don't offer. When Elliott wrote about the wave principle in his monograph, *Nature's Law* (1946), he stated that the Fibonacci sequence was the mathematical basis for the wave principle. Elliott waves, both impulsive and corrective,

adhere to specific Fibonacci proportions, as illustrated in *Figure 3*. For example, common objectives for wave 3 are 1.618 and 2.618 multiples of wave 1. In corrections, wave 2 typically ends near the .618 retracement of wave 1, and wave 4 often tests the .382 retracement of wave 3. These high-probability price targets allow traders to set profit-taking objectives or identify regions where the next turn in prices will occur.

5. Finally, the wave principle helps you know when you are wrong by providing points of ruin. At what point does a trade fail? Many traders use money management rules to determine the answer to this question, because technical studies simply don't offer one. Yet the wave principle does in the form of Elliott wave rules.

• Rule 1: Wave 2 can never retrace more than 100 percent of wave 1.
• Rule 2: Wave 4 may never end in the price territory of wave 1.
• Rule 3: Out of the three impulse waves, 1, 3 and 5, wave 3 can never be the shortest impulse wave.

A violation of one or more of these rules implies that the operative wave count is incorrect. How can traders use this information? If a technical study warns of an upturn in prices and the wave pattern is a second-wave pullback, the trader knows specifically at what point the trade will fail—a move beyond the origin of wave 1. That kind of guidance is difficult to come by without a framework like the wave principle.

Trades To Make vs. Trades To Ignore

So the wave principle identifies trend, countertrend moves, maturity of trend, price targets, and specific points of ruin. But can the wave principle also identify high-probability trades over trade setups that traders should ignore? That's where the rubber meets the road, and the answer to this question is yes, specifically by exploiting waves 3, 5, A, and C.

Why? Because five-wave moves determine the direction of the larger trend, three-wave moves offer traders an opportunity to join the trend. So in *Figure 4*, waves 2, 4, 5, and B are actually the setup for

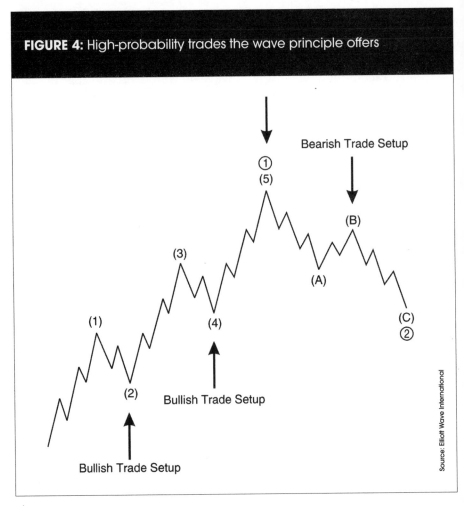

FIGURE 4: High-probability trades the wave principle offers

Bearish Trade Setup

① (5)

(B)

(3)

(A)

(1)

(4)

(C) ②

(2)   Bullish Trade Setup

Bullish Trade Setup

Source: Elliott Wave International

high-probability trades in waves 3, 5, A, and C. For example, a wave 2 pullback provides traders an opportunity to position themselves in the direction of wave 3, just as wave 5 offers them a shorting opportunity in wave A. By combining the wave principle with traditional technical analysis, traders can improve their trading by increasing the probabilities of a successful trade.

Technical studies can pick out many trading opportunities, but the wave principle helps traders discern which ones have the highest probability of being successful. This is because the wave principle is the framework that provides history, current information, and a peek at the future. When traders place their technical studies within this strong framework, they have a better basis for understanding current price action.

The wave principle works on any market and any timeframe. However, here's a word of caution for futures traders. At times, the wave principle can be difficult to apply to commodity futures versus individual stocks, because the psychology behind commodity markets is very different from that of the stock market. For example, a sudden freeze in Florida would have no impact on Microsoft's stock price. However, it would send OJ futures through the roof. Another example would be that conflict in a Third World nation would likely have no impact on Johnson & Johnson's stock price. Yet, as we've seen in recent years, conflict in the Ivory Coast has dramatically affected cocoa futures.

The key to success in using the wave principle in the commodity futures markets is patience. Traders need to wait and trade on only the classic or textbook wave patterns for set-ups. Look for and trade off of only very clear five-wave rallies or three-wave declines. Make sure that the wave count adheres to the rules for the wave principle discussed above. It can still work well in the futures arena, but traders need to be patient and should trade only very clearly defined wave patterns.

How to Use the Wave Principle to Place Stops

One important requirement for many traders is a method to place their protective stops. Unfortunately, before he died, Ralph Elliott did not address how to trade the wave principle. However, much of the information that traders require, such as where to place protective or trailing stops, can be gleaned from its three cardinal rules.

Let's begin with the first rule and see how traders could apply it to stop placement: wave 2 may never retrace more than one hundred percent of wave 1. For example, in *Figure 5*, we have a five-wave advance followed by a three-wave decline, which we will call waves (1) and (2). [In order to clarify, waves (1) and (2) are seen as the start of a larger five-wave advance.] An important thing to remember about second waves is that they often retrace more than half of first waves, most often a .618 retracement. So, in this case, we are anticipating a third-wave rally, which is where prices normally travel the farthest in the shortest amount of time, and traders should look to buy at or near the .618 retracement of wave (1). And once a long position is initiated, a protective stop can be placed one tick below the origin of wave (1).

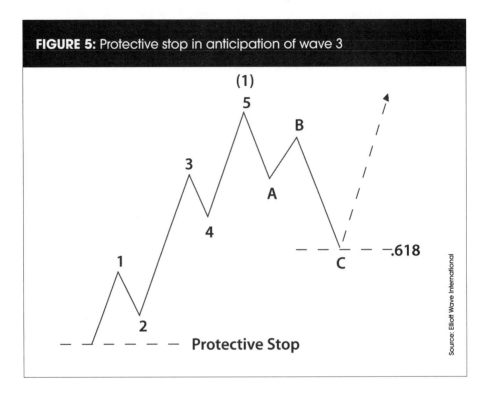

FIGURE 5: Protective stop in anticipation of wave 3

That's because if wave (2) retraces more than one hundred percent of wave (1), the move no longer can be labeled wave (2).

Now let's examine rule number two: wave 4 may never end in the price territory of wave 1. This rule is useful to traders because it can help them set protective stops in anticipation of catching a fifth-wave move to new highs. The most common Fibonacci retracement for fourth waves is a .382 retracement of the third wave. Thus, after a sizeable advance in price in wave (3), traders should look to enter long positions following a three-wave decline that ends at or near the .382 retracement of wave (3). Where would the protective stop on such a long position go? As shown in *Figure 6*, the protective stop should go one tick below the extreme of wave (1), because something is wrong with the wave count if what a market participant has labeled as wave (4) heads into the price territory of wave (1).

Last but not least, rule number three: wave 3 may never be the shortest impulse wave of waves 1, 3, and 5. This also offers some guidance for stop placement. Typically, the third wave is the wave

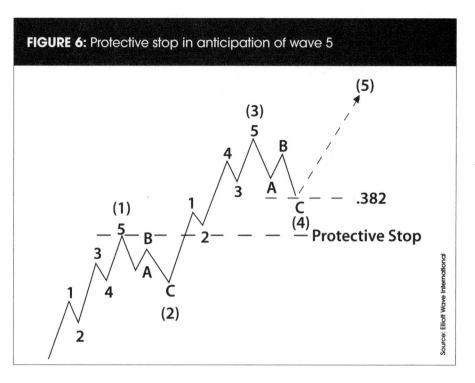

FIGURE 6: Protective stop in anticipation of wave 5

Source: Elliott Wave International

that travels the farthest in an impulse wave or five-wave move, but not always. In certain situations (such as within a pattern called a diagonal triangle), wave 1 travels farther than wave 3. When this condition occurs, a short position can be considered with a protective stop one tick above the point where wave 5 becomes longer than wave 3 (see *Figure 7*). Why? If the labeling of the price action is correct, wave 5 will not surpass wave 3 in length, because if wave 3 is already shorter than wave 1, it cannot also be shorter than wave 5. If wave 3 does become the shortest wave, thus breaking cardinal rule number three, then it's time to rethink the wave count.

Putting It All Together

By simply following the three cardinal rules of the wave principle, traders can figure out where to place protective stops as they trade, which is the beginning of a more defined trading system. I've often wondered what discoveries R.N. Elliott would have made about how to trade the wave principle had he begun his work ten or twenty years earlier. Even so, for the passionate Elliott wave student, many of the

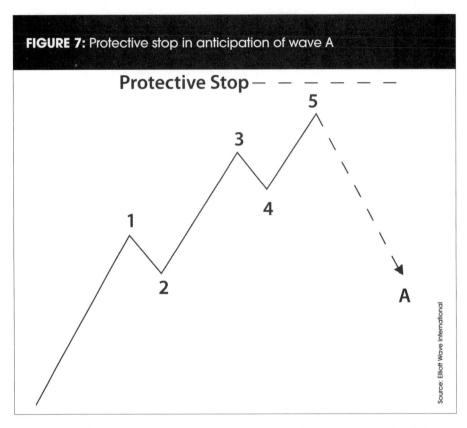

FIGURE 7: Protective stop in anticipation of wave A

Source: Elliott Wave International

unanswered questions concerning how to apply the wave principle successfully and profitably in real time are waiting to be discovered in his original works.

Jeffrey Kennedy is a senior financial analyst at Elliott Wave International (www.elliottwave.com) with more than fifteen years of experience as an analyst and trader. He writes and edits Futures Junctures, EWI's premier commodity forecasting package that includes Daily Futures Junctures, The Weekly Wrap-Up and *Monthly Futures Junctures*. EWI has published two volumes of *The Trader's Classroom Collection*, which present Jeffrey's trading insights, market analysis and advice on how to apply the wave principle in real time. Versions of this article originally appeared in *SFO* in April 2005 and February 2006.

SECTION FIVE
Technical Trading in Action

This section focuses on implementing technical analysis and using the tools you've mastered in tandem to improve your trading practice. You'll gain insight into long-term charts, sentiment-based indicators, intermarket analysis, and special qualities to be aware of using technical analysis in the forex markets.

First, we'll look at timeframes. Two or more timeframes can be better than one. Experimenting with using a combination of timeframes can give you a new perspective on trading and work as a sanity check on your objectivity. Considering long-term charts can also improve your overall trading strategy.

The vast majority of technical indicators—even the most complex—are usually a function of price. Sometimes going back to simple supply and demand can help you spot early market turns to make objective, profitable trading and investing decisions.

Forex markets are good technical markets but have some distinct characteristics not found in other venues. Every currency pair has unique qualities. Understanding which technical indicators work best on which market can create opportunities for better profitability. Brian Dolan writes about the personalities associated with each currency pair and tells you how this affects which tools you should choose to evaluate charts and forecast price moves.

Renowned technical analyst John Murphy looks at the major intermarket relationships characterizing the financial markets over the last thirty years. Gain fresh insights into your own market by looking at trends in other markets.

And lastly, even in this information-laden computer age, looking back at what worked in the past makes sense. Consider incorporating some fundamental strategies into your trading methodologies. It is possible and can be profitable to combine elements of old-fashioned fundamental analysis with cutting-edge technical modeling.

FOCUS ON TRUE SUPPLY AND DEMAND TO SPOT TURNS

BY SAM SEIDEN

Noted economist Adam Smith suggested hundreds of years ago that when supply exceeds demand at a price level, prices will decline and vice-versa. Isaac Newton suggested in his three laws of motion that an object will remain in motion until it is met with an equal or greater force. These two simple, yet brilliant principles have stood the test of time and are directly responsible for the movement of price in the markets we trade today. There is no doubt in my mind that the two of them would have made excellent traders.

Getting down to business, the focus of this article is on what conventional technical analysis refers to as support (demand) and resistance (supply). We'll be digging deeper into what support and resistance really are, how we identify and quantify them on a price chart, and how we use them to make objective, profitable trading and investing decisions. The trade examples used in this piece are real trades executed by our capital management firm.

Think Corporate Profits

The way traders and investors derive profits from the markets is very similar to the way corporations profit in their marketplace. Microsoft, for example, identifies demand for a type of software, estimates the cost of production, and determines what price the consumer will pay for that software. If the company's projections are reasonably accurate and they are on target with supply and demand, they can estimate their price and profit. Microsoft clearly has been very successful in this regard, enjoying large profit margins on many of their products.

As in any other marketplace, the financial markets reflect human action in response to an ongoing supply and demand relationship. Unfortunately, when the average person enters the world of trading and investing, operating in these markets becomes a kind of art, based on subjective indicators and oscillators, news-driven perceptions, and pictures of conventional price patterns that are more valuable with a frame around them on a person's wall than they are in his financial statement!

Traders need to remember that the markets are nothing more than pure supply and demand at work, with human action reacting to that ongoing supply and demand relationship. This is ultimately what determines price, and opportunity emerges when this simple and straightforward relationship is out of balance. When we simply look at the ongoing supply and demand relationship, identifying where prices are most likely to turn is really not that difficult.

Yes, this is basic, but why not begin at the start to get this right? Support (demand) is a price level where there are more willing buyers than available supply at a specific price level. Resistance (supply) is a price level where there is more supply available than there are willing buyers to purchase the supply at a specific price level. Let's take a look at *Figure 1* to identify what constitutes truly objective demand and why.

Area A in *Figure 1* represents a price level where supply and demand are in relative balance or equilibrium. Everyone who wishes to buy and sell at that price level is able to do so, and prices are stable. On the close of the candle B, the supply and demand relationship in area A is no longer in balance. We now know that there is much more demand at price level A than there is available supply. How do we know this to be true?

The only thing that can cause prices to rise as they did is a shift in the supply-demand relationship. In other words, when candle B closes, we can objectively conclude that some willing buyers were left behind. Area A can now objectively be labeled demand (support). The area labeled C represents a decline in price to our objective demand level. And, this is where we would find opportunity for a low-risk/high-odds trade as price revisits an area of imbalance. We'll discuss how to take advantage of this opportunity shortly.

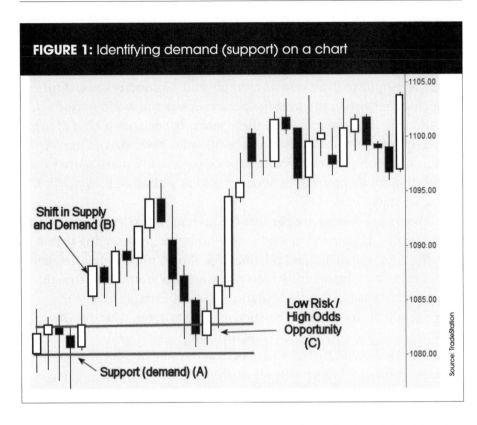

FIGURE 1: Identifying demand (support) on a chart

Now simply stand that previous example on its head for identifying supply (resistance) and quantifying it on a chart. Just apply and reverse the criteria and logic from the prior demand example to *Figure 2.*

Identifying true demand (support) and supply (resistance) price levels is typically what complicates most trading decisions. Specifically, finding where prices are likely to turn and why consumes most traders' thoughts. The demand and supply definitions are all that needs to be considered when identifying turning points in price. Smith kept things simple, logical, and real. When applying his theory to the trading markets, nothing breaks down.

Let's face it. The only truly objective information available to us is price and volume. Everything else is either subjective or a derivative of price and volume, so why not go right to the source? Most trading books and so-called market professionals will talk about moving averages, Fibonacci retracement levels, and so on, as being demand (support) and supply (resistance) areas. This could not be

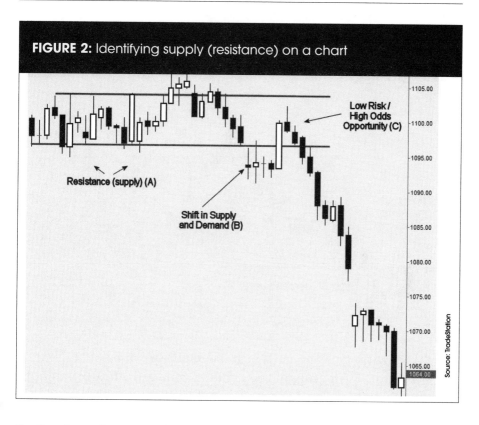

FIGURE 2: Identifying supply (resistance) on a chart

further from the truth. Any indicator or oscillator that someone touts as a tool for identifying support and resistance is just that, an indicator or oscillator, not demand and supply. These will appear to work only at times when they line up with true supply and demand levels on a chart. Can you imagine Microsoft directors sitting in a meeting talking about head and shoulders patterns and cup and handles? Not likely.

Don't Forget about the Human Element

Let's take Smith's theory a step further and add the element of human behavior to our supply and demand analysis. To do this, let's look at a tick chart instead of a time-based chart, as it is made up of trades and price, not time. This is the most objective way to view any market. Each candle represents a specific number of trades (human action), not a time interval. After all, the goal in analyzing any market is to determine the buying and selling activity at each price level.

The light gray dots on *Figure 3* are a proprietary indicator we created (and use) that identifies extreme selling. Area A is a side-

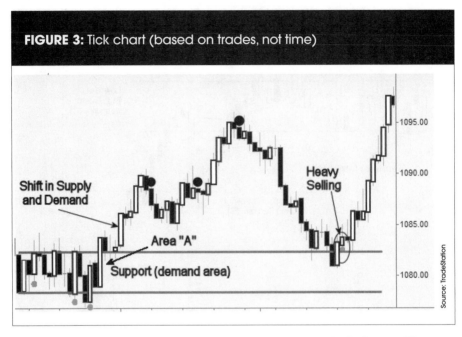

FIGURE 3: Tick chart (based on trades, not time)

1095.00
1090.00
Heavy
Selling
Shift in Supply
and Demand
1085.00
Area "A"
Support (demand area)
1080.00

Source: TradeStation

ways trading range where supply and demand are in balance. Next, there is a shift in the supply and demand equation when prices rally out of price-level A, as noted on *Figure 3*. Now, one can objectively conclude that there are now more willing buyers at price-level A than available supply. This level now, of course, becomes a demand (support) level. Traders need to refocus their thought process. The breakout of area A actually just gave the astute trader all of the objective information he needs for a potentially low-risk/high-odds trade if and when prices revisit that area. It's faulty to think that you have just missed a breakout.

Again, the light gray dots in the demand area in Figure 3 tell us objectively that there was heavy selling during that period of sideways trading. With that much selling, one would think prices would fall, but they rose instead. This suggests there is strong demand at price level A.

The light gray dot that appears when prices revisit this demand level means that aggressive sellers have taken action (sold) after a decline in price and into an area of demand. The laws of supply and demand tell us that novice sellers have entered the market and that prices are likely to rise. Someone who sells after a period of selling and into an area of objective demand is likely to consistently lose according to the laws and principles of supply and demand. Therefore, we simply need to identify the novice seller and take the other side of that trade each and every time we see it.

Like Mass into Motion

When determining the strength of a demand or supply level, there are two important factors that need to be considered. First, we must determine the amount of trading activity in the level of demand or supply. This is no different from how the great physicist Isaac Newton incorporates mass into his three laws of motion. For traders, mass would simply equal volume. The higher the volume in a demand or supply area, the stronger that area will be if and when prices reach it. If there is a willing buyer of one hundred shares of stock at a price level where there are one thousand for sale, prices can't move higher until all one thousand shares are bought (supply absorbed). When they all are bought, more buyers are needed for prices to rise and so on.

Second, we must determine objectively how many times prices revisit a demand or supply level. The highest-odds buying opportunity, for example, is when prices revisit an objective demand area for the first time, not the second, third, or fourth. Remember what demand is—some buyers who wanted to buy were not able to because prices rose. Each time prices revisit the demand level, more buyers that were left behind are now able to buy. This logically weakens the strength of the demand level in question each time it is revisited simply because there are fewer buyers. Think of chopping down a tree. Each time the tree is struck by the axe, the likelihood of the tree falling increases, as there is less mass in the trunk.

Executing entries and exits and determining protective stops properly and objectively can only be accomplished by identifying true demand and supply areas and taking advantage of imbalances when they occur. If one can accomplish a trade entry into true demand and supply price levels, it solves the two most important tasks in trading. First, it allows the trader to enter a full position very close to his protective stop and to take advantage of sound money management strategies.

Second, it allows a trader to enter and be a part of the reversal in price that then invites others in to pay the trader! Price reversals that end up as white candles after a number of black candles at demand

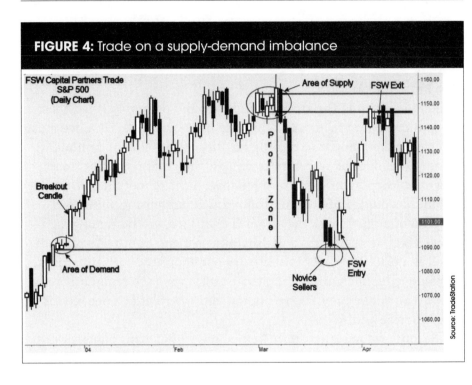

FIGURE 4: Trade on a supply-demand imbalance

areas on a chart, for example, invite the masses to buy. Smart traders consistently strive to be a part of that invitation (the first white candle) that goes out to the masses.

Knowing when It's Real

Let's now develop an objective set of rules and criteria for entering and exiting consistently profitable trades and investments. The low-risk/high-odds trade seen in *Figure 4* incorporated an entry based on identifying an objective supply and demand imbalance.

How did we know this area was demand? Simply, the breakout from the area of price stability objectively told us so. Prices eventually revisited that demand area, which we had flagged as an entry point for a long position because of the supply-demand imbalance. Once prices reached that level, we concluded that the sellers in that area were novice traders who consistently lose. But how does one know this? Again, the laws of supply and demand tell us that someone who sells after a period of selling and into an objective area of demand will consistently lose, which was exactly the scenario at hand with this opportunity.

The profit zone (or profit margin in the case of Microsoft) is the distance between the demand area and the supply area, as seen on the chart. Based on this information, the trade was taken. The risk was low as the trade was taken near the demand level (very close to the protective stop). We also became a part of the reversal candle, or the invitation to the masses to buy after we do—which is ideal. Profits were taken into the area of supply, identified prior to entry.

A common question among traders is how far to look back on a chart to identify demand and supply areas. The answer is always the same. Traders searching for demand and supply levels should look back as far as need be in order to find the true demand or supply level. Much of the time a few days will suffice. Occasionally, the market being traded is at a multi-day/week high or low. In some cases, we must look back further. To limit the look-back search for true supply and demand in a given market to a specific number of days is a case of form-fitting the market to fit a convenient need; it is not real and objective. The key is to eliminate time from the equation completely.

Why Is It So Difficult?

It all seems pretty simple. But why then do so few traders and investors enter properly into demand and supply areas? The answer is simple: human emotion. The fear of a potential break of a demand level is stronger than the benefit a low-risk entry at a demand or supply area offers. But traders need to remember that opportunity always lies where the majority is afraid to go.

However, anyone can do this. The key is to have a set of rules based on the laws of supply and demand and the human behavior relationship that is responsible for the movement of price. The only two books one really needs are the old econ 101 and psych 101 books.

As we've discussed, it is the origin of the movement of price that serves as the demand (support) or supply (resistance). The origin is actually where the equation becomes out of balance, which in essence is the definition of demand (support) and supply (resistance).

Don't watch an initial advance or decline in price and get upset. It isn't actually a missed opportunity. In reality, this simply gives traders the objective information that is needed for a low-risk/high-odds opportunity. Or put in another way, breakouts and breakdowns from areas of congestion show us exactly where the shift in supply and demand has taken place.

Do true support and resistance areas always hold and produce turns? Most of the time the answer is yes, when the analysis is objective. However, we actually don't always need them to produce a turn in price. After all, our trading objective is increasing the odds of success, not guaranteeing certainty. Simply identifying an area of price congestion above or below current prices is not enough. The area in question must meet the definition of true demand or supply. Trade what is real, not what you feel.

Sam Seiden is a trader, research analyst, and instructor with more than ten years of experience, including trading his personal account and fund management. Mr. Seiden provides research and guidance to clients through speaking engagements, workshops, magazine articles, and advisory services via www.samseiden.com. He can be reached at sam@samseiden.com. This article originally appeared in *SFO* in January 2005.

INCREASE YOUR ODDS WITH MULTIPLE TIMEFRAME ANALYSIS

BY BRIAN SHANNON

We have all heard the market cliché "the trend is your friend" for good reason. Making big money in the markets is accomplished by entering a position at the onset of a new trend and then having the patience to hold the position long enough to allow the profit to accumulate into a large winner. Participation in a long-term trend is the dream of every investor. To have a huge winner that we believed in and held well beyond the point where most participants would have been shaken out on a short-term pullback is what allows successful investors to reap large gains.

Many investors may find their most satisfying winners in a three-year hold. But that timeframe does not fit all market participants. There are those of us who believe that long-term capital gains should be recognized after just a few days. For those traders, three years seems like a lifetime! Short-term trading can produce outsized returns, as long as losers are properly managed and winners are larger than the losers (but then again, that is true for any timeframe).

In order to attain larger winners than losers, the easiest way to get the odds in your favor is to trade with the primary trend, regardless of whether you are an investor or a trader. Think of the most basic definition of an up-trend, which is price making higher highs and higher lows. In an up-trend, the sum of the rallies will always be greater than the sum of the declines; otherwise the trend would not be intact. The opposite is true for a down-trend; the sum of the declines will always be greater than the sum of the rallies, which obviously makes the short side more profitable in a down-trending stock. The simple math of trends is the biggest argument for why it makes sense to participate in moves that are aligned with the direction of the primary trend, rather than trying to pick tops and bottoms. Even if one can accurately predict turning points in a market, the reward will not be as great as it would be if one were participating in the trend.

Market Corrections

The way that markets correct is another factor that stacks the odds against those who attempt to profit by trading against the trend. For those who are beginning technical traders, there are two ways markets can correct after a move in either direction.

The first type of correction is one that occurs by price. For example, an up-trending market will experience a pullback in price, or a down-trending stock will experience a short-term rally before the primary trend re-exerts its dominance. The other way a market corrects is through time, meaning that instead of a countertrend move, the market will trade sideways as the buyers and sellers battle it out for control. A correction through time is typically marked by low volatility in a tight range, which can frustrate the person anticipating a reversal. Because numerous trends are often prevalent in a given market, the surest way to stack the odds in your favor is to use multiple timeframe analysis for trend alignment, before risking your capital.

In theory, trend trading is simple: buy low and sell high for longs, and sell high and buy back low for short positions. In reality, many traders find trend trading frustrating because they are not focusing on the right trend. A little over one hundred years ago, Charles H. Dow wrote a series of editorials in the *Wall Street Journal* in which he laid out his views of how the stock market works; collectively these writings are referred to as the Dow theory. The work of Dow is still referred to today and is the underlying premise of technical analysis.

Three Types of Trends

One of the foundations of the Dow theory is the identification of three types of price trends: the primary trend, the secondary trend, and minor trends. The primary movements were compared to oceanic tides. They are the main trend of the market and can last from a few months to several years. Primary trends cannot be manipulated, as the forces of supply and demand are too large for any one participant to successfully influence the collective reasoning of the crowd. Secondary movements were referred to as waves and they are known as reactionary moves, trends that typically last from two weeks to three months. The secondary movements are often created by a large participant (mutual fund, hedge fund, etc.) exiting all or a significant part of their position; once that supply (in an up-trend) is absorbed by the market, the buyers regain control and the stock continues higher in the primary trend. Finally, minor (or short-term) trends were viewed as insignificant ripples, which lasted less than two weeks and were given little significance because they represent fluctuations in the secondary trend. The short-term ripples in the market can be difficult to predict because they are often driven by emotions. However, skilled day traders thrive on this type of emotional short-term movement.

One of the most important elements in successful trend trading is to determine which trend to focus on. Deciding which timeframe to engage the market is largely determined by individual factors. These include time available to commit to the markets, capital base, experience level, risk tolerance, and even one's level of patience. Investors are naturally attracted to the primary movement, while the secondary moves are going to be the focus of a more intermediate-term participant (swing traders). And, the minor trends will be the obvious choice of day traders. Even as simple as that concept may seem, it becomes more complicated because technical analysis is about timing, and you must look at more than one timeframe if you are truly to have the odds in your favor:

TABLE 1: Know your timeframe

	INVESTOR	SWING TRADER	DAY TRADER
Primary Trend	Week	Day	60 Minute
Secondary Trend	Day	60 Minute	10 Minute
Minor Trend	60 Minute	10 Minute	2/1 Minute

The investor, swing trader, and day trader will look at different timeframes for their analysis of primary, secondary, and minor trends.

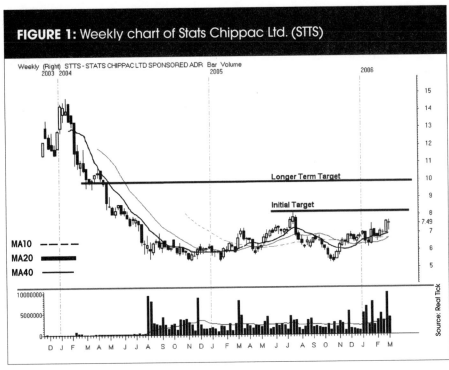

FIGURE 1: Weekly chart of Stats Chippac Ltd. (STTS)

In order to make timing decisions that will allow you to determine a low-risk area to get involved and still have large profit potential, it is essential to conduct your analysis on multiple timeframes. We will now explore three different timeframes that investors, swing traders and day traders should consider. To make this analysis real we will use an example of a current setup in the market as if we were going to enter an investment or a swing trade. Because of the short-term nature of a day trade we will outline the timeframes to consider but will not study an actual trade setup (see *Table 1*).

Whether you are an investor, swing trader, or day trader, the first timeframe that you should study is one that represents the primary trend. The longer, more powerful trends are the ones that you want to be sure not to fight, as mistakes can be quite costly. The long-term timeframe is not about timing—it is about idea generation. For an investor, the timeframe to start with is a weekly chart that encompasses at least two years worth of data. Looking at *Figure 1*, the weekly chart of Stats Chippac Ltd. (STTS) shows the stock has been bottoming out over the last eighteen months. The recent increased volume suggests the stock may be ready for a sustained move higher that could see

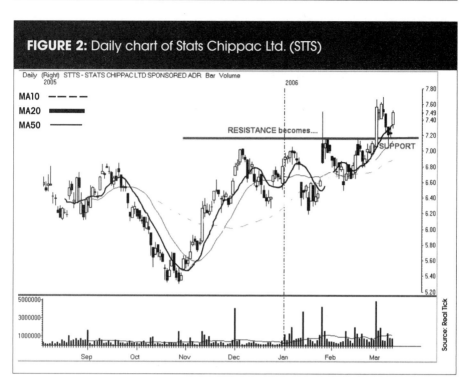

FIGURE 2: Daily chart of Stats Chippac Ltd. (STTS)

the stock trade near the 10-level. This is the type of chart that should get an investor interested in further study on shorter timeframes (of course, having a fundamental reason for being involved—in this case increased earnings and revenues—is always a bonus).

The primary trend for a swing trader will not be quite as long term as it would be for an investor; this is why the swing trader's analysis of a long-term trend should take place on a daily chart, which shows at least 150 days of data. A swing trader would have good reason for being bullish on the daily trend of STTS, as the stock is in a strong up-trend, which is defined by a strong volume pattern and the stock holding above rising key moving averages (see *Figure 2*). It is also encouraging to bullish traders that the stock found support at the prior level of resistance near $7.20 on a recent low-volume pullback.

Drilling Down

Day traders will find it necessary to bring their analysis of a long-term trend to an even shorter period of time. That can be accomplished by studying price action on a 60-minute chart, which shows price movement over at least 25 days. The 60-minute chart of STTS

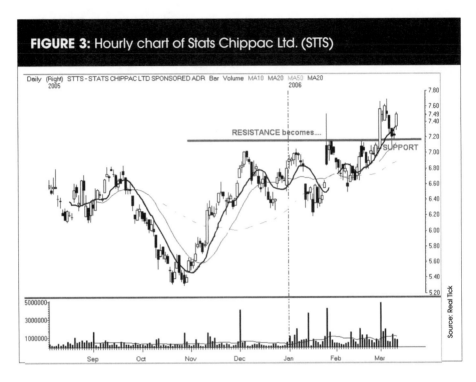

FIGURE 3: Hourly chart of Stats Chippac Ltd. (STTS)

(see *Figure 3*) is telling day traders a similarly bullish message as was seen on the weekly and daily timeframes. The 60-minute timeframe shows that the buyers have once again taken control of the stock by pushing past the short-term resistance at $7.30. Notice how this action has also turned the moving averages higher, confirming that the short, intermediate, and longer-term trends of this timeframe are now higher.

The units of time studied in these examples are starting points. It is often necessary to look further to the left to see older data that may be relevant to the primary trend. The goal of the long-term timeframe is to allow the participant to recognize signs of a new trend or a stock that appears to be early on in an established trend, and then move to a shorter timeframe for further confirmation of a reason to get involved in an actual trade.

Once the stock has been identified as a viable candidate for a commitment of capital, the next step is to determine key levels of support and resistance, which brings our analysis to the secondary timeframe. A trader must first identify the existence of a primary trend, using the appropriate longer-term timeframe. The next step for a trade set-up is to determine if there is sufficient potential for reward relative to the perceived risk—essentially this is where we plan our trade. The evaluation of the risk-reward scenario should take place on an inter-mediate-term timeframe that allows for easier recognition of levels of support and resistance, which might not have been visible on the longer-term timeframe.

To view the secondary trend, an investor would study the ac-tion on the daily timeframe of STTS (*Figure 2*). On the daily chart, the investor should notice that the stock recently rallied from 7.00 to 7.60 on heavy volume and then experienced a lower volume pullback to previous resistance at 7.20. At this point, it appears the 7.20 level is where there should be good support for the stock, but the investor may want to set a stop under the rising 20-day moving average (MA), which is now at approximately 7.10. This would give the investor a theoretical risk of approximately $0.40. Setting the stop under the 20-day MA instead of under the support at 7.20 exposes the trade to more risk, but it also reduces the chance of getting stopped out of the position prematurely.

Coming up with an upward price objective could not be done on the daily timeframe because of the limited price action above 7.00, so the investor would have to revert back to the weekly timeframe (*Figure 1*) to come up with an initial target near 8.20, which is the high for the stock in 2004. Because the stock had limited trading history at the 8.20 level it is unlikely that resistance would be very strong, thus making a target closer to 10.00 more feasible. Even the 10.00 level could prove to be conservative, as there is further potential for the stock to rally up toward 12.00, which was a support level broken in late 2003. Whether the stock eventually rallies up toward 10 or 12, the risk of getting involved with a stop of just $.40 makes this a very at-tractive long-side candidate.

Finding Support and Resistance

After identifying STTS as a good potential swing trade candidate on a daily timeframe, the intermediate-term trader would then drill down the analysis of support and resistance by looking at the hourly timeframe (*Figure 3*). The way a swing trader should interpret action seen on the hourly chart is that the stock is in an ideal area for pur-chase, as the buyers have just regained control of the trend on this

FIGURE 4: Ten-minute chart of Stats Chippac Ltd. (STTS)

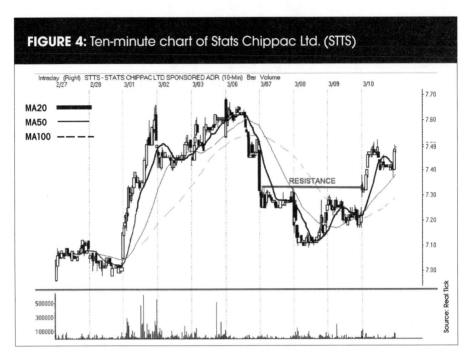

timeframe. By clearing the short-term resistance at 7.30, the buyers are back in control of the intermediate-term trend, and the stock now has strong upward momentum, making it an excellent candidate for a swing trade. The minimum upward objective for the swing trade would be the recent high of 8.20, and determination of where to set the stop would come from an examination of the minor trend, which can be seen in *Figure 4*.

The final timeframe to be studied is the minor trend. The goal on this timeframe is to capture a more accurate entry price. The minor trend for the investor is found in *Figure 3*, the hourly timeframe. If the investor is looking to enter the stock while it exhibits upward strength, he may choose to enter at the same level the swing trader was targeting, 7.30.

A swing trader should analyze the short-term trend by studying price action on a ten-minute chart, which covers ten days of trading activity. As we saw on the 60-minute chart, the ideal purchase would have occurred as the buyers gained control of the short-term trend when they pushed the stock past short-term resistance at $7.30 (the 10-minute timeframe shows this level in greater detail). While the 10-minute timeframe does not offer any particular advantage over the

60-minute timeframe in the case of STTS, it does often provide greater detail that allows us to fine tune not only our entry price but also where to place our initial protective stop.

Multiple Timeframe Analysis Can Help

The concept of using multiple timeframes for trading is one every market participant should consider because it allows for a greater level of objective analysis of what the market is actually doing, rather than relying on our opinions to make important trading decisions. Using three different timeframes allows market participants in all timeframes to find the idea (primary trend), create a plan of action (secondary trend), and capture more accurate entries (minor trend). In the end, multiple timeframes allow us to become better at holding our winners and cutting our losers, a goal common to all investors.

Brian Shannon is an independent trader and highly regarded market educator. His work can be viewed at www.alphatrends.blogspot.com Brian can be reached at alphatrends@gmail.com This article originally appeared in SFO in May 2006.

DAYS OF THE LONG-TERM TRADER

BY MICHAEL KAHN

Think back to your college days when all of your efforts and thoughts were directed toward the big picture. Saving the world. Inventing the next great thing. Contemplating the higher being. The daily battles with everyday life were more distraction than primary focus—unlike today when fighting traffic, programming a cell phone and scheduling your kids' travel for soccer games dominate your attention. Fighting fires crowds out long-term planning, and when we are in that mode there is little real progress to be made.

In the investment world, no matter how hard we try to follow investment plans, we are still caught up in the frenzy of Wall Street and the constant bombardment of stock tickers, earnings news, and the not-too-infrequent scandal. Trade online for low commissions! Real-time tools to manage your portfolio! Get the edge with up-to-the-second bids and asks to see who is moving the market! If you are an investor with better things to do than worry about squeezing an extra penny out of your one hundred-share purchase, there is salvation from broker noise and media hype. Long-term portfolio management is possible using charts and technical analysis, and it will let you sleep at night while helping you with your long-term goals.

Technical Analysis Works across All Timeframes

Wait a minute! Technical analysis? That stuff day traders use to scalp in and out of the market every five minutes? Those pictures that look like mountains that professional traders use to try to make a nickel per trade? I don't want to be tied to a quote machine.

The good news is that technical analysis (which, by the way, is an awful name for using charts to gauge the mood of the market) works in all timeframes from minute-by-minute, to day-by-day, to month-by-month. Analysis that applies to day traders using five-minute charts applies to long-term investors using weekly charts that cover years worth of data. Math majors might call chart patterns fractal, as every wave, action, and reaction in the market can be broken down into smaller units that look just like the larger unit. Engineering majors might call it scalable. The point is that what works in one timeframe for traders works in other timeframes for investors, and that makes chart watching a valuable tool for everyone.

Before the stock market bubble popped in 2000, the long-favored investment model was buy and hold. Historical returns in the market were ten percent per year on average—not including the bubble years when it was twice that—so short-term declines were mere speed bumps in a multi-year investment journey. Given enough time, the market would bounce back and bail out investors who made poorly timed purchases. Stocks of good companies would always be welcome in any portfolio. But that thinking had one major flaw: the long term can be so long that it becomes impractical for many investors. After the debacle of 1987, it took two years for the market to recapture its peak levels. Is that too long to wait for the market to bail us out? Maybe not.

In 1972, the Dow Jones Industrial Average crossed the 1,000 mark for the first time, but not long thereafter the great bear market of 1973-1974 set in. It would be ten years before the Dow was able to get back above 1,000 again. Is that too long to wait? It is if you don't have a lifetime left to earn money for retirement. After the crash of 1929, it took more than two decades for the Dow to recapture its peak levels. Is that too long to wait for the market to return to its historical average return? You bet your backside it is, and that is the point. Buy and hold only works when you have multiple decades to ride out the bear markets that are a normal part of market life. Buy and hold should be renamed buy and hope.

We've all heard the arguments that market timing does not work and missing the ten best days in the market costs thousands upon thousands of dollars in lost profits. What they don't tell us is that avoiding the ten worst days saves many times that amount in losses. So what do we do about it? First of all, continue to use whatever tools you already use when making decisions to buy and sell stocks. If you use fundamental analysis, keep on using it. If you like quantitative analysis, keep using that. If you don't know what you use and just take recommendations from your broker, make no changes. All you need to do is add one additional step to see if the conclusions you have made fit with what the market is saying. Take a look at a long-term chart. Think of it as a sanity check.

While long-term investors can choose from a wide array of technical analysis tools, only a few are necessary for our purposes, namely making sure the market agrees with our other conclusions. Forget about the alphabet soup of momentum indicators such as RSI, MACD, and CCI. While advanced chart watchers can employ them to hone their analyses, we do not need them here. All we need to know are four basic concepts:

1. How the stock got to where it is right now (its trend and patterns);
2. Whether money is flowing into the stock (demand);
3. A comparison to past performance;
4. A comparison to the market.

These concepts can be analyzed with one single chart—a weekly price chart with volume, a 40-week moving average, and a relative performance ratio to the broad market.

Let's start with a recent example in the market of how to stay out of trouble: General Motors. For years, this was the market bellwether and not coincidently the phrase, "What's good for General Motors is good for the country," was well known. It was a solid company and a solid investment—so when its price started to pull back in 2004 it seemed to be a good stock to buy (see *Figure 1*).

Reading the Chart

In fact, between April and July of that year, with the stock hovering in the low 40s, several analysts from major firms upgraded their opinions and price targets so things seemed to be back on track. Load up the truck. This blue chip is ready to move! But *Figure 1* shows several

FIGURE 1: Weekly General Motors (GM) chart

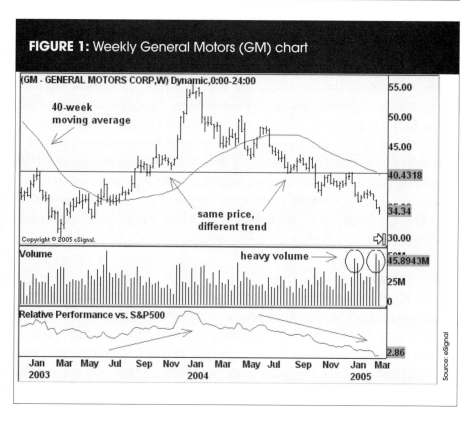

bits of technical evidence to the contrary. For space reasons, all of these are shown on one chart, but the reader can easily maintain two or three versions of the chart to reduce clutter. First, the stock was now in a declining trend. What was cheap during the rising trend in 2003 is no longer considered that way, and that means the mindset of the market is the opposite of what it once was.

To drive this point home, price dipped below the forty-week moving average on two occasions in the summer of 2004. While this is not always the best trading signal, it does indicate that at least some investors who bought shares within the past forty weeks are now underwater. Keep in mind that those investors holding losing positions will often seek to sell those positions as soon as they can break even. It creates a source of supply in the market and as we all know, supply and demand rule. Price cannot help but follow, and in this case that means there is a built-in ceiling for the market to fight. The volume measurement in 2004 did not provide additional clues, because it was not signaling anything unusual.

However, we'll reserve this indicator for later to see how it really adds value to the analysis.

Finally, GM had changed from outperforming the market to underperforming the market as the year was starting to unfold. This performance indicator is simply a ratio of the price of GM to the price of the Standard & Poor's 500; when the ratio is rising it means that GM is rising faster than the market (assuming a rising trend, which was the case in 2004). Conversely, when it is falling, it means that GM is not rising as fast as the market (again, assuming the rising trend). There was a fairly substantial body of evidence saying that General Motors was not the stock people thought it was. Six months later, the stock had shed an additional fifteen percent.

Using Volume

On the right side of *Figure 1*, we can see that volume has two periods of unusually high levels. Both times, prices were falling, so we can assume that the sellers were more aggressive than the buyers and supply was still outpacing demand despite the new "cheap" price. Two more analysts weighed in with stock upgrades during January, but the trend was clearly down at this point. Not shown on the chart is action from the very next week when the stock shed almost six points on news that it was slashing its own earnings outlook. The charts did not tell us this was going to happen, but there was enough there to keep us from buying into the myth that humans know better than the market that a stock is in trouble.

Even though avoiding a bad investment is just as important as making a good one, if not more so, let's look at an example in which the analysts were right. In the middle of 2002, the stock market was, unbeknownst to investors, undergoing a basing process after a long bear market. The oil services stock Schlumberger (SLB) was in a bear market of its own and was guided lower from its August 2000 peak by a nicely formed trendline (see *Figure 2*).

However, unlike the broad market, which was gyrating wildly, Schlumberger was already stabilizing in a small base, preparing for the breakout it was going to make in May 2003. *Figure 2* shows a move through the bear market trendline and the forty-week average within a week of each other. That's good! But the entire market was moving higher, so it seemed that Schlumberger was just going

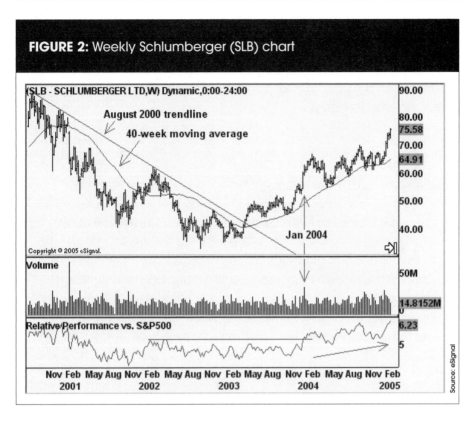

FIGURE 2: Weekly Schlumberger (SLB) chart

along for the ride. It was pacing the market, as evidenced in its flat relative performance line at the time. There was nothing remarkable in its volume chart, either. Still, for investors listening to Wall Street, the parade of upgrades seemed to be encouraging and the charts did not say otherwise.

But as the market started to peak in January 2004, something kicked it up a notch for Schlumberger. Volume began to get heavy and the relative performance chart broke through its own resistance level to show that money was flowing into this stock at the same time the rest of the market was stalling. That's very good! With rising trends in price, volume and relative performance, not to mention a rising 40-week moving average guiding higher, this stock was firing on all burners. Every criterion was now in play, and the stock went from the 40s at its breakout to the 120s without violating any of the criteria we used to find it.

A long-term investor could have held on without worrying about the news of the day, stock market corrections, or simply the desire to cash in with only a modest profit—all because technical chart analysis and Wall Street analysts agreed that the stock was a winner. Again, keep all your other decision-making tools. Add a simple chart to the mix and watch your results go up while your stress level goes down.

Michael Kahn is a well respected technical analyst. He writes the *Getting Technical* column for Barron's Online (www.barrons.com), the daily *Quick Takes Pro* technical newsletter (www.QuickTakesPro.net) and is a regular contributor to *SFO*. Kahn is the author of two books on technical analysis, most recently *Technical Analysis: Plain and Simple: Charting the Markets in Your Language* (Financial Times Prentice Hall, 2006), and was chief technical analyst for BridgeNews. He also is on the board of directors of the Market Technicians Association www. mta. org. This article originally appeared in *SFO* in June 2006.

OPTIONS-BASED SENTIMENT INDICATORS: Directional Clues for Equities

BY LAWRENCE McMILLAN

In the option market, there are two very useful and quite popular sentiment-based indicators: the volatility index ($VIX) and the put-call ratio. In this chapter, we'll take a little different look at how these might be used and what they might be saying about the future course of the broad stock market.

What the $Vix Measures

Most option traders are familiar with the volatility index, but for those who aren't, the $VIX measures the implied volatility of S&P 500 Index ($SPX) options that trade on the Chicago Board Option Exchange (CBOE). The formula for the calculation of $VIX recently was changed, as it had previously measured the implied volatility of representative options on the S&P 100 Index ($OEX). The "old" $VIX can now be quoted under the symbol $VXO. In either case, both volatility measures reflect the anticipation of option traders. If traders are nervous, or if they expect the market to be volatile, they will bid up the prices of options, and this will be reflected in a high $VIX reading. On the other hand, if traders feel that the market will be dull and not move much, then they will sell options or will not bid aggressively for them, and $VIX will trade down to low levels.

In general, $VIX shoots up to high levels during serious market declines, as traders panic and rush to buy puts at very expensive prices. At the opposite end of the spectrum, $VIX trades down to very low levels during quiet markets. At the extremes, $VIX is a contrary indicator: when it shoots up to a peak and pulls back rapidly, that is usually a buy signal for the broad stock market. That is, the majority of people are panicking and buying puts right at the bottom of the market (contrary theory). Hence, the peak in $VIX coincides with the market turnaround to the up-side.

At the other extreme, when $VIX reaches very low levels, that means that the average option trader figures nothing is going to happen in the market. Perhaps this average trader even decides to sell some naked puts and calls. Because the market acts in contrary fashion, the opposite of nothing happening is for a big market explosion to happen. And that's what usually follows a bottom on the $VIX chart, especially if that bottom is at a fairly low level—a market explosion. In recent years, such explosions have been on the down-side because of the bear market, but in the 1990s, many of the explosions were on the up-side during the bull market. The conclusion that one can draw is that a bottom on the $VIX chart precedes a market explosion—probably in the direction of the major market trend in force at the time.

These thoughts on using $VIX are more or less standard ones, but there is another approach that some traders find usable. That is to look at the seasonality of volatility, for it tends to follow a rather set pattern. *Figure 1* shows the composite $VIX, using all data from the past thirteen-plus years. This chart purports to show how volatility behaves, on average, during the trading year. The CBOE has data going back to 1986, but we chose not to include 1987, because it was such an outlier that it would distort the chart without providing any useful information.

From the chart in *Figure 1*, one can draw several conclusions. Following the points marked on the chart as A through H, it is evident that there is a modest peak in volatility in January (point A). Then, $VIX is rather dull and well contained until there is another minor peak in April. From there, $VIX usually goes into a long slide, culminating at the yearly low on about July 1. At that point, things begin to change, as volatility increases during July, holds those gains in August, and then starts to rise rapidly into the yearly peaks in late September and October—even into early November. After that, $VIX experiences a rather steep slide all the way into the end of the year.

It should be understood that any one year can deviate from this chart, but the data from all the years averaged together produces the

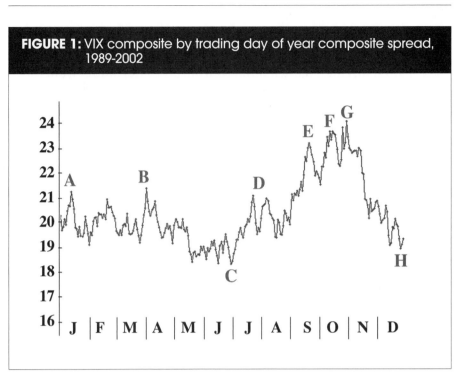

FIGURE 1: VIX composite by trading day of year composite spread, 1989-2002

pattern just described. This can be very valuable information for option traders. For example, if you prefer to buy straddles, then you'd want to be most aggressive, in general, at about point C on the chart in *Figure 1*. Straddle buyers might also want to get busy near the end of the calendar year (point H), looking to take advantage of the increase in volatility in January and later in the spring. On the other hand, if you're an option seller, then you'd want to curtail your activity at point C and get aggressive near the peaks at points E, F and G—and maybe be aggressive in April (at point B) as well.

Obviously, any trader would want to use other criteria before selling naked options or buying straddles, but the knowledge of how volatility behaves seasonally can be invaluable to the option strategist and might provide a bit of information that you wouldn't normally consider.

Some New Thinking about the Put-Call Ratio

The put-call ratio is another contrary indicator that uses option prices and/or volume to help identify extremes in investor sentiment. Put-call ratios also are contrary indicators: if everyone is bullish (i.e., they are all buying calls), then the astute trader will want to do the opposite, buy puts or establish short sales. Conversely, if everyone is bearish and buying puts, then the contrarian trader would want to buy stock or buy calls. The way we normally determine when the put-call ratio is giving a signal is to observe the chart of its 21-day moving average. If that average makes a peak (put buyers are exhausting themselves), then as a contrarian we'd buy calls or stock. On the other hand, if the put-call ratio moving average is making a relative low, we look to buy puts or sell short.

Sometimes, however, the normal interpretation of the ratios is not the best one—often due to the fact that hedging activity can distort the ratios, and what we are really looking for is speculative activity (to act against, contrarily).

Both the equity-only ratios—standard and weighted—gave sell signals in September 2003, yet the market continued to rally. When a trusted indicator seems to be giving incorrect signals, we look behind the scenes. A similar situation arose in July 2002. At that time, the put-call ratios were giving buy signals, but the market was plummeting.

The put-call ratio is, of course, stated as:

$$\text{Put-call ratio} = \frac{\text{put volume}}{\text{call volume}}$$

A ratio can increase when either 1) the numerator increases, or 2) the denominator declines. Conversely, a ratio can decrease when either 1) the numerator decreases, or 2) the denominator increases.

Recall that put-call ratio buy signals are given when the ratio peaks and begins to decline, and that's what happened in July 2002. The ratio peaked and began to decline (a contrarian buy signal), but the market continued to plummet. Upon further inspection in July 2002, it was deduced that the reason for the incorrect put-call ratio signal was that call volume had increased dramatically. The put-call ratio thus declined because call volume increased in the denominator of the fraction. However, it is much more classic for a buy signal to be given in a bear market when put volume reaches a maximum and then declines—not when call volume increases (both situations cause the put-call ratio to decline).

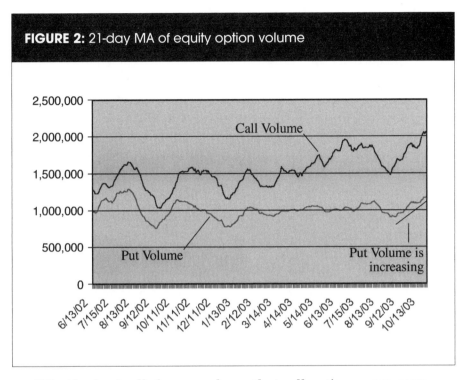

FIGURE 2: 21-day MA of equity option volume

What had actually happened was that call options were very expensive, and some of the major brokers had been recommending that their clients sell covered calls. So they did, and thus greatly increased the volume of calls traded—enough to make the put-call ratio decline and give a false buy signal. Once we identified the problem, we correctly stated that the best buy signal would be a peak in put volume, and it turned out to be a very accurate buy signal, occurring near the August 2002 bottom.

U.S. Equities

September 2003 saw an analogous situation. The put-call ratios gave sell signals—that is, they began to rise—even while the market itself was rising. What can cause the put-call ratio to rise? Either the traditional case of a decrease in call volume from an extreme level—which is usually what happens at a sentiment-based market top—or, less frequently, an increase in put volume.

What in the world would cause an increase in put volume while the market was rising? Not speculation, that's for sure. But what if stockholders became aware, en masse, that put premiums were cheap, and therefore represented good protection for stock holdings? In fact, that's exactly what has happened: a lot of cheap put options have been bought as protection. Thus, an increase in put volume is what led to a put-call ratio sell signal, even though it was not accompanied by a decline in call volume—which all speculative market tops should be.

In fact, the chart in *Figure 2* shows call volume continuing to increase. The true sell signal will thus occur when that call volume peaks, because the current sell signal is distorted by the hedging activity of those who bought puts.

The factors mentioned above are all longer-term projections and should not override short-term signals. However, they can prove to be a general guide for approaching the market. For example, if your own trading systems issue a buy signal, then the fact that the longer-term indicators are bullish should induce you to be sure to take your signal—perhaps aggressively. On the other hand, however, you may want to view sell signals with some caution as long as these longer-term bullish signals are still in effect.

Lawrence G. McMillan, author of several books, including the best-selling *Options as a Strategic Investment,* 4th ed. (Prentice Hall Press, 2001), is president of McMillan Analysis Corp. (www.optionstrategist.com). McMillan Analysis publishes several option trading newsletters, has a wide array of option research material, educational material and seminars available, and manages individual accounts in the option markets as well as a hedge fund. The company also sells software, such as a stand-alone version of the Black-Scholes model. McMillan formerly was a proprietary trader for the brokerage firms, Thomson McKinnon Securities and Prudential-Bache Securities, prior to founding McMillan Analysis Corp. in 1991. He has a BS in math from Purdue University and a Masters in applied math and computer science from the University of Colorado. This article originally appeared in *SFO* in January 2004.

TAILORING YOUR TECHNICAL APPROACH TO CURRENCY PERSONALITIES

BY BRIAN DOLAN

Much has been written about the suitability of technical analysis for trading in the currency markets. While this is undoubtedly true, it can leave traders, particularly those new to the currency markets, with the impression that all technical tools are equally applicable to all major currency pairs. Perhaps most dangerous from the stand-point of profitability, it can also seduce traders into searching for the proverbial silver bullet: that magic technical tool or study that works for all currency pairs, all the time. However, anyone who has traded forex for any length of time will recognize that, for example, dollar/yen (USD/JPY) and dollar/Swiss (USD/CHF) trade in distinctly different fashions.

Why, then, should a one-size-fits-all technical approach be expected to produce steady trading results? Instead, traders are more likely to experience improved results if they recognize the differences between the major currency pairs and employ different technical strategies to them. This article will explore some of the differences between the major currency pairs and suggest technical approaches that are best suited to each pair's behavioral tendencies.

The Biggie

By far the most actively traded currency pair is euro/dollar (EUR/USD), accounting for twenty-eight percent of daily global volume in the most recent Bank for International Settlements (BIS) survey of currency market activity. EUR/USD receives further interest from

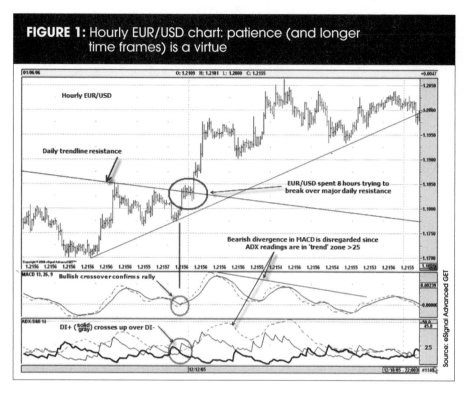

FIGURE 1: Hourly EUR/USD chart: patience (and longer time frames) is a virtue

Hourly EUR/USD

Daily trendline resistance

EUR/USD spent 8 hours trying to break over major daily resistance

Bearish divergence in MACD is disregarded since ADX readings are in 'trend' zone >25

Bullish crossover confirms rally

DI+ (solid) crosses up over DI- (gray)

Source: eSignal Advanced GET

volume generated by the euro-crosses (e.g., euro/British pound (EUR/GBP), euro/Swiss franc (EUR/CHF), and euro/Japanese yen (EUR/JPY), and this interest tends to be contrary to the underlying U.S. dollar direction. For example, in a U.S. dollar-negative environment, the euro will have an underlying bid stemming from overall U.S. dollar selling. However, less liquid dollar pairs (e.g., USD/CHF) will be sold through the more liquid euro crosses, in this case resulting in EUR/CHF selling, which introduces a euro offer into the EUR/USD market.

This two-way interest tends to slow euro movements relative to other major dollar pairs and makes it an ideal market for short-term traders, who can exploit backing and filling. On the other hand, this depth of liquidity also means EUR/USD tends to experience prolonged, seemingly inconclusive tests of technical levels, whether generated by trend-line analysis or Fibonacci or Elliott-wave calculations. This suggests breakout traders need to allow for a greater margin of error: 20-30 pips. (A pip is the smallest increment in which a foreign currency can trade with respect to identifying breaks of technical levels.) Another way to gauge whether EUR/USD is breaking out is

FIGURE 2: Daily USD/JPY: candlesticks light the way

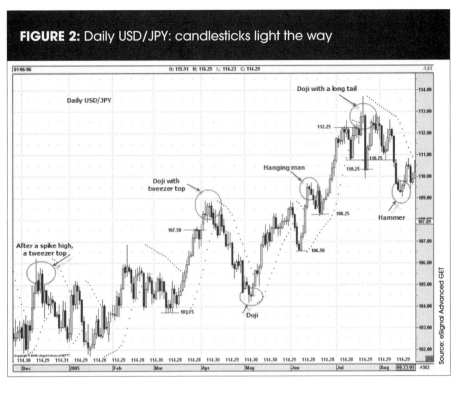

to look to the less liquid USD/CHF and GBP/USD. If these pairs have broken equivalent technical levels, for example recent daily highs, then EUR/USD is likely to do the same after a lag. If "swissy," (the Swiss franc) and "cable" (popular name for British pound) are stalling at those levels, then EUR/USD will likely fail as well.

In terms of technical studies, the overwhelming depth of EUR/USD suggests that momentum oscillators are well-suited to trading the euro, but traders should consider adjusting the studies' parameters (increase time periods) to account for the relatively plodding, back-and-fill movements of EUR/USD (see *Figure 1*). In this sense, reliance on very short-term indicators (less than 30 minutes) exposes traders to an increased likelihood of whipsaw movements. Moving average convergence divergence (MACD) as a momentum study is well-suited to EUR/USD, particularly because it utilizes exponential moving averages (greater weight to more recent prices, less to old prices) in conjunction with a third moving average, resulting in fewer false crossovers. Short-term (hourly) momentum divergences routinely occur in EUR/USD, but they need to be confirmed by breaks of price levels identified though trend line analysis to suggest an actionable trade. When larger moves are underway, traders are also likely to find the directional movement indicator (DMI) system useful for confirming whether a trend is in place, in which case momentum readings should be discounted. They might choose to rely on DI+/DI- crossovers for additional trade entry signals.

Second Place

The next most actively traded currency pair is USD/JPY, which accounted for seventeen percent of daily global volume in the 2004 BIS survey of currency market turnover. USD/JPY has traditionally been the most politically sensitive currency pair, with successive U.S. governments using the exchange rate as a lever in trade negotiations with Japan. While China has recently replaced Japan as the Asian market evoking U.S. trade tensions, USD/JPY still acts as a regional currency proxy for China and other less-liquid, highly regulated Asian currencies. In this sense, USD/JPY is frequently prone to extended trending periods as trade or regional political themes (e.g., yuan revaluation) play out.

For day-to-day trading, however, the most significant feature of USD/JPY is the heavy influence exerted by Japanese institutional investors and asset managers. Due to a culture of intra-Japanese collegiality, including extensive position and strategy information-sharing, Japanese asset managers frequently act in the same direction on the yen in the currency market. In concrete terms, this frequently manifests itself in clusters of orders at similar price or technical levels, which then reinforce those levels as points of support or resistance. Once these levels are breached, similar clusters of stop-loss orders are frequently just behind, which in turn fuel the breakout. Also, as the Japanese investment community moves en masse into a particular trade, they tend to drive the market away from themselves for periods of time, all the while adjusting their orders to the new price levels, for instance raising limit buy orders as the price rises.

An alternate tactic frequently employed by Japanese asset managers is to stagger orders to take advantage of any short-term reversals in the direction of the larger trend. For example, if USD/JPY is at 115.00 and trending higher, USD/JPY buying orders would be placed at arbitrary price points, such as 114.75, 114.50, 114.25, and 114.00, to take advantage of any pullback in the broader trend. This also helps explain why USD/JPY frequently encounters support or resistance at numerically round levels, even though there may be no other corresponding technical significance.

Turning to the technical side of USD/JPY, the foregoing discussion suggests trend line analysis as perhaps the most significant technical tool for trading USD/JPY. Because of the clustering of Japanese institutional orders around technical or price levels, USD/JPY tends to experience fewer false breaks of trend lines. For example, large-scale selling interest at technical resistance will need to be absorbed if the technical level is to be broken. This is likely to happen only if a larger market move is unfolding, and this suggests any break will be sustained. This makes USD/JPY ideal for breakout traders who employ stop-loss entry orders on breaks of trend line support or resistance. Short-term trend lines, such as hourly or 15 minutes, can be used effectively, but traders need to operate on a similarly short-term basis; daily closing levels hold the most meaning in USD/JPY. In terms of chart analysis, Japanese institutional asset managers rely heavily on candlestick charts (which depend on daily close levels), and traders would be well-advised to learn to recognize major candlestick patterns, such as doji, hanging man, tweezer tops and bottoms, and the like (see *Figure 2*). When it comes to significant trend reversals or pauses, daily close (5 p.m. EST) candlesticks are highly reliable leading indicators.

The yen discussion above also highlights the factors behind the propensity of USD/JPY to trend over the medium-term (multi-week). This facet suggests traders should look to trend-following tools, such as moving averages (21- and 55-day periods are heavily used), DMI, and J. Welles Wilder, Jr.'s parabolic system stop and reverse (Parabolic SAR). Momentum oscillators, such as relative strength index (RSI), MACD, or stochastics should generally be avoided, especially intraday, due to the trending and institutional nature driving USD/JPY. While a momentum indicator may reverse course, typically suggesting a potential trade, price action often fails to reverse enough to make the trade worthwhile due to underlying institutional interest. Instead of reversing along with momentum, USD/JPY price action will frequently settle into a sideways range, allowing momentum studies to continue to unwind, until the underlying trend resumes.

Finally, Ichimoku analysis (roughly translated as one-glance cloud chart) is another largely Japanese-specific trend identification system that highlights trends and major reversals.

A Look At Some Illiquid Currencies

Having looked at the two most heavily traded currency pairs, let's now examine two of the least liquid major currency pairs, USD/CHF and GBP/USD, which pose special challenges to technically oriented traders. The so-called swissy holds a place among the major currency pairs due to Switzerland's unique status as a global investment haven; estimates are that nearly one-third of the world's private assets are held in Switzerland. The Swiss franc has also acted historically as a so-called safe-haven currency alternative to the U.S. dollar in times of geo-political uncertainty, but this dimension has largely faded since the end of the Cold War. Today, USD/CHF trades mostly based on overall U.S. dollar sentiment, as opposed to Swiss-based economic fundamentals. The Swiss National Bank (SNB) is primarily concerned with the franc's value relative to the euro, since the vast majority of Swiss trade is with the European Union, and Swiss fundamental developments are primarily reflected in the EUR/CHF cross rate.

Liquidity in USD/CHF is never very good, and this makes it a favorite whipping horse for hedge funds and other speculative interests looking to maximize the bang for their buck. The lower liquidity and higher volatility of swissy also makes it a significant leading indicator for major U.S. dollar movements. *Figure 3* illustrates an example of a recent break of major daily trend line support in USD/CHF that took place a full day before EUR/USD and USD/JPY broke equivalent levels. Swissy will also lead the way in shorter-term movements, but the overall volatility and general jitteriness of USD/CHF price action makes false breaks of technical levels common. These false breaks are frequently stop-loss driven and it is not unusual for prices to trade 15-25 points through a support or resistance level before reversing after the stop losses have been triggered. In strong directional moves, USD/CHF price action tends toward extreme one-way traffic, with minimal backing and filling in comparison to EUR/USD.

Cable (GBP/USD), or sterling, also suffers from relatively poor liquidity, in part due to its higher pip value (U.S. dollars) and the rela-

FIGURE 3.1: Daily USD/CHF

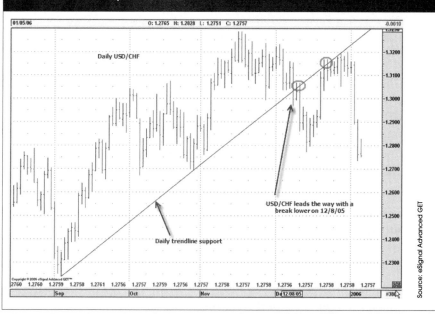

FIGURE 3.2: Daily EUR/USD

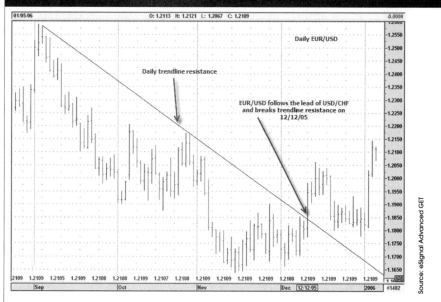

Swissy and sterling are leading indicators for EUR/USD. The less liquid and more volatile USD/CHF breaks major daily support levels on Thursday, 12/8/05 along with sterling (not shown). EUR/USD broke the equivalent trendline the following Monday, 12/12/05. Also, note swissy then retests the break and briefly exceeds the level, an example of its tendency for false breaks and overshoots.

tively Euro-centric basis of U.K. trade. Sterling shares many of the same trading characteristics of swissy outlined just above, but cable will also react sharply to U.K. fundamental data as well as to U.S. news. Sterling's price action will also display extreme one-way tendencies during larger moves, as traders caught on the wrong side chase the illiquid market to the extremes.

Focus on Risk Management
The volatility and illiquidity of swissy and sterling suggests traders need to use a more proactive overall approach to trading these pairs, particularly concerning risk management (i.e., position size in relation to stop levels). With regard to technical tools, the tendency for both pairs to make short-term false breaks of chart levels suggests breakout traders need to be particularly disciplined concerning stop entry levels and should consider a greater margin of error on the order of 30-35 points. In this sense, trend line analysis of periods less than an hour tends to generate more noise than tradable break points, so a focus on longer time periods (four hours daily) is likely to be more successful in identifying meaningful breaks. By the same token, once a breakout occurs, surpassing the margin of error, the ensuing one-way price action favors traders who are quick on the trigger, and this suggests employing resting stop-loss entry orders to reduce slippage. For those positioned with a move, trailing stops with an acceleration factor, such as parabolic SAR, are well suited to riding out directional volatility until a price reversal signals an exit.

The volatility inherent in cable and swissy makes the use of short-term (hourly and shorter) momentum oscillators problematic, due to both false crossovers and divergences between price and momentum that frequently occur in these time frames. Longer-period oscillators (four hours and more) are best used to highlight potential reversals or divergent price action, but volatility discourages initiating trades based on these alone. Instead, momentum signals need to be confirmed by other indicators, such as breaks of trend lines, Fibonacci retracements or parabolic levels, before a trade is initiated.

With regard to Fibonacci retracement levels, the greater volatility of cable and swissy frequently sees them exceed 61.8-percent retracements, only to stall later at the 76.4-percent level, by which time most short-term Elliott-wave followers have been stopped out. Short-term spike reversals of greater than 30 points also serve as a reliable way to identify when a directional surge, especially intraday, is completed, and these can be used as both profit-taking and counter-trend trading signals. For counter-trend, corrective trades based on spike reversals, stops should be placed slightly beyond the extreme of the spike low and high. A final technical study that is well suited to the explosiveness of swissy and sterling is the Williams %R, an overbought/oversold momentum indicator, which frequently acts as a leading indicator of price reversals. The overbought and oversold bands should be adjusted to -10 and -90 to fit the higher volatility of cable and swissy. As with all overbought and oversold studies, however, price action needs to reverse course first before trades are initiated.

Traders who seek to apply technical trading approaches to the currency market should be aware of the differences in the trading characteristics of the major currency pairs. Just because the euro and the pound are both traded against the dollar does not mean they will trade identically to each other. A more thorough understanding of the various market traits of currencies suggests that certain technical tools are better suited to some currency pairs than others. A currency-specific approach to applying technical analysis is more likely to produce successful results than a one-size-fits-all application across all currency pairs.

Brian Dolan is the director of research at forex.com, a division of GAIN Capital Group. A pioneer in online foreign exchange, GAIN Capital Group provides forex trading and asset management services to clients in more than 140 countries. The company's flagship service, GAIN Capital (gaincapital.com) supports the needs of institutional investors. FOREX.com, the company's retail division, provides individual investors of all experience levels with 24-hour, commission-free trading, lower account minimums, and extensive education and training. GAIN Capital Group and FOREX.com are registered with the CFTC as Futures Commission Merchants. This article originally appeared in *SFO* in March 2006.

NO MARKET IS AN ISLAND: Take Off Your Blinders and Peer at Other Markets

BY JOHN MURPHY

No market is an island. No market trades in isolation. Every market traded anywhere on the globe has some bearing on something else, hence the need for intermarket analysis. Intermarket analysis, of course, simply refers to looking at the relationships between markets. This type of analysis focuses on the relationships among stocks, bonds, commodities, and currencies, both on a global and domestic basis. I originally introduced this subject in my 1991 book, *Intermarket Technical Analysis: Trading Strategies for the Global Stock, Bond, Commodity, and Currency Markets* (Wiley). Historically and more recently, economic events, such as the threat of deflation in 2003, had a big impact on the financial markets, and normal intermarket relationships shifted due to that threat.

Traders can benefit by looking at trends in related markets as an indicator for the individual market that is being traded. Because of this important linkage, traders in one market need to know what's happening on the other side of the market fence. Why? Because each market is just one link in a much bigger financial chain. Should a trader ignore events in related markets, he will leave himself without valuable information that could affect trading decisions. That said, let's take a look at some traditional relationships and how these markets actually affect each other.

Falling Buck Is Bullish for Commodities

It's generally known, for example, that a falling dollar usually is bullish for commodity prices. That's especially true for gold. From 2002 to

2004, a falling dollar pushed gold prices to its highest level in seven years. Rising gold bullion made gold stocks one of the hottest sectors in the stock market. The falling dollar also helped account for the major bull market in most other commodity markets, as seen in *Figure 1*.

The CRB Index of seventeen commodities also rallied to its highest level since 1996. Because the dollar and commodity prices trend in opposite directions, it's important for commodity traders to watch the trend of the dollar. Any sudden rally in the greenback most likely would lead to profit-taking in commodity markets, especially gold. Because a bull market in commodities is normally associated with a bear market in the dollar, it also follows that bull markets in commodities coincide with bull markets in foreign currencies. That's especially true for the currencies of natural-resource countries like Australia and Canada.

But, that's only the tip of the intermarket iceberg. There's a lot more to it than that. There's the relationship of commodities to bonds, the relationship of bonds to stocks, and the relationship of the dollar to bonds and stocks. Each of the four markets has an impact on the other three.

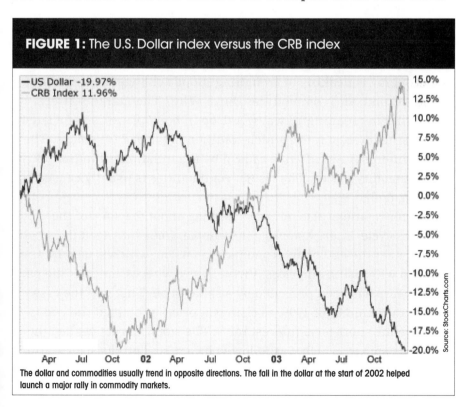

FIGURE 1: The U.S. Dollar index versus the CRB index

The dollar and commodities usually trend in opposite directions. The fall in the dollar at the start of 2002 helped launch a major rally in commodity markets.

Asset Allocation and Sector Rotation

From an asset allocation standpoint, it's important to know which asset classes are the strongest and which are the weakest. Intermarket analysis is especially helpful in that regard. From the start of 2000 to the end of 2002, bonds were a better place to be than stocks as the economy weakened. From the end of 2002 to the end of 2003, stocks did better than bonds as the economy strengthened.

Within the stock market, sector rotations also are influenced by intermarket trends. During 2003, for example, rising commodity prices gave a big boost to basic-material and natural-resource stocks tied to those commodities. Thus, for example, gold affects the direction of gold stocks. Energy prices affect the direction of energy stocks. And so on. Economically sensitive cyclical stocks are affected by the direction of industrial metals like copper. During 2003, the strongest part of the commodity world was industrial metals. That's usually a sign of global economic growth, which favors stock investments over bonds. The direction of industrial metals is closely tied to trends in Asia. And so it goes.

Intermarket relationships also shed light on the state of the economy, and that's done in two ways. Bonds, stocks, and commodities usually peak and trough in a predictable order that tells us whether the economy is peaking or troughing. Bonds change direction first, stocks second, and commodities third. Why? The markets affect each other in meaningful ways. A drop in bond prices is associated with rising interest rates, which traditionally is bad for stocks. The rise in interest rates often is caused by the inflationary impact of rising commodity prices. The rise in commodities is usually caused by a falling dollar.

Sector rotations also tell us something about the state of the business cycle. Energy stocks, for example, frequently lead the stock market near the end of an economic expansion, which is usually associated with rising oil prices. Virtually every recession over the past thirty years has been preceded by a spike in oil. That was the case during the summer of 1999, as rising oil prices prompted the Fed to start raising short-term interest rates. The stock market peaked the following spring, which was followed by a recession the spring after that. At market bottoms, small stocks and technology usually lead the market higher, as was the case during 2003.

There's one basic difference, however, between traditional economic analysis and intermarket analysis. While economists rely on lagging economic indicators to predict the economy, the intermarket analyst takes his or her cues from the financial markets—which anticipate trends as far out as six months into the future. Intermarket work also relies heavily on the use of charts.

Keeping a Global Perspective

It's important to remember that global trends are especially important in intermarket relationships. Deflationary forces coming from Asia during 1997 became the dominant theme for the next five years and changed some key intermarket relationships. The threat of global deflation explains why U.S. interest rates fell to forty-five-year lows and took so long to benefit the stock market. Deflationary tendencies also explain why bond prices rose after 2000 while stock prices fell. The Fed's stated intention during May 2003 to battle deflation helps explain the continuing weakness of the U.S. dollar and the rise in commodity prices. The dollar was allowed to drop in an attempt to reflate the economy. Why? The best way to fight deflation is to create a little inflation.

That's why rising commodity prices during 2003 were actually beneficial to the stock market. Ironically, Asia became a driving force behind the economic recovery of 2003. Most of that came from China. The rising tide in Asia helped boost commodity prices, which were reflective of global economic growth. Rising commodity prices during 2003 also gave a big boost to emerging markets in Asia and Latin America, which export those commodities. Stock market sectors like semiconductors, which also are closely tied to trends in Asia, became market leaders during 2003 and helped spearhead a strong recovery in the Nasdaq market.

The years since 1997 made it dramatically clear why American investors needed to know what was going on in foreign markets. That's because they were driving financial markets in the U.S. Trends in the dollar, commodities, bonds, and stocks were largely determined by trends in Asia.

These then are the main intermarket relationships that have characterized the financial markets over the last thirty years:

• The dollar trends in the opposite direction of commodity prices;

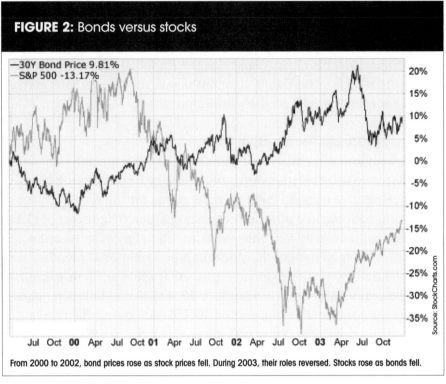

FIGURE 2: Bonds versus stocks

—30Y Bond Price 9.81%
—S&P 500 -13.17%

Jul Oct **00** Apr Jul Oct **01** Apr Jul Oct **02** Apr Jul Oct **03** Apr Jul Oct

Source: StockCharts.com

From 2000 to 2002, bond prices rose as stock prices fell. During 2003, their roles reversed. Stocks rose as bonds fell.

- Commodity prices trend in the opposite direction of bond prices;
- Bond prices normally trend in the same direction as stock prices;
- Bond prices, however, usually change direction before stocks;
- During a deflation, bonds and stocks decouple—bonds rise while stocks fall;
- A falling dollar becomes bearish for bonds when it pushes commodities higher;
- A falling dollar becomes bearish for stocks when it pushes interest rates higher;
- Rising commodity prices boost stock sectors tied to those commodities;
- Rising commodity prices are good for emerging markets; and
- Trends in commodities, interest rates, and stocks are global in scope

Deflation Changed the Mix

This intermarket model stayed pretty constant until the late 1990s. The threat of deflation, however, changed some of those relationships. In early- and mid-2002, the U.S. Fed began to discuss the potential for deflation in the U.S. and possible ways it could combat it.

This new dynamic actually changed the relationship between bonds and stocks.

A secondary change was the relationship between stocks and commodities. Normally at the end of an economic expansion, bond prices turn down before stocks, as interest rates rise. That was the case during 1999 when rising oil prices put downward pressure on bonds. After the stock market peaks, bond and stock prices normally fall together until lower interest rates have their beneficial effect on both markets.

During 2000, however, bond prices soared as stocks collapsed. It took a dozen easings by the Federal Reserve Board to finally turn things around. In the past, rising bond prices were considered to be bullish for stocks. Starting in 2000, however, rising bond prices were actually bearish for stocks. That's what happens in a deflationary environment. The last time a decoupling of that magnitude occurred was during the early 1930s (see *Figure 2*).

The second intermarket change was the relationship of stocks to commodities. When the economy is recovering from recession, stocks usually turn up well before commodities. Basically that's because it takes awhile for inflationary forces to start building. During the second half of 2002, however, stocks and commodities bottomed together and rose together throughout 2003. That also happened during the early part of the deflationary 1930s. In that situation, rising commodity prices are a sign that deflationary pressures are easing, which is bullish for stocks. It was these intermarket changes, which began in the late 1990s, that prompted me to write a second book on the subject. The period after 1991 is covered in my second book, *Intermarket Analysis: Profiting from Global Market Relationships* (Wiley Trading, 2004).

Intermarket Analysis Points to Higher Rates

During 2003, the two strongest asset classes were stocks and commodities, and the dollar and bonds were the two weakest. The falling dollar produced a major rally in commodity markets, which was symptomatic of global economic recovery that aided the rally in stocks.

Early in 2004, the main wild card is interest rates. Interest rates usually rise during a period of economic recovery, especially if that recovery is accompanied by a falling dollar and rising commodity prices.

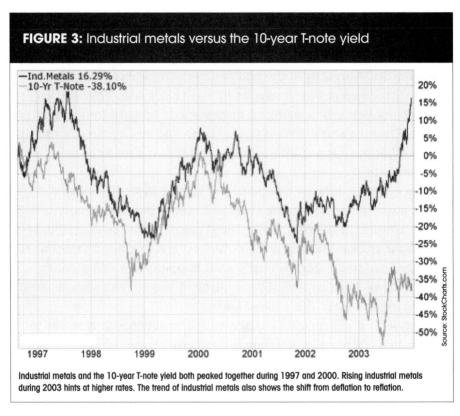

FIGURE 3: Industrial metals versus the 10-year T-note yield

—Ind.Metals 16.29%
‑‑10-Yr T-Note -38.10%

Industrial metals and the 10-year T-note yield both peaked together during 1997 and 2000. Rising industrial metals during 2003 hints at higher rates. The trend of industrial metals also shows the shift from deflation to reflation.

One of the intermarket principles listed earlier was that a falling dollar becomes bearish for bonds when it pushes commodities higher. Long-term rates jumped during the summer of 2003 and appear to have bottomed. However, the Fed's commitment to keeping short-term rates from rising has kept long-term rates relatively flat during the second half of 2003. That has been one of the bullish props under the stock market, which posted a strong rally through year-end.

A second intermarket principle is that a falling dollar becomes bearish for stocks when it pushes interest rates higher. That may be the Achilles heel for stocks in the coming year. In the past, the stock market has been able to ignore a falling dollar as long as interest rates stayed low.

From Deflation to Reflation

During 2003, the global pendulum swung from deflation to reflation, and that carried good news for the global economy and global stock markets. It may, however, translate into bad news for bonds. Why?

Take a look at *Figure 3*, which compares the direction of industrial metals to the yield on 10-year Treasury notes since 1997. Traders should notice that they normally trend in the same direction. That's because both markets are barometers of economic strength or weakness. Both markets peaked together during 1997 as the Asian currency crisis raised the first fears of global deflation.

Commodity prices fell significantly that year and pulled global interest rates along with them. A second peak in both markets occurred again during the first half of 2000. The peak in industrial metals coincided with a peak in the stock market and forewarned of a coming recession. Interest rates fell as the deflationary impact of falling commodity prices caused money to rotate from stocks into bonds. That situation continued until 2002.

Rising industrial metals during 2002 (and a falling dollar) was symptomatic of a recovering global economy and helped pave the way for a stock market bottom in the fourth quarter of that year. The trend of industrial metals shows how the deflationary trend that began during 1997 changed to a more reflationary environment during 2003 as industrial metals soared to a six-year high.

That's where interest rates come in. Given the historic link between industrial metals and long-term interest rates, it may be just a matter of time before interest rates follow industrial metals higher. The bigger question may be how the stock market fares if and when rates do start to climb.

John J. Murphy, former technical analyst for CNBC, is the author of *Technical Analysis of the Financial Markets* (Prentice Hall, 1999), widely regarded as the standard reference in the field. His latest book, *Intermarket Analysis: Profiting from Global Market Relationships* (Wiley, 2004), is an updated version of the 1991 original. Murphy is the technical analyst for StockCharts.com. In 1992, he received the first award for outstanding contribution to global technical analysis by the International Federation of Technical Analysis and was the recipient of the 2002 Market Technicians annual award. This article originally appeared in *SFO* in November 2005.

THE TECHNOFUNDAMENTAL REVOLUTION

BY PHILIP GOTTHELF

For anyone over the age of forty-five, there may be faint memories of such antiquities as slide rules. Personal computers did not exist, let alone hand-held calculators. Those over fifty may recall that technical analysis once was in the same category as tarot cards, Ouija boards, and crystals. Virtually every professor espoused the random walk theory and proclaimed the efficient market principle. The 20th century was a different world, with different rules and different disciplines when it came to investments. However, by the 1960s there were hints of changing tides.

The scientific establishment laughed when Galileo broached the possibility that the Earth was round and our planets circled the sun. So too, were eyebrows raised with scorn when renegade market "technicians" had the audacity to suggest price movements might not be random and, more ridiculously, markets also might not be efficient. Heaven have mercy on any student who dared suggest that technical analysis might work under any circumstances. Prior to the 1970s, anyone seeking a job as a market analyst or economist was better off keeping any interest in technical analysis a personal secret. It would not have been wise to divulge such a transgression—even to a spouse!

Personally, I have been on the wrong side of the technical analysis debate under many circumstances. In college during the 70s, I made the egregious mistake of writing a term paper on technical tools for identifying trends and filtering profits. The professor scoffed at my entire premise with the boldly written comment, "Nonsense!"

scrawled across the page in red next to a C- grade. Undaunted, I persevered in my quest to find technical solutions to market timing. Eventually, I was pleasantly surprised to find myself among a growing movement toward technical analysis, as the personal computer has gained popularity, power, sophistication, and affordability.

Shockingly, by the mid-1980s, technical analysis had almost gained equal status with the fundamentalists. And amazingly, within another five years, fundamentalists became the dinosaurs placed on the defensive.

At the height of the technical evolution, I recalled my old college professor and the "Nonsense" he had written on my term paper. I wondered if there was merit to his criticism. After all, he was the professor, and I was the student. His market approach had been proven over centuries, while technical analysis was an emerging science, or at least an emerging technology.

I recalled my father's statements that every major commodity or stock trend had a basis in fundamental fact. Either supply changes or demand changes. If neither changes, there can be no real price change. A trend in the absence of fundamental change could only represent a secular movement based on changing monetary values associated with inflation. Other fluctuations were, indeed, market noise as predicted by the random walk theory.

Unquestionably, there has been enormous progress in quantitative analysis that has spawned effective technical trading models. However, this same technology has paved the way toward more efficient fundamental market evaluations as well. Equally important, the premise that fundamental information is inequitably distributed has been challenged by the Internet, cable television, and satellite imaging. We now have the ability to receive information in real time and analyze, interpret, and react within moments. Even our reactions in the market are reflected by real-time systems to permit reactions to reactions in a continuous chain of market-influencing events.

Fundamental, Technical, or Both?

This phenomenon raises an interesting question. Given any fundamental market event impacting supply or demand, which market reactions are fundamentally based and which are technical? This is to say that an initial reaction to something like Hurricane Katrina may be fundamental, like a shutdown of U.S. refining capacity. The resulting upward spike in gasoline prices would be associated with this decrease in supply. But at some stage the reaction in the market will trigger technical participation that can carry prices further and faster than the fundamentals might justify. Under such circumstances, an investor or trader still would want to participate in any upward movement. However, trading decisions or triggers would need to be based upon technical analysis rather than a fundamental measurement of supply versus demand.

In the late 1980s I wrote my first book, *Technofundamental Analysis* (Irwin), which is now out of print. The foundation of the book was my theory that new quantitative and qualitative approaches to technical analysis could be retrofitted into traditional fundamental analysis. The result was a melding of a technical interpretation with fundamental measurements.

A simple example might be the corn cycle whereby farmers plant increasing amounts to expand returns. At some point, corn prices will fall relative to expanding supplies, and farmers will be discouraged from increasing production. As planting slows, corn becomes more scarce and prices firm up. How would this appear on a chart of corn supply? We would see a rising supply line until supplies hit technical resistance—meaning the price-to-cost ratio becomes a disincentive to plant. The corn supply line then falls until it reaches support, i.e., the point at which prices firm sufficiently to encourage more planting. Assuming that prices trend higher, there will be an increasing incentive to plant until the cycle repeats. Thus, the corn supply chart can be interpreted in a similar way as its price chart.

Why is this helpful? Obviously, if we know price levels that promote or discourage planting, we can predict price ranges, price cycles, potential contingencies for drought or perfect weather, and future planting patterns. This method uses technical imagery to derive fundamental pictures. It represents a new synergy between fundamental supply and demand statistics and technical price forecasting. Because fundamental analysis enjoyed prominence prior to the rise of technical analysis, any return to a fundamentally based market approach should be considered a revolution. In contrast, any new market technique that has no basis in prior science should be labeled an evolution.

Human Emotion Meets Cold, Hard Cash

When powerful, high-speed personal-computing platforms became reasonably affordable, new market approaches evolved to provide a different trading paradigm that challenged both the random walk theory and fundamental pricing assumptions. This inspired the concept of a new market revolution that truly tries solving the perplexing equations that combine human emotions with objective logic.

Traditional technical analysis relies on a basic assumption that prices in motion will remain in motion unless acted on by some altering force. Some may recognize this phraseology as similar to a law of physics. As in the physical world, where an object must be set in motion, markets require a force to set prices in a direction. The force that moves markets is money in the form of human intervention. This means that traders act upon their market interpretations by committing money to a market or withdrawing money from a market. Here we have two distinct components of human emotion and cold, hard cash. The cash can be quantified simply by measuring the change in position and the change in price. For stocks, bonds—and even real estate—the objective formula can be expressed as follows:

$M = P \times V$ (where M is money, P is price, and V is velocity or volume)

Assuming we were observing a stock with a value of $10 that moved to $11 on a volume of 5,000 shares, the formula would yield an M of $5,000. In other words, $5,000 entered the market. That seems simple enough; however, some may argue that the $1 rise also must be applied to static shares that did not trade, because they, too, increased in value by $1. However, because there was no action taken regarding static shares, they cannot be considered the motivating force behind the price movement. Some might consider static shares a form of inertia that must be overcome to alter price direction. This adds complexity beyond the scope of this brief review.

Algebra tells us that we can solve for price by dividing money by velocity. This suggests that we can construct a matrix of possible volume and money combinations to determine the price change. This is where the quantitative models become interesting because they call upon substantial computing power to derive a precursor to possible future price movements. Clearly, our problem is that we do not know the price change until it has occurred, nor do we know the volume until shares have traded. This does not prevent us from taking observations and extrapolating possible outcomes.

Commodity futures and options give a slightly better window on M because we can use the direct relationship between initial margin and maintenance margin in our formula. The equation is as follows:

M = P x OI (where OI = open interest)

Open interest is the number of contracts (positions) existing between buyers and sellers. Unlike stocks and bonds, where the number of shares or issues is fixed, open interest is variable. For every position established, initial margin must be deposited. We know the approximate amount of this margin because exchanges establish minimums. Thus, if open interest increases by 10 and the price rises by $1, M = $10. By the same logic, if the price rises by $10 and open interest changes by $1, the same M of $10 results. We see that open interest and price share the same influence on money flow into and out of specific futures or options markets.

Again in contrast to stocks and bonds, the static component (existing open interest) carries more significance, because a variation margin actually moves from the losing positions to the winners. This is because variation margin actually is subtracted from the losers and placed into the winners' accounts. This is shown below:

M = (P x OI) + (P x OI)

Here, M represents total cash flow in the form of initial and maintenance margin. The existing open interest and the delta open interest are combined. It is a more precise measurement that simply uses volume as an indication of the amount of money needed to move prices a certain distance.

Having quantified cash flows, technical analysis examines behavioral indications by identifying price formations and patterns. As chartists know, a formation is a reflection of a singular market response. For example, prices may reach a high point—a top—from which they retreat. By itself, a single top tells very little about potential behavior because prices can continue lower or retrace back above the original turning point. However, if a top is seen more than once at the same price level (a top followed by a correction, followed by a retracement back to the same top), we observe a pattern called a double top, consisting of two top formations.

A pattern suggests market psychology by showing that resistance occurs at the same price more than once. We can deduce that when we approach this price level (the top), buyers no longer will be willing to pay a higher price, and sellers will only be able to sell if they accept lower prices—thus, resistance. When we observe a bottom pattern (more than one bottom formation), we can assume that sellers no longer are willing to accept lower prices and, hence, buyers must offer better prices to acquire the position. This, of course, is support, and support and resistance are the foundation of technical interpretation. There are dozens of recognized patterns, including flags, pennants, triangles, trend lines, head and shoulders, and more. But regardless of the pattern, each still seeks to reveal where we can expect support or resistance.

A More Exacting Measurement

By combining behavioral patterns with the amount of money measured by the formula, we have a new technofundamental derivation that matches support or resistance with changes in market cash flows. We are making a fundamental measurement of M and correlating it with behavior that is reflected by technical chart patterns. This is different from the model that observes corn supply and demand as a technical chart. It is an adjunct to the new concept of technofundamentals.

Skeptics and cynics will criticize this as being no more than a formularized version of plotting volume bars and an open interest line on a price chart. Given the vast amount of writing that attempts to explain how to use price, volume, and open interest, this criticism is valid—to a point. The difference is that the formula provides a more exact numerical measurement that is more objective.

Suppose we see that whenever crude inventories exceed anticipated consumption by ten percent, production meets resistance. This would be a supply and demand comparison. *Figure 1* illustrates how that might appear on a chart.

As with the corn example, charting crude oil inventory against consumption can yield formations and patterns that allow us to pre-

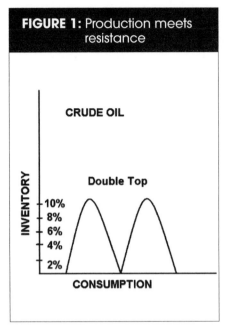

FIGURE 1: Production meets resistance

dict support and resistance for production. By inverting *Figure 1*, we can observe support and resistance for consumption, too. For example, the chart illustration may suggest that when inventories fall below two percent of consumption, production is stimulated. The missing ingredient is price.

When we combine this with a price picture, we can derive a price reference point that tells us where the inventory-to-consumption ratio influences prices to move in a direction, at a speed, and toward an objective. Understand that the incentives for the inventory-to-consumption ratio may not simply be correlated to price. For example, crude inventory can be limited by storage capacity or transportation. Consumption may be influenced by seasonal changes and weather or by refining capacity. Clearly, price is not the only factor in determining if or when the ratio can change.

Focusing back on corn, farmers can be limited by the price of seed and fertilizer or a government subsidy program. Weather can force a farmer out of corn and into soybeans. Again, price is not the only incentive to produce more or less.

Technofundamentals become interesting and challenging when the imagery is combined with statistical correlation and extrapolation. If we see technical patterns in supply and demand that are highly correlated with price incentives, while isolating the non-price influences, we can develop a highly accurate quantitative forecasting model—the ultimate objective.

Technofundamentals in Action

Some actual examples of technofundamentals in action can be seen in three back-to-back crude oil option trades recently placed during the raging bull market. All were bull option ratio spreads that

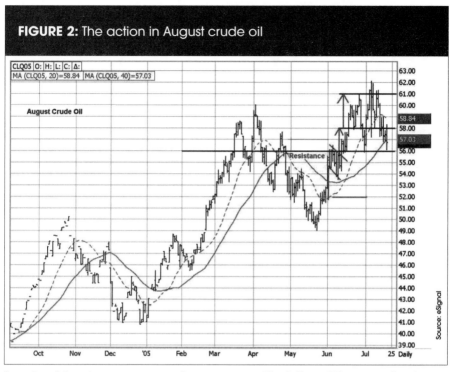

FIGURE 2: The action in August crude oil

involved buying a near-to-the-money call while selling two farther out calls for a credit.

The first trade recommended buying an August crude 55 call, while selling two 56 calls at 80, and buying an August 57 call, while selling two 58 calls at 95. Then I added a long 59 call with two short 60 calls at 115. Positions were added as prices were rising in June and July. The formulae showed that crude oil inventories were building to the point where refiners "should" dump positions on or before expiration.

There was the technical indication that 56 would offer resistance as a consolidation formed (as seen in *Figure 2*). We see a pole extending from 5200 to 5600 in the first week of June, with a downward flag. Technically, a breakout above 5600 defines the formation as a continuation pattern, with a first up-side objective equal to 50 percent of the pole's distance and a second objective equal to the $4 from 5200 to 5600.

For those who can discern the tendency toward 5800 through the June-July gyrations, the technical interpretation was reasonable. Admittedly, fear gripped traders as prices moved to 6200 and newscasts called for $70/bbl before contract expiration. However, crude oil inventories had reached June 2000 levels, a time when prices were appreciably lower. Refinery runs implied that the August delivery might not be well received above 6000. In the meantime, technical rules called for former resistance of 5600 to act as support. Assuming a 50-percent retracement before expiration, we were in good technical shape, backed up by the propensity for prices to decline when inventories are above consumption, as reflected by refinery numbers.

Indeed, as expiration approached, the futures slid to 5706, and we were redeemed, as expected. The initial strategy was to have options expire between 5500 and 5600 to collect the net premium on the first ratio while picking up profit between the strikes. When the rally took prices well above our initial technical interpretation, we took advantage of fatter premiums at higher strikes. The last spread was an insurance move—at best. We collected all premiums plus the 100 points between 5500 and 5600, less the exposure from 5600 to 5700.

On Thursday, July 28, we recommended buying the September crude 60 call while selling two 61 calls for 75 or better. Crude rallied for Friday's open, and the spread was done at 110. We added a long 62 call with two short 63 calls at 70. The 61 calls expired in the money, placing us short at a net 6390. Crude futures dropped, and we covered for an approximate $690 profit on the trade on August 19.

On Thursday, August 25, we recommended buying the October crude 71 call while selling two 72 calls for $0.50 or better. By Friday's open, crude rallied and the spread was placed at 110! After another bout of tension during the Katrina aftermath, crude dropped like a stone, and we were redeemed. The technical patterns confirmed 7100 as the probable resistance, and crude was backing up against shut refineries. Once again, the technofundamental approach proved profitable.

Crude oil is not a unique example of combining patterns and formations in both price charts and supply-demand plots. These correlations also are proven in grains, meats, softs, and metals. There is even applicability in financial contracts like Treasuries, currencies, and stock indexes—although inventory is a bit more difficult to assess. Whether I deserved a C- grade for attempting to introduce technical analysis to a die-hard fundamentalist professor can be debated. I am grateful to my professor for stimulating my interest in revisiting the potential value fundamental analysis can have in an

age when everyone seems to have gone techno-crazy. In reality, using patterns and formations to define supply and demand relationships is obvious and not a new methodology. It is the computer age
that allows us to combine this old-fashioned approach with cutting-
edge technical modeling.

Philip Gotthelf is publisher of the COMMODEX, the longest-running
daily futures trading system published anywhere, and president of
EQUIDEX Inc. and EQUIDEX Brokerage Group. Known for his extensive work in the futures industry, Gotthelf's works have appeared in
major industry and business publications. He is quoted regularly in
Barron's, the *Wall Street Journal*, the *New York Times*, *Fortune*, and
Forbes, among others. Gotthelf has written several books, including *Precious Metals Trading: How to Forecast and Profit from Major
Market Moves* (Wiley, 2005), *Currency Trading: How to Access and
Trade the World's Biggest Market* (Wiley, 2002), and *Techno Fundamental Trading* (Probus Press/McGraw-Hill, 1994). This article was
originally published in *SFO* in November 2005.

GLOSSARY OF TERMS

A

Algorithm: An advanced mathematical model that can be used in a trading system to make transaction decisions in the financial markets.

American Stock Exchange (AMEX): A stock exchange; a private, not-for-profit corporation, located in New York City and founded in 1842. Also called AMEX and the curb exchange.

Arbitrage: The simultaneous purchase of one asset against the sale of the same asset (usually in different exchanges or marketplaces) in an attempt to profit from different prices for the same security, commodity, or financial instrument in different markets.

Ask: The price a seller is willing to accept for a security, futures contract or other financial instrument. Also called the offer.

At or better: (1) In a buy order for securities, futures, or other financial instruments, a purchase at the specified price or under it (2) For a sell order, a sale at the specified price or above it.

At-the-money: An option with a strike price equal to the current price of the instrument, such as a stock, upon which the option was granted.

At-the-opening order: An order that specifies it is to be executed at the opening of the market or of trading or else it is to be canceled. The order does not have to be executed at the opening price, but within the opening range of prices.

B

Backspread: A type of options spread in which a trader holds more long positions than short positions. The premium collected from the sale of the short option is used to help finance the purchase of the long options. This spread can be created using either all call options or all put options.

Bear market (bear, bearish): A market in which prices are declining. A period of generally falling prices and pessimistic attitudes.

Beta: A measure of an investment's volatility. The lower the beta, the less risky the investment.

Bid: The price a buyer is willing to pay for a security, futures contract or other financial instrument.

Beta coefficient: A means of measuring the volatility of an individual market (security, future, financial instrument) in comparison with the market as a whole.

Black-Scholes Model: A widely used option pricing equation developed in 1973 by Fischer Black and Myron Scholes. Used to evaluate OTC options, option portfolios, or option trading on exchanges.

Board of Trade: Any exchange or association of persons engaged in the business of buying or selling a commodity. Usually an exchange where commodity futures and/or options are traded. Sometimes referred to as Contract Market or Exchange.

Bollinger bands: A method used by technical analysts that indicates if a market is overbought or oversold. The bands are comprised of fixed lines above and below a simple moving average. As volatility increases, the bands widen.

Bond: A debt instrument that pays a set amount of interest on a regular basis. The issuer promises to repay the debt on time and in full.

Book value: The value of a financial instrument as shown by accounting records, often not the same as the instrument is valued by the market.

Booked: The point at which a transaction is processed. Though funds may not yet be available, the system has posted it and marked it as having a value date in the future.

Booking date: The date the payment is to be booked and executed. The date the payment will be passed to the automated system to book.

Bookings: A collection of records of financial transactions processed by automated systems. Booking are also called postings.

Bracket order: A three-part order, including the entry order, stop exit order and target exit order. When one exit order is fulfilled, the other is cancelled.

Break: A rapid and sharp price decline.

Break-even point: (1) The point at which gains equal losses. (2) The price a market must reach for an option buyer to avoid a loss if he or she exercises.

Broker: (1) An individual or firm that charges a fee or commission for executing buy and sell orders placed by another individual or firm. (2) A floor broker in commodities futures trading, a person who actually executes orders on the trading floor of an exchange.

Brokerage: A fee charged by a broker for execution of a transaction.

Bear spread: A simultaneous purchase of one option, hedged by the sale or another option, where the options have the same expiration month but different striking prices and will profit from a decrease in prices. Also called a vertical spread.

Bull spread: A simultaneous purchase of one option, hedged by the sale or another option, where the options have the same expiration month but different striking prices and will profit from an increase in prices. Also called a vertical spread.

Bull market (bull, bullish): A market in which prices are rising. A trader who believes prices will move higher is called a bull.

Buy in: A purchase to offset, cover, or close a short position.

Buy stop order: An order to buy a market that is entered at a price above the current offering price and that is triggered when the market price touches or goes through the buy stop price.

C

Calendar spread: See horizontal spread.

Call option: Publicly traded contract granting the owner the right, but not the obligation, to buy a commodity or other financial instrument at a specified price at a stated future date.

Candlestick Chart: A price chart that includes information on the opening price, closing price, and direction of movement during a trading session. Also called a Japanese candlestick chart, since the method was developed to analyze rice markets in 17th century Japan.

Cap: An investment product that compensates the holder when interest rates rise above a certain level.

Carrying broker: A member of a commodity exchange, usually a clearinghouse member, through whom other brokers or customers clear all or some trades.

Carrying charges: Costs incurred in warehousing the physical commodity, generally including interest, insurance, and storage.

Cash market: The underlying commodity, security, currency, or money market in which transactions for the purchase and sale of cash instruments which futures and derivative contracts relate to are carried out.

Charting: The use of graphs and charts in the technical analysis of markets to plot trends of price movements, volume, and open interest.

Chicago Board Options Exchange (CBOE): An exchange at the Chicago Board of Trade to trade stock options. The CBOE has markets in equities, options, and over-the-counter securities.

Chicago Board of Trade (CBOT or CBT): The oldest futures exchange in the United States, established in 1848. The board announced their intention (in late 2006) to merge with the Chicago Mercantile Exchange (and operate under the name of the CME). The exchange lists agricultural commodity futures such as corn, oats, and soybeans, in addition to financial instruments—e.g., Treasury bonds and Treasury notes.

Chicago Mercantile Exchange (CME): The exchange announced their intention (in late 2006) to merge with the Chicago Board of Trade to become the largest futures exchange in the world. The Exchange operates the International Monetary Market (IMM), the Index and Options Market (IOM), and the Growth and Emerging Markets (GEM), and will eventually operate Chicago Board of Trade agricultural commodity futures such as corn, oats, and soybeans, as well as financial instruments such as Treasury bonds and Treasury notes.

Clear: The formal completion of a trade.

Close: The period at the end of a trading session during which all transactions are considered to be made at the close.

Closing balance: The balance of entries posted to the account at the close of the statement period.

Closing price: The price at which transactions are made just before the close on a given day.

Closing range: A range of closely related prices at which transactions took place at the closing of the market; buy and sell orders at the closing might have been filled at any point within such a range.

Commission: (1) A fee charged by a broker to a customer for performance of a specific duty, such as the buying or selling of futures contracts. A commission must be fair and reasonable, considering all the relevant factors of the transaction. (2) Sometimes used to refer to the Commodity Futures Trading Commission (CFTC).

Commodity: An entity of trade or commerce, services, or rights in which contracts for future delivery may be traded. Some of the contracts currently traded are wheat, corn, cotton, livestock, copper, gold, silver, oil, propane, plywood, currencies, Treasury bills, Treasury bonds, and stock indexes.

Commodity Channel Index (CCI): An oscillator used in technical analysis to help determine when an investment vehicle has been overbought and oversold. The index quantifies the relationship between the asset's price, a moving average (MA) of the asset's price, and normal deviations (D) from that average.

Commodity Exchange of New York (CMX): A division of the New York Mercantile Exchange.

Commodity Futures Trading Commission (CFTC): The federal agency established by the Commodity Futures Trading Commission Act of 1974 to ensure the open and efficient operation of the futures markets.

Conditional order: An order that is automatically submitted or cancelled only when specified criteria are met.

Congestion: Sideways movement in the market.

Consolidation: A technical analysis term. A pause in trading activity in which price moves sideways, setting the stage for the next move. Traders are said to evaluate their positions during periods of consolidation.

Contract date: Date on which the contract is agreed between the parties.

Contract month: The month in which deliveries are to be made in accordance with a futures contract.

Contract: (1) An agreement between at least two parties to buy or sell, on certain conditions, a certain product, as a result of which a legal status concerning rights and duties of the parties exists. (2) A term of reference describing a unit of trading for a commodity.

Cookie: A small text file of information that certain Web sites attach to a user's hard drive while the user is browsing the Web site. A Cookie can contain information such as user ID, user preferences, or archived shopping cart information.

Corner: To secure control of a market so that its price can be manipulated.

Correction: A technical analysis term. A price reaction against the prevailing trend of the market. Sometimes referred to as a retracement.

Cover: The action of offsetting a futures securities or other financial instrument transaction with an equal and opposite transaction. Short covering is a purchase to offset an earlier sale of an equal number of the same delivery month. Liquidation is a sale to offset the obligation to take delivery.

Covered: An investment strategy in which the seller owns the underlying security.

Credit spread: The simultaneous purchase of one option, hedged by the sale of another option, when payment comes into the account when the spread is initially established.

Cross hedging: The hedging of a cash instrument on a different, but related, futures or other derivatives market.

D

Day order: An order that if not executed expires automatically at the end of the trading session of the day it was entered.

Day trader: Traders who take positions in the market and then liquidate them prior to the close of the trading day.

Dead Cat Bounce (DCB): A chart pattern that occurs when a price drops 30 percent to 70 percent in one session, then bounces upward before the decline resumes.

Dealer option: A put or call on a physical commodity, not originating at or subject to the rules of an exchange, written by a firm which deals in the underlying cash commodity.

Dealer: An individual or company that buys and sells financial instruments for its own account and customer accounts.

Debit spread: The simultaneous purchase of one option, hedged by the sale of another option, when payment comes into an account when the spread is expended.

Defrag: Short for Defragment. The process of collecting fragments of computer files and sorting them into contiguous sections on the hard drive, thus speeding up file management, and facilitating faster online trading.

Delta hedge: The partial offset of the exchange risk of a currency option by an opposite open currency spot position in the same foreign currency.

Delta: A measure of the relationship between an option price and its underlying futures contract or stock price. Measures how rapidly the value of an option moves in relation to the underlying value.

Demand: A consumer's desire and willingness to pay for a good or service.

Derivative: A complex investment whose value is derived from or linked to some underlying financial asset, such as a stock, bond, currency, or mortgage. Derivatives may be listed on exchanges or traded privately over-the-counter. For example, derivatives may be futures, options, or mortgage-backed securities.

Diagonal spread: A simultaneous purchase of one option, hedged by the sale of another option, where the two options have different striking prices and different expiration months.

Discount brokers: Brokers who charge lower commissions than full-service brokers.

Discount rate: The interest rate charged by the Federal Reserve on loans to member banks. This rate influences the rates these financial institutions then charge to their customers.

Divergence: A situation in which the price of an asset and an indicator, index or other related asset move in opposite directions. Can be positive or negative and is used in technical analysis to make investment decisions.

Doji: A pattern in candlestick charting that indicates the opening and closing price are the same.

Double tops: A price chart pattern where the trend is up and forms two peaks that top out near the same price.

Dow theory: An investment philosophy developed in the late 1800s on which modern technical analysis is based. The theory was outlined in a series of editorials in the Wall Street Journal by Charles Dow and posits that stocks and futures trade in trends and have common, predictable patterns.

Drawdown: The peak-to-trough decline during a specific record period of a trade, usually quoted as the percentage between the peak and the trough.

E

Earnings per share (EPS): The portion of a company's profit allocated to each outstanding share of common stock. EPS serves as an indicator of a company's profitability and is often considered the single most important variable in determining the price of a share.

Equity curve: A chart that plots the ups and downs of the value of an account.

Equivolume charts: A charting technique that combines price and volume into one bar on the chart.

Elasticity: A characteristic which describes the interaction of supply, demand, and price. A commodity is said to be elastic in demand when a price change creates an increase or decrease in consumption. Inelasticity of supply or demand exists when either supply or demand is relatively unresponsive to changes in price.

Electronic trading: The computerized matching of buyers and sellers of financial instruments. GLOBEX, Project A, and Access are examples.

Elliott wave theory: a technical approach to market analysis that suggests that markets move in well-defined, repetitive five-wave moves, followed by a three-wave corrective move.

Equity: The dollar value of a futures account if all open positions were offset at the current market price. In securities markets, it is the part of a company's net worth that belongs to shareholders.

Exchange: An association of persons or entities engaged in the business of buying and selling futures and/or options, usually involving an auction process. Also called a board of trade or contract market.

Execution date: The date on which a trader wishes to exercise an option.

Execution: (1) The completion of an order for a transaction. (2) The carrying out of an instruction.

Exercise date and striking price: The last day on which the option can be exercised, as well as the currency and price at which the market can be purchased or sold, on or before that date.

Exercise date: The date on which the buyer of an option chooses to exercise the buyer's right under the option contract with the seller of the option.

Exercise price: The price at which the buyer of a call (put) option may choose to exercise his right to purchase (sell) the underlying futures contract. Also called strike price or strike.

Exercise: By exercising an option, the buyer elects to accept the underlying market at the option's strike price.

Expiration date: Generally the last date on which an option may be exercised or a transaction made.

Exposure: A possible loss of value caused by changes in market value, interest rates, or exchange rates.

F

Fed: The short name for the U.S. Federal Reserve Banks.

Federal Open Market Committee (FOMC): A committee of the Federal Reserve Banks that makes decisions concerning the Fed's operations to control the money supply. Their primary purpose is the purchase and sale of government securities, which increases or decreases the money supply. It also sets key interest rates, such as the discount rate and Fed fund rate.

Federal Reserve: The central bank of the United States that sets monetary policy. The Federal Reserve and FOMC oversee money supply, interest rates, and credit with the goal of keeping the U.S. economy and currency stable. Also called the Fed.

Fibonacci numbers (or sequence): The sequence of numbers, used in technical analysis, discovered by the Italian mathematician Leonardo de Pise in the 13th century. The first two terms of the sequence are 0 and 1, and each successive number is the sum of the previous two numbers (0, 1, 2, 3, 5, 8, 13, 21, 34, 55, 89, 144, . .).

Fill: The act of completing an order (such as buy or sell) for a security or commodity.

Financial instruments: Also known as financial products or simply as instruments; includes bonds, stocks, derivatives, and other financial representations of assets.

Flag: A chart formation that results from the market's tendency to pause between impulse moves.

Floor broker: An individual who executes orders on the trading floor of an exchange for any other person or entity.

Floor traders: Members of an exchange who are personally present, on the trading floors of the exchanges, to make trades for themselves.

Floor: (1) The lowest rate a financial market is allowed to fall. (2) The trading floor of an exchange.

Forward: A rate or the price of a financial instrument or event which is in the future.

Friction: The implicit and explicit costs associated with market transactions.

Fundamental analysis: An approach to the analysis of markets which examines the underlying factors which will affect the supply and demand of the market, overall economy, industry conditions, etc.

Futures contract: A standardized, binding agreement to buy or sell a specified quantity or grade of a commodity at a later date. Futures contracts are freely transferable and can be traded only by public auction on designated exchanges.

Futures option: An option on a futures contract.

G

Gap: In technical analysis, a trading day during which the daily price range is completely above or below the previous day's range

Gap theory: A form of technical analysis that predicts price action by classifying gaps, or situations where there is no overlap in price between one session and another, based on the underlying trend.

Globex: A global, after-hours electronic system for trading in derivatives, futures and commodity contracts. A Reuter's system for the Chicago Mercantile Exchange.

Good 'Til Cancelled (GTC) order: An order to buy or sell an asset at a set price that remains active until the customer cancels it, or it is filled.

H

Head and shoulders: A technical analysis chart pattern that has three peaks resembling a head and two shoulders. A head and shoulders top typically forms after a substantial rise and indicates a market reversal. A head and shoulders bottom (an inverted head and shoulders) indicates a market advance.

Hedge: An investment made in order to reduce the risk of an adverse price movement.

Hedging: A transaction strategy used by dealers and traders in foreign exchange, commodities, and securities, as well as farmers, manufactures, and other producers, to protect against severe fluctuations in exchange rates and market prices. A current sale or purchase is offset by contracting to purchase or sell at a specified future date.

Horizontal spread: A simultaneous purchase of one option, hedged by the sale of another option, where the two options have the same striking price but different expiration months. Also called a calendar spread.

I

Implied Volatility (IV): The estimated volatility of a security or commodity's price.

In-the-money: An option having intrinsic value. A call is in-the-money if its strike price is below the current price of the underlying futures contract. A put is in the money if its strike price is above the current price of the underlying futures contract.

Inelasticity: A characteristic that describes the interdependence of supply, demand, and price. A commodity is inelastic when a price change does not create an increase or decrease in consumption; inelasticity exists when supply and demand are relatively unresponsive to changes in price.

Initial margin: Customers' funds required at the time a futures or forex position is established, or an option is sold. Margin in futures or forex markets is not a down payment, as it is in securities.

Insider trading: (1) The legal trading of securities by corporate officers based on information available to the public. (2) The illegal trading of securities by any investor based on information not available to the public.

Intercommodity spread: A trade involving the same (or close) delivery times and related commodities, generally on the same exchange.

Interdelivery spread: A trade involving the same commodity, usually at the same exchange, but different delivery times.

Intermarket spread: A trade involving the same commodity on different exchanges but with the same delivery time.

International Securities Exchange (ISE): The world's largest electronic equity options exchange.

Interest: The charge or cost for using money; expressed as a percentage rate per period.

International Options Market (IOM): A division of the Chicago Mercantile Exchange.

Introducing Broker (IB): A firm or individual that solicits and accepts commodity futures orders from customers but does not accept money, securities, or property from the customer.

L

Level I: An online trading service consisting of real-time bid/ask quotes.

Level II: An online trading service consisting of quotes from individual market participants.

Leverage: The use of borrowed assets to enhance the return to the owner's equity, allowing an investor to establish a position in the marketplace by depositing funds that are less than the value of the contract.

Limit move: A price that has advanced or declined the limit permitted during one trading session as fixed by the rules of a contract market.

Limit order: An order to buy or sell as a specified price or better.

Liquid market: A market where selling and buying can be accomplished easily due to the presence of many interested buyers and sellers.

Liquidity: The ease of converting an asset to cash

Long hedge: Buying futures contracts to protect against possible increased prices of commodities. See also Hedging.

Long position: An excess of assets (and/or forward purchase contracts) over liabilities (and/or forward sale contracts) in the same currency. A dealer's position when net purchases and sales leave him or her in a net-purchased position.

Long: To own (buy) to a security, currency, futures contract, commodity, or derivative.

Long-term Equity Anticipation Security (LEAPS) options: Options that expire more than nine months from the current date.

M

Margin call: A call from a brokerage firm or clearing house to a customer or clearing member firm to bring margin deposits back up to minimum levels required by exchange regulations.

Margin: (1) In the futures industry, the amount of money deposited by both buyers and sellers of futures contracts to ensure performance against the contract. (2) In the stock market, the amount of cash that must be put up in a purchase of securities.

Market: (1) Any area or condition where buyers and sellers are in contact for doing business together. (2) The generic term for a financial instrument.

Market arbitrage: The simultaneous purchase and sale of the same security, futures, or other financial instrument in different markets to take advantage of a price disparity between the two markets.

Market impact cost: The price difference between the level at which an order is filled and the price level at it was optimally requested to be filled.

Market order: An order to buy or sell securities, futures contracts, or other financial instruments to be filled immediately at the best possible price. A limit order, in contrast, may specify requirements for price or time of execution.

Market Technicians' Association: A national organization of market analysis professionals incorporated in 1973, which was instrumental in establishing technical analysis as a legitimate and profitable form of market analysis.

Markup: The difference between the lowest current offering price among dealers and the higher price a dealer charges a customer.

Match trading: Financial transactions made outside of an auction or negotiation process. Buy and sell orders for the same financial instrument, at the same price, are paired and executed, often by computer.

Matching orders: Simultaneously entering identical (or nearly identical) buy and sell orders for a financial instrument to create the appearance of active trading in that market.

Measured Move Up (MMU): A chart pattern that signals a continuing upward price trend.

Mechanical system: A method of buying and selling stocks according to a screen based on results from predetermined indicators and other criteria.

Minis or E-Minis: Mini-sized versions of stock index futures traded electronically. Contracts are available on a wide range of indices such as the Nasdaq 100, S&P 500, S&P MidCap 400 and Russell 2000.

Momentum indicator: A line that represents the difference between today's price and the price of a fixed number of days ago. Momentum can be measured as the difference between today's price and the current value of a moving average. Often referred to as momentum oscillators.

Moving average: An average of prices over a fixed period. The value changes over time, eliminating fluctuations in data. Moving averages emphasize the direction of a trend, confirm trend reversals, and smooth out price and volume fluctuations that can confuse interpretation of the market.

Moving average convergence divergence (MACD): A trend-following momentum indicator that shows the difference between two moving averages.

N

New York Stock Exchange (NYSE): The largest stock exchange in the United States. It is a corporation, operated by a board of directors, responsible for administering the Exchange and member activities, listing securities, overseeing the transfer of members' seats on the Exchange, and determining whether an applicant is qualified to be a specialist.

Normalizing: Adjusting data, such as a price series, to put it within normal or more standard range. A technique sometimes used to develop a trading system.

NYFE: New York Futures Exchange.

Nymex: New York Mercantile Exchange.

O

Offer: An indication of willingness to sell at a given price, also referred to as an ask, or asking price. The opposite of bid.

Offset: (1) The liquidation of a purchase of a futures contract, forward, or other financial instrument through the sale of an equal number of the same delivery months; (2) The covering of a short sale of futures forward or other financial instrument through the purchase of an equal number of the same delivery month. Either action transfers the obligation to make or take delivery of the actual financial instrument to someone else.

On-balance volume (OBV): A volume momentum indicator that correlates volume to price change. Originally developed by Joe Granville.

One-day reversal (ODR): A one-day change in the direction of price of a stock, commodity or derivative.

Online broker: A retail securities, futures or options broker that provides services over the Internet.

Online trading: Using a computer and an Internet connection to place your buy and sell trading orders with an online brokerage firm, without the physical inclusion of a broker. Orders are entered and returned electronically via computer terminals.

Open: The period at the beginning of a trading session during which all transactions are considered made "at the open."

Open interest: The total number of options or futures contracts that have not closed or been delivered.

Opening range: The range of closely related prices at which transactions took place at the opening of the market; buying and selling orders at the opening might be filled at any point within such a range.

Option contract: The right, but not the obligation, to buy or sell a specific quantity of an underlying instrument on or before a specific date in the future. The seller of the option has the obligation to sell the underlying instrument (in a put option) or buy it from the option buyer (in a call option) at the exercise price if the option is exercised.

Option period: The period between the start date and the expiry date of an option contract.

Option premium: The money, securities, or property the buyer pays to the writer (grantor) for granting an option contract.

Option seller/writer: The party who is obligated to perform if an option is exercised by the option buyer.

Option: An agreement that represents the right to buy or sell a specified amount of an underlying security, such as a stock, bond, futures contract, at a specified price within a specified time. The purchaser acquires a right, and the seller assumes an obligation.

Order execution: The handling of an order by a broker, including receiving the order verbally or in writing from the customer, transmitting it to the trading floor of the exchange, and returning confirmation of the completed order to the customer.

Order to buy: An instruction to buy a given quantity of an identified financial instrument under specified conditions.

Order to sell: An instruction to sell a given quantity of an identified financial instrument under specified conditions.

Oscillator: A technical analysis tool that attempts to determine when an asset has become over- or under-priced. As the value of the oscillator approaches the upper extreme value the asset is deemed to be overbought, and as it approaches the lower extreme it is deemed to be oversold.

Out-of-the-money: A call option with a strike price higher, or a put option with a strike price lower, than the current market value of the underlying asset.

Over-the-counter-market (OTC): Trading in financial instruments transacted off organized exchanges, including transactions among market-makers and between market-makers and their customers.

Overbought: A technical analysis term that the market price has risen too steeply and too fast in relation to underlying fundamental or other factors.

Oversold: A technical analysis term for a market price that has experienced stronger selling than the fundamentals justify.

Over-the-counter (OTC) derivative: A financial instrument whose value is designed to track the return on commodities, stocks, bonds, currencies or some other benchmark that is traded over-the-counter or off organized exchanges.

P

Parity: Equal standing.

Pip: Unit that expresses differences between exchange rates. The minimum incremental price change in the inter-bank markets.

Pit: A specially constructed arena on the trading floor of some exchanges where trading is conducted by open outcry. On other exchanges, the term "ring" designates the trading area.

Platform: A computer interface that provides the user with information and the means to place trades electronically.

Pledging: The act of putting up security for a loan or other financial transaction.

Point: The minimum fluctuation in prices or options premiums. Also called ticks.

Point and figure charts: A method of plotting price on a chart that eliminates time and better reflects changing market conditions.

Portfolio: A selection of financial instruments held by a person or institution, often designed to spread investment risk.

Position trader: A trader who buys or sells financial instruments and holds them for an extended period of time, as distinguished from the day trader, who will normally initiate and liquidate positions within a single trading session.

Position: A market commitment. For example, a buyer of futures contracts is said to have a long position, and, conversely, a seller of futures contracts is said to have a short position.

Premium: (1) The amount that an option buyer pays to an option seller. (2) The difference between the higher price paid for a financial instrument and the financial instrument's face amount at issue. (3) The additional payment allowed by exchange regulations for delivery of higher-than-required standards or grades of a commodity against a futures contract.

Price limit: Maximum price advance or decline from the previous day's settlement price, permitted for futures in one trading session by the rules of the exchange.

Price-to-earnings ratio (P/E): A measure of comparison of the value of different common stocks that is calculated by dividing the market price of the stock by the earnings per share.

Protective stop: An order to exit a trade if a price reaches a predetermined level, placed to defend against extreme loss.

Pullback: A fall in price from its peak.

Put (option): An option that gives the option buyer the right, but not the obligation, to sell the underlying financial instrument at a particular price on or before a particular date.

Put spread: The selling of a put at a lower strike price to pay for a put at a higher strike.

Quote: The actual price, or the bid or ask price, of a security, commodity, futures, option, currency, or other financial instrument at a particular time.

R

Rally top: The point where a rally stalls.

Rally: An upward movement of prices.

Random walk theory: The theory that the past movement or direction of the price of a stock or other market cannot be used to predict its future movement or direction.

Range: The difference between the high and low price during a given period.

Ratio spread: An options strategy in which an investor simultaneously holds an unequal number of long and short positions.

Reaction: A short-term countertrend movement of prices.

Relative Strength Index (RSI) or (RS): A technical momentum indicator that compares the magnitude of recent gains to recent losses in an attempt to determine overbought and oversold conditions of an asset.

Resistance: The price level where a trend stalls. The market stops rising because sellers start to outnumber buyers. The opposite of a support level.

Retracement: In technical analysis, price movement in the opposite direction of the prevailing trend. Also described as a correction.

Retrenchment: A decline in price.

Return on equity: A calculation of a corporation's profitability, specifically its return on assets, calculated by dividing after-tax income by tangible assets.

Reversion to the mean: The concept that most natural fluctuations tend to center around a normal or average value over time.

Risk management: Management to control and monitor the risks of a bank, financial institution, business entity, or individual.

Risk: The potential to lose money.

S

Securities and Exchange Commission (SEC): The Federal agency created by Congress to regulate the securities markets and protect investors.

Security: A note, stock, bond, investment contract, debenture, certificate of interest in profit-sharing or partnership agreement, certificate of deposit, collateral trust certificate, pre-organization certificate, option on a security, or other instrument of investment.

Sell-off: A period of intensified selling in a market that pushes prices sharply lower.

Settlement price: (1) The closing price, or a price within the range of closing prices, which is used as the official price in determining net gains or losses at the close of each trading session. (2) Payment of any amount of money under a contract.

Short covering: Trades that reverse, or close out, short-sale positions.

Short: One who has sold a cash commodity, a commodity futures contract, or other financial instrument; a long, in contrast, is one who has bought a cash commodity or futures contract.

Slippage: The difference between estimated transaction costs and the amount actually paid, usually attributed to a change in the spread.

Speculator: One who attempts to anticipate price changes and make profits through the sale and/or purchase of financial instruments.

Spinning top: A small real body in candlestick charting that indicates a small difference between the open and close price of the day.

Spread: (1) The purchase of one futures against the sale of another futures contract, to take advantage of and profit from the distortions from the normal price relationships that sometimes occur. (2) In a quote, the difference between the bid and the ask prices of a market. (3) The difference between two or more prices.

Spyware: Software that companies place on a user's PC without permission that slows down the computer by collecting data on the user's practices and generating ads.

Stochastics: A technical momentum indicator that compares the closing price of a commodity, security or option contract to its price range over a given time period.

Stop limit: An order that becomes a limit order once the specified price is hit.

Stop order or stop: A dormant order that is triggered and becomes active only when a stock or commodity hits a price specified by the customer. A sell stop is placed below the market; a buy stop is placed above the market. Sometimes referred to as a stop loss order.

Strike price: A specified price at which an investor can buy or sell an option's underlying financial instrument. The exchange rate, interest rate, or market price that is guaranteed by an option transaction.

Straddle: An options strategy of purchasing a put and a call with the same strike price and expiration date. The strategy is generally used if the investor believes the price will move significantly but is unsure of the direction.

Supply: The total amount of a good or service available for purchase by consumers.

Support: A price level at which, historically, a declining market has difficulty falling below. Once this level is reached, the market trades sideways for a period of time or rebounds. It is the opposite of a resistance price range.

Synthetic stop: An order to exit the trade held either on your own computer or an intermediary computer, rather than at the exchange level. When the price touches the level of the stop, the order is then fired off to the exchange server for execution.

T

Tail: A chart pattern that shows a long, one-day price spike with a close near the intraday low.

Technical analysis: An approach to analysis of markets that anticipates trends of market prices based on mathematical patterns. Technicians normally examine patterns of price range, rates of change, changes in volume of trading, and open interest. Data are charted to show trends and formations which serve as indicators of likely future price movements.

Technical stop: An order to exit a trade at a predetermined price level that uses technical analysis to determine placement of the level.

Theta: Measures the change in the theoretical value of an option when the outstanding time before it expires is changed.

Three falling peaks: A price chart pattern of three peaks, each lower than the previous one, beginning with the highest high on the chart that occur in downward price trends and at major bearish turning points.

Tick: A minimum upward or downward movement in the price of a securities, futures, or other financial instruments. Also called points.

Tick chart: A candlestick price chart that removes the element of time, with each candle representing a specific number of trades.

Traders: Individuals who negotiate prices and execute buy and sell orders, either on behalf of an investor or for their own account.

Trading system: A method of buying and selling stocks according to a screen based on results from predetermined indicators and other criteria.

Trailing stop: An order to exit a trade at a predetermined price level. Trailing stops automatically follow the stock tick-by-tick by a specified amount as the market moves in a trader's favor, ensuring that a winner does not turn into a loser.

Transaction costs: (1) The costs of negotiating, monitoring, and enforcing a contract. (2) The total cost of executing a financial transaction.

Trend line: A line that connects either a series of highs or lows in a trend. The trendline can represent either support (a positive trendline) or resistance (a negative trendline).

True range: A determination of range (high of the bar minus the low of the bar) that accounts for price gaps by adding the range of the gap to the calculation.

V

Vega: The amount that the price of an option changes as compared to a one-percent changes in volatility.

Vertical spread: A simultaneous purchase of one option, hedged by the sale of another option, where the two options have the same expiration month but different striking prices. Also called a bull or bear spread.

Volatility: (1) A measure by which an exchange rate is expected to fluctuate over a given period. (2) A measure of a commodity's tendency to move up and down in price based on its daily price history over a period of time.

Volume: The number of contracts, shares, or other financial instruments traded during a specified period of time.

W

Whipsaw: a short-term trade with a small loss.

Y

Yield: The annual rate of return on an investment, as paid in dividends or interest. It is expressed as a percentage.

CONTRIBUTORS

Gerald Appel is president of Signalert Corporation and the inventor of the moving average convergence divergence (MACD) indicator. He has published numerous books, articles and videotapes related to technical analysis.

John Bollinger is the president and founder of Bollinger Capital Management and the inventor of Bollinger bands. He is a regular contributor on CNBC and a speaker at financial seminars. Bollinger is the author of a best-selling book on Bollinger bands.

Thomas Bulkowski is a private investor and author of several books on technical analysis. He was formerly a hardware design engineer at Raytheon and a senior software engineer for Tandy Corporation.

Nina Cooper is the president and principal of Pendragon Research Inc. She is an instructor at the Chicago Mercantile Exchange and a founding member and past president of the American Association of Professional Technical Analysts.

Brian Dolan is the director of research at forex.com, a division of GAIN Capital Group. A pioneer in online foreign exchange, GAIN Capital Group provides forex trading and asset management services to clients in more than 140 countries.

Philip Gotthelf is publisher of the COMMODEX, the longest-running daily futures trading system published anywhere, and president of EQUIDEX Inc. and EQUIDEX Brokerage Group. He is the author of several books on trading and investing.

Adam Grimes is the head trader and system designer at Level Partners, LLC, a hedge fund in Columbus, Ohio. He is an active trader in futures, equities and options markets.

Michael Kahn is a well respected technical analyst. He writes the Getting Technical column for Barron's online, the daily Quick Takes Pro technical newsletter, and has written two books on technical analysis.

Peter Kaplan is the co-founder of Nexus Capital Management, LLC. He is a securities trader specializing in intermediate and longer-term trading, with a comprehensive approach to the equities market.

Cynthia Kase is founder and president of Kase and Company, Inc., a hedging and trading solutions firm serving the corporate and institutional energy sector. She started her career as a chemical engineer, was Chemical Ba nks' first commodity derivatives trader, and later consulted with the Saudi oil ministry.

Jeffrey Kennedy is a senior financial analyst at Elliott Wave International (EWI) with more than fifteen years of experience as an analyst and trader. He writes and edits Futures Junctures, EWI's premier commodity forecasting package.

Tracy Knudsen is the senior market strategist at Candlecharts.com. She is co-author of Illuminations, a daily market commentary that combines the insights of both Eastern and Western technical analysis.

Steven Landis is the founder of Landis Financial & Investment Services and a past president and chairman of the National Association of Active Invstment Managers (NAAIM), an organization for professional, active investment managers.

Kira McCaffery Brecht is a senior editor at SFO magazine. She has been writing about the financial markets for sixteen years as a former Chicago bureau chief at Futures World News, a market analyst at Bridge News, and technical analyst at MMS International.

Lawrence McMillan is founder and president of McMillan Analysis Corp., which publishes option-related educational material, manages individual options accounts, and administers a hedge fund. He is the author of several trading books.

Bernard Mitchell is the president of PBSP, LLC. He is a systems developer and has trained more than 800 traders in his trading methodologies.

John Murphy is the technical analyst for StockCharts.com. He is the author of several books, including Technical Analysis of the Financial Markets, widely regarded as the standard reference in the field.

Steve Nison is the president of Candlecharts.com, which provides educational products and services to institutions and private traders. He is acknowledged as the Western word's leading authority on candlesticks.

Mark Pankin is the founder and owner of MDP Associates LLC. Before becoming a registered investment advisor, he taught math at the university level and worked as an operations research analyst.

Sam Seiden is a trader, research analyst, and instructor with more than a decade of experience. He provides research and guidance to clients through speaking engagements, workshops, magazine articles, and advisory services via www.samseiden.com

Ken Shaleen is the founder of Chartwatch, which provides technical research on financial instruments and grain futures. He has taught the technical analysis course for the Chicago Mercantile Exchange since 1974 and is the author of several books on technical analysis.

Brian Shannon is an independent trader and highly regarded market educator. His work can be viewed at www.alphatrends.blogspot.com.

Christopher Terry is a full-time professional trader with LBR Group, specializing in index futures and equities markets. He speaks regularly at derivatives conferences and has written articles for several publications.

Ken Tower is former chief market strategist at CyberTrader, Inc., a Charles Schwab company. He is a former president of the Market Technicians Association and is a frequent lecturer on technical analysis.

Russell R. Wasendorf, Sr., is chairman and CEO of Peregrine Financial Group, Inc., publisher of SFO, and author of the Complete Guide to Single Stock Futures and All About Futures.

INDEX

R

Raschke, Linda Bradford, 30, 141-142
Relative Strength Index (RSI) or Relative Strength (RS), 123, 144, 157, 161-162, 170, 210, 225
Risk, 15, 21, 29, 76, 84-85, 87-92, 100, 105, 107, 110, 151, 175, 191, 194-198, 200-201, 203-205, 228, 229
Roth, Philip, 3, 5, 122

S

Schabacker, Richard, 17
Seiden, Sam, 190, 198
Shaleen, Ken, 39, 43, 93, 99
Shannon, Brian, 122-124, 126-127, 199, 207
Shaw, Alan, 32-33, 35-36
Stochastics, 71-75, 120, 123, 169-177, 179-180, 225
Stop(s), 50-53, 72, 76, 87, 103-109, 131-136, 143, 148, 151, 178, 182, 185-187, 195, 197, 205-207, 224-226, 228-229

T

Terry, Christopher, 17, 31
Tower, Ken, 57, 63
Trend following, 12-13, 18-22, 77-92, 199-207

V

Volatility, 55, 58-59, 61, 86-87, 147, 151, 153-154, 163, 200, 215-217, 226, 228-229
Volume, 1, 22-24, 27-28, 40-43, 59, 63, 96-97, 99, 111-117, 120-128, 130-131, 160, 162-168, 188, 192, 195, 202-203, 205, 210-213, 218-222, 224, 241-243

W

Wasendorf, Sr., Russell R., ix

NOTES

NOTES

NOTES

NOTES

NOTES

NOTES

NOTES